X-O MANOWAR

EMPEROR

MATT KINDT | CLAYTON CRAIN | RENATO GUEDES

D1511939

CONTENTS

Collection Cover Art: Lewis LaRosa
with Brian Reber

Assistant Editor: David Menchel (#10)
Assistant Editor: Charlotte Greenbaum
Editor: Warren Simons

VALIANT

X-O Manowar® (2017): Emperor. Published by Valiant Entertainment LLC. Office of Publication: 350 Seventh Avenue, New York, NY 10001. Printed in the U.S.A. First Printing. ISBN: 9781682152355.

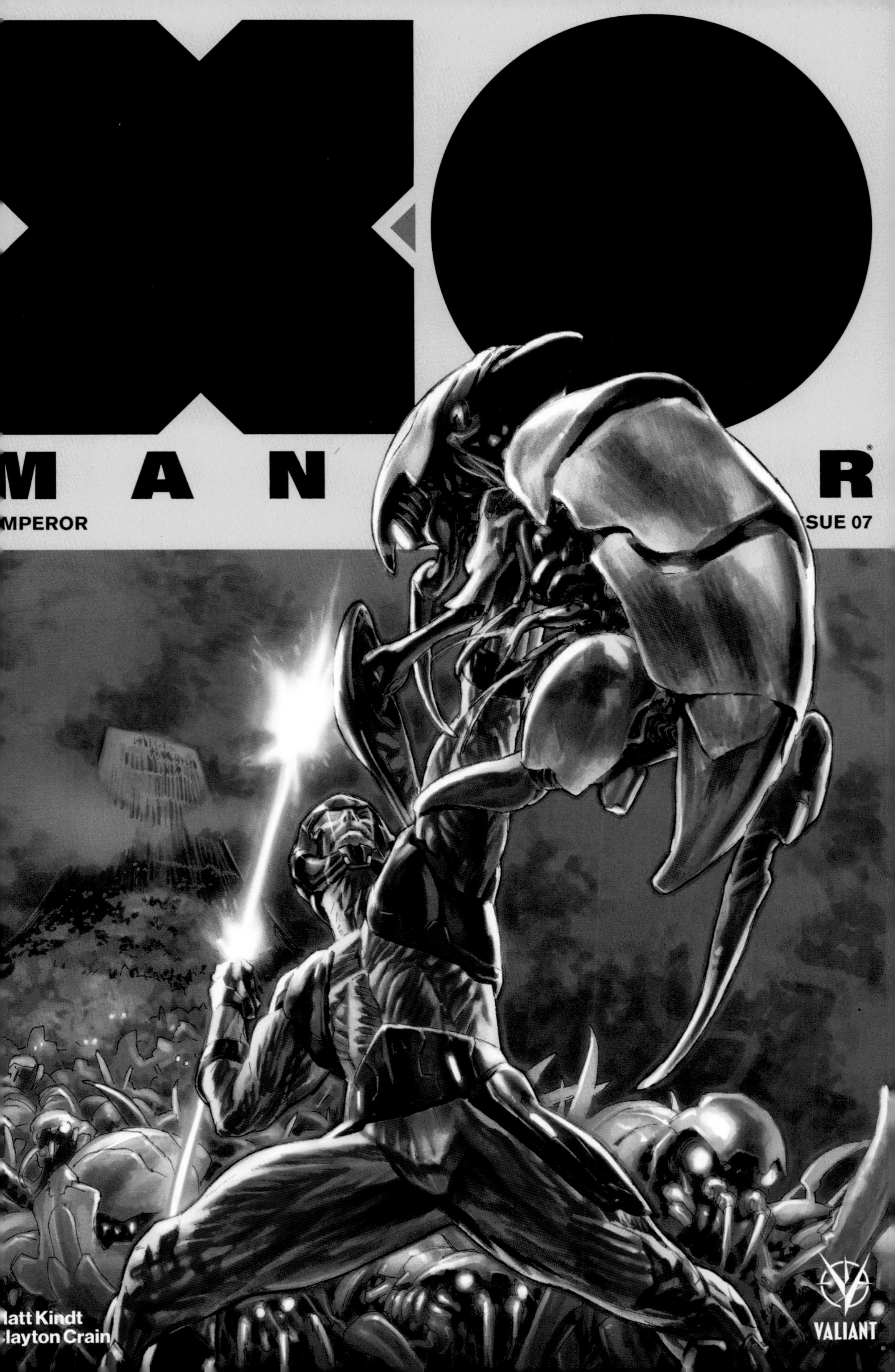
M A N
R
MPEROR
SUE 07
latt Kindt
layton Crain
VALIANT

X-O MANOWAR

The skies of planet Gorin are filled with fire -- the monolith, a strange floating pillar that rains destruction down from above, has attacked. Though Aric has proven that the late general colluded with the mysterious ships, there is no true indication of why they're here or what they're after. Only one thing is clear: their arrival on planet Gorin is no coincidence, and neither is their genocide of the Burnt.

Now, with the planet hanging in the balance, Aric must ward off the alien armada and save his new home, charging forward from one war directly into the next...

ARIC OF EARTH

With the power of his own growing army at his back, Aric has achieved the rank of General. No longer allied with Azure, Aric can only trust those closest to him.

SHANHARA

Aric has so far refused to don the X-O armor, but the war has escalated, and so has Aric's dependency on Shanhara.

ARIC'S TEAM

Comprised of Ironside, Wynn, Catt, and Bruto, these soldiers have fought beside Aric since the initial assault on the Cadmium. With each battle, their devotion and respect for their leader increases.

SCHON

An Azure citizen who took Aric in and made a life with him. Since he joined the war against the Cadmium, Schon has had to house the ghostly Shanhara armor as it awaits Aric's return.

THE EMPEROR

Hungry for planetary dominance, the Emperor will stop at nothing to subjugate the Burnt.

THE MONOLITH

Strange visitors from off world, the monolith rains fire down on Planet Gorin, but why are they here? And what are they looking for?

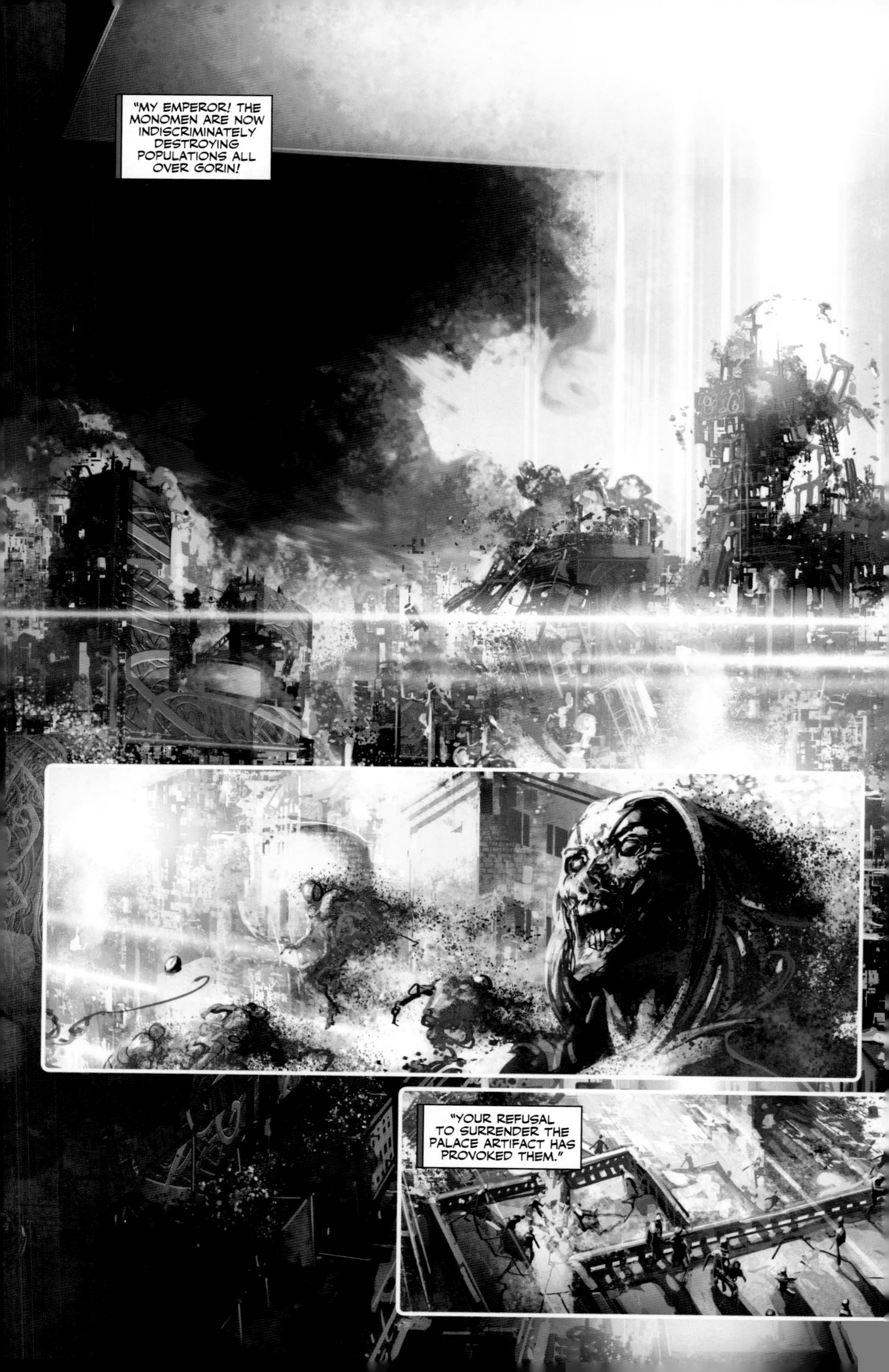
"MY EMPEROR! THE MONOMEN ARE NOW INDISCRIMINATELY DESTROYING POPULATIONS ALL OVER GORIN!
"YOUR REFUSAL TO SURRENDER THE PALACE ARTIFACT HAS PROVOKED THEM."

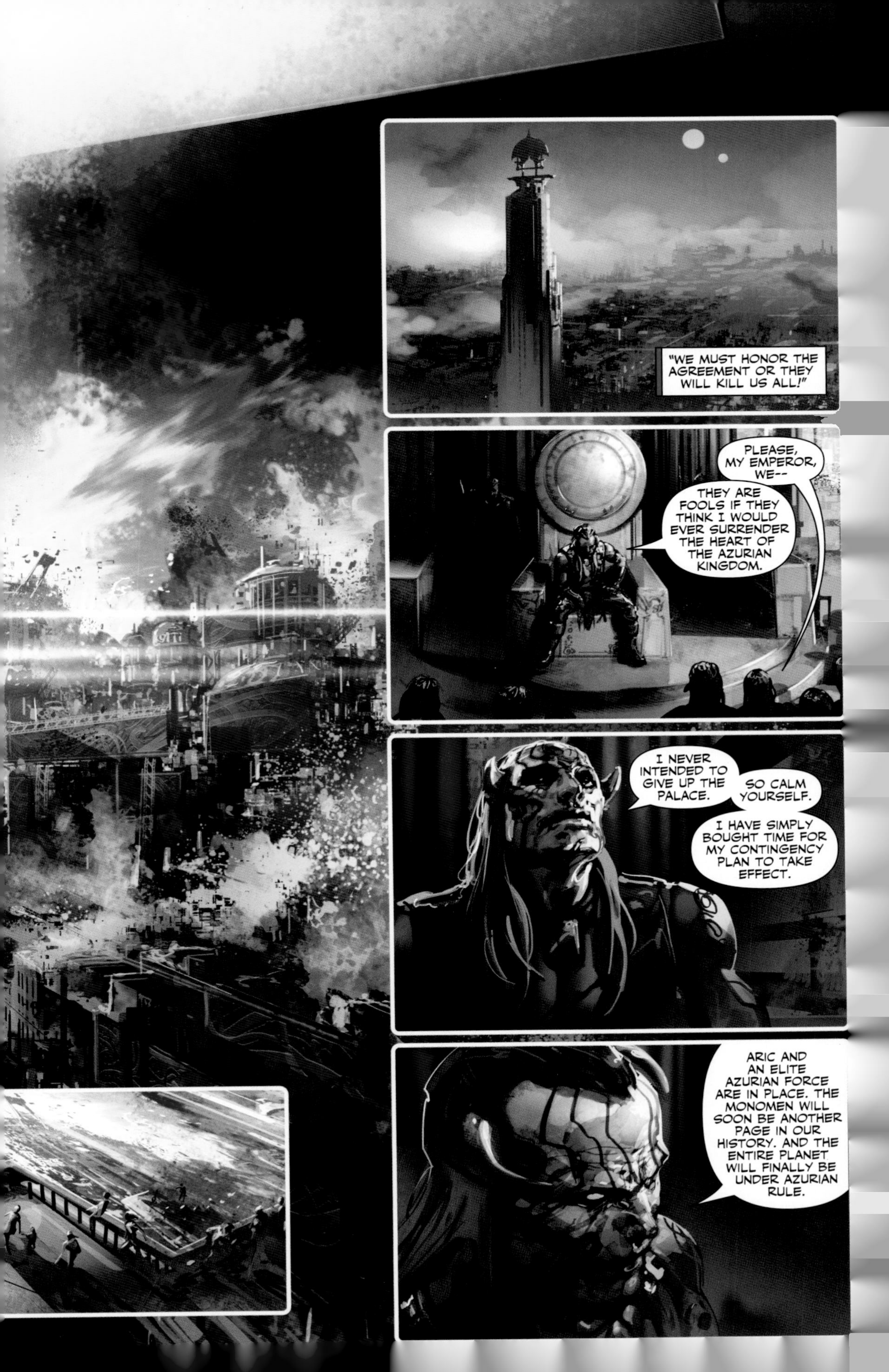
"WE MUST HONOR THE AGREEMENT OR THEY WILL KILL US ALL!"
PLEASE, MY EMPEROR, WE--
THEY ARE FOOLS IF THEY THINK I WOULD EVER SURRENDER THE HEART OF THE AZURIAN KINGDOM.
I NEVER INTENDED TO GIVE UP THE PALACE.
SO CALM YOURSELF.
I HAVE SIMPLY BOUGHT TIME FOR MY CONTINGENCY PLAN TO TAKE EFFECT.
ARIC AND AN ELITE AZURIAN FORCE ARE IN PLACE. THE MONOMEN WILL SOON BE ANOTHER PAGE IN OUR HISTORY. AND THE ENTIRE PLANET WILL FINALLY BE UNDER AZURIAN RULE.

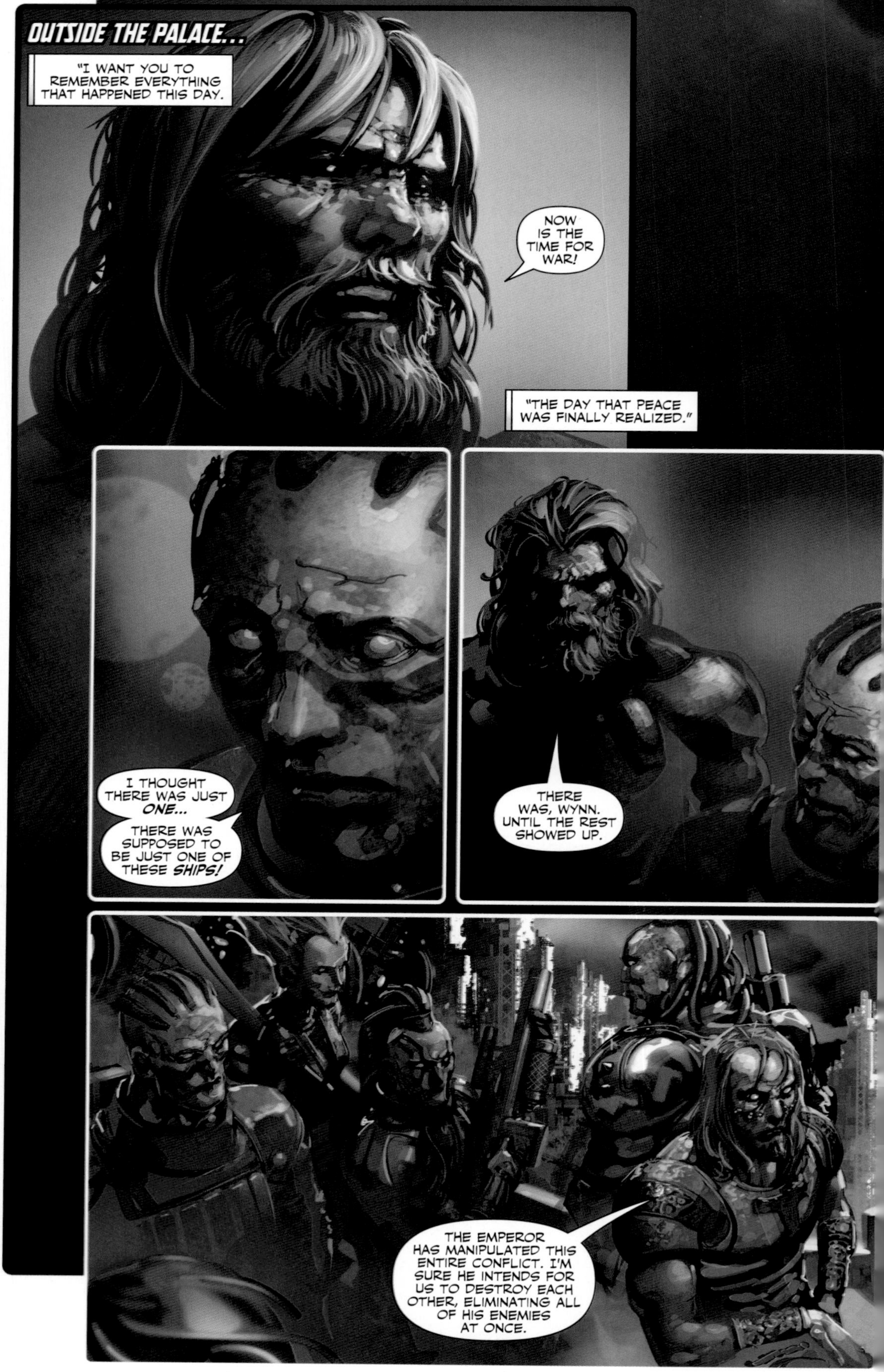
OUTSIDE THE PALACE...
"I WANT YOU TO REMEMBER EVERYTHING THAT HAPPENED THIS DAY.
NOW IS THE TIME FOR WAR!
"THE DAY THAT PEACE WAS FINALLY REALIZED."
I THOUGHT THERE WAS JUST *ONE...*
THERE WAS SUPPOSED TO BE JUST ONE OF THESE *SHIPS!*
THERE WAS, WYNN. UNTIL THE REST SHOWED UP.
THE EMPEROR HAS MANIPULATED THIS ENTIRE CONFLICT. I'M SURE HE INTENDS FOR US TO DESTROY EACH OTHER, ELIMINATING ALL OF HIS ENEMIES AT ONCE.

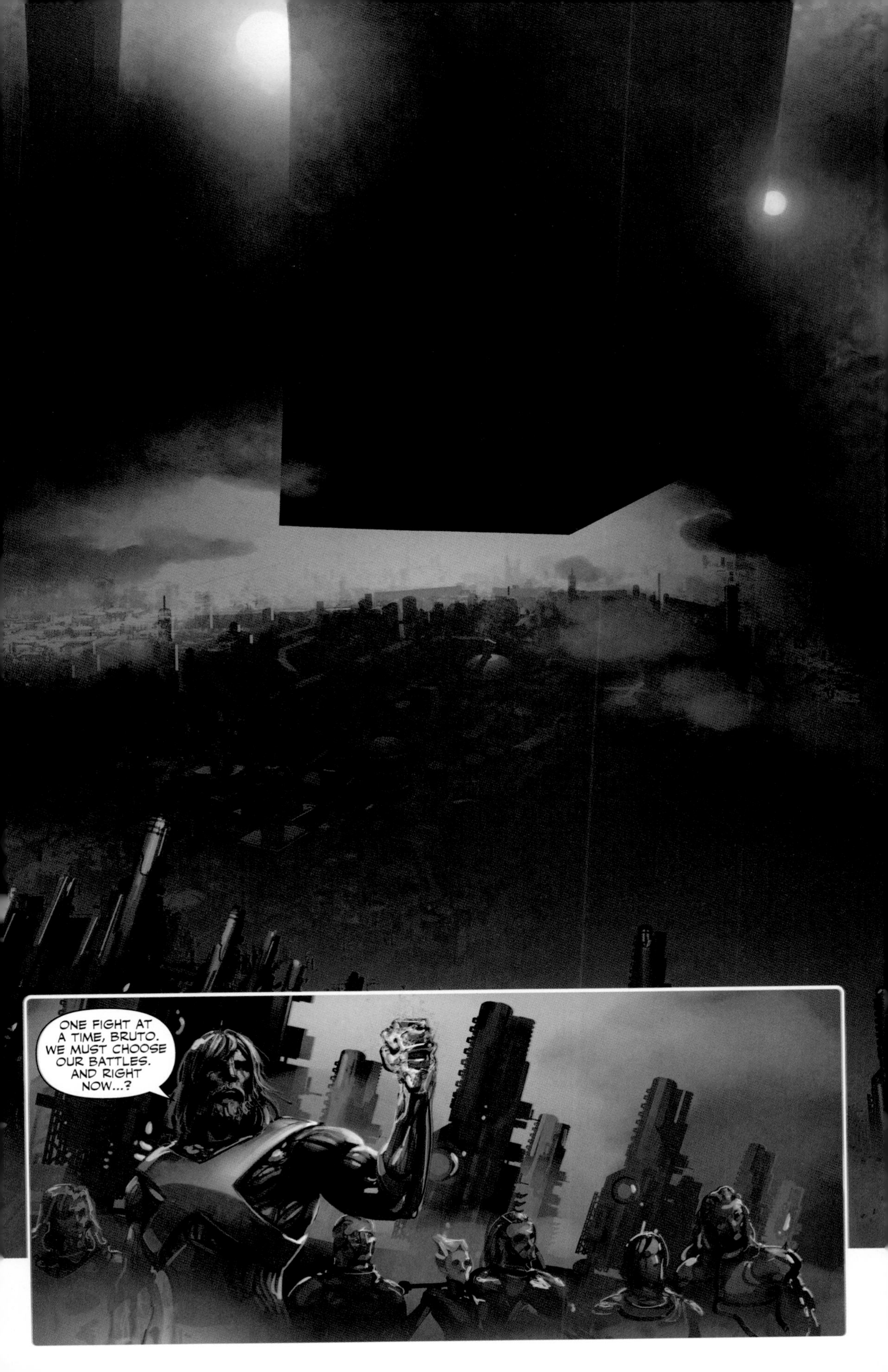
ONE FIGHT AT A TIME, BRUTO. WE MUST CHOOSE OUR BATTLES. AND RIGHT NOW...?

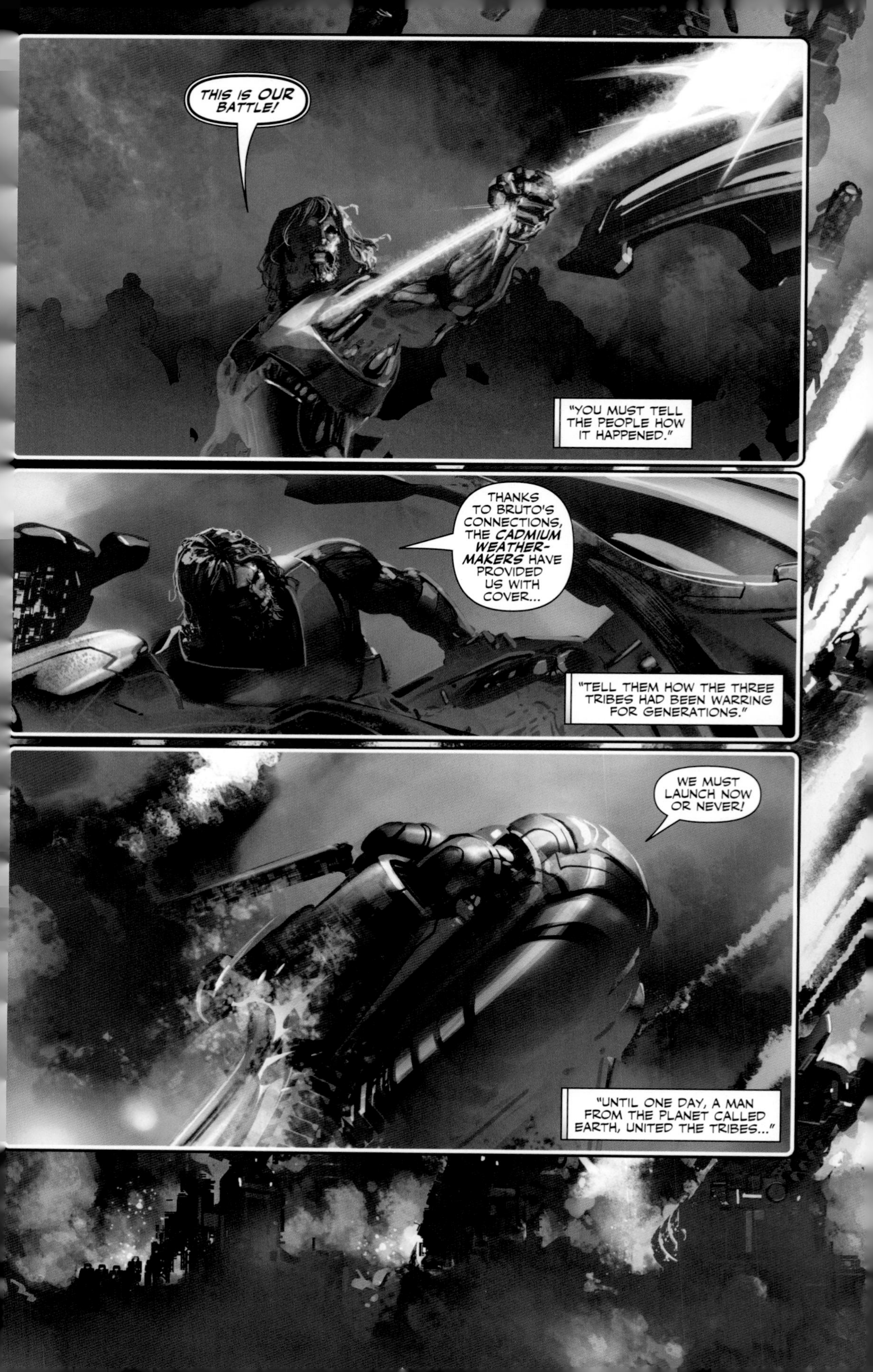
THIS IS OUR BATTLE!
"YOU MUST TELL THE PEOPLE HOW IT HAPPENED."
THANKS TO BRUTO'S CONNECTIONS, THE CADMIUM WEATHER-MAKERS HAVE PROVIDED US WITH COVER...
"TELL THEM HOW THE THREE TRIBES HAD BEEN WARRING FOR GENERATIONS."
WE MUST LAUNCH NOW OR NEVER!
"UNTIL ONE DAY, A MAN FROM THE PLANET CALLED EARTH, UNITED THE TRIBES..."

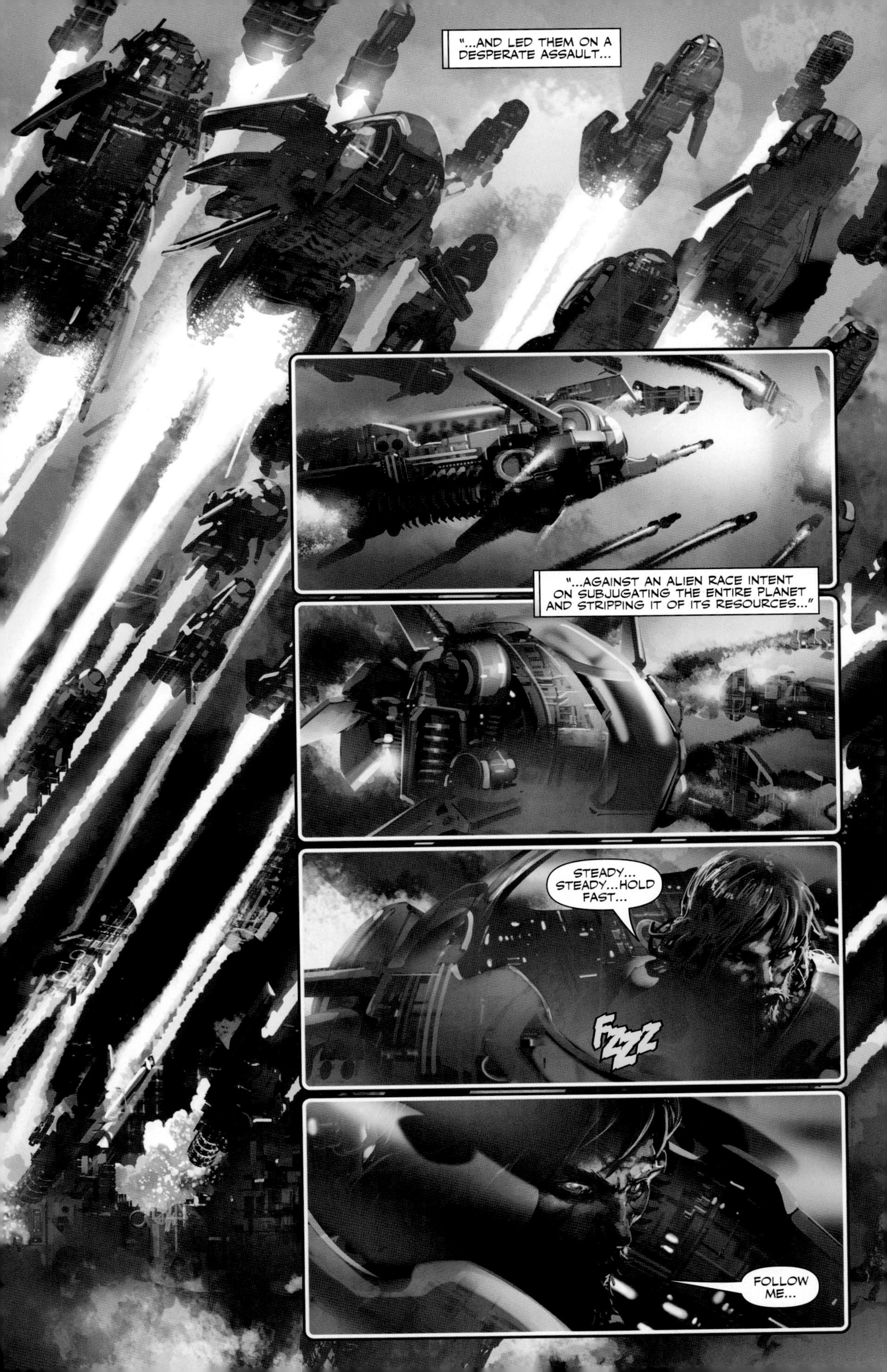
"...AND LED THEM ON A DESPERATE ASSAULT...
"...AGAINST AN ALIEN RACE INTENT ON SUBJUGATING THE ENTIRE PLANET AND STRIPPING IT OF ITS RESOURCES..."
STEADY... STEADY...HOLD FAST...
FZZZ
FOLLOW ME...

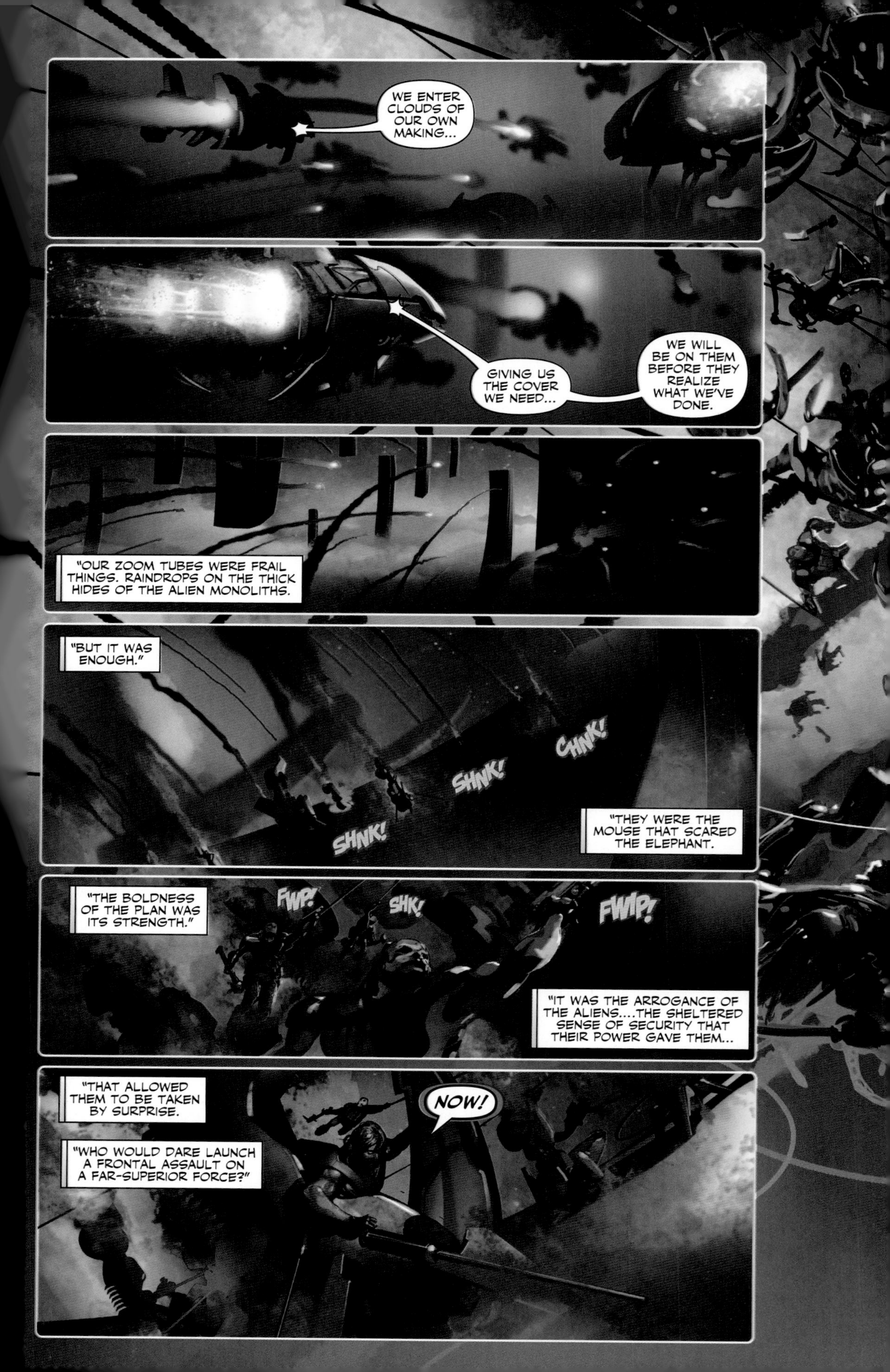
WE ENTER CLOUDS OF OUR OWN MAKING...
GIVING US THE COVER WE NEED...
WE WILL BE ON THEM BEFORE THEY REALIZE WHAT WE'VE DONE.
"OUR ZOOM TUBES WERE FRAIL THINGS. RAINDROPS ON THE THICK HIDES OF THE ALIEN MONOLITHS.
"BUT IT WAS ENOUGH."
CHNK!
SHNK!
SHNK!
"THEY WERE THE MOUSE THAT SCARED THE ELEPHANT.
"THE BOLDNESS OF THE PLAN WAS ITS STRENGTH."
FWP!
SHK!
FWIP!
"IT WAS THE ARROGANCE OF THE ALIENS....THE SHELTERED SENSE OF SECURITY THAT THEIR POWER GAVE THEM...
"THAT ALLOWED THEM TO BE TAKEN BY SURPRISE.
NOW!
"WHO WOULD DARE LAUNCH A FRONTAL ASSAULT ON A FAR-SUPERIOR FORCE?"

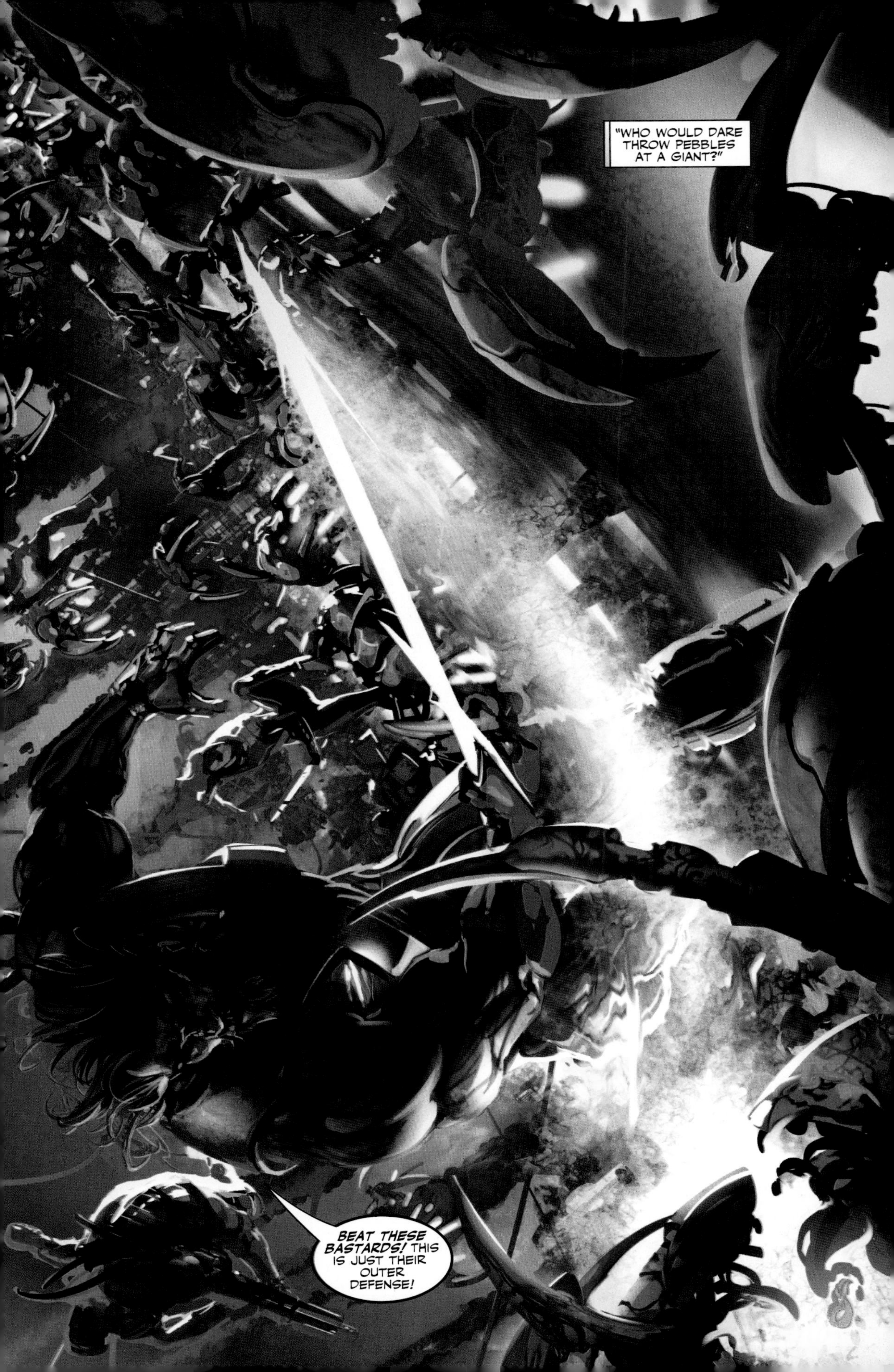
"WHO WOULD DARE THROW PEBBLES AT A GIANT?"
BEAT THESE BASTARDS! THIS IS JUST THEIR OUTER DEFENSE!

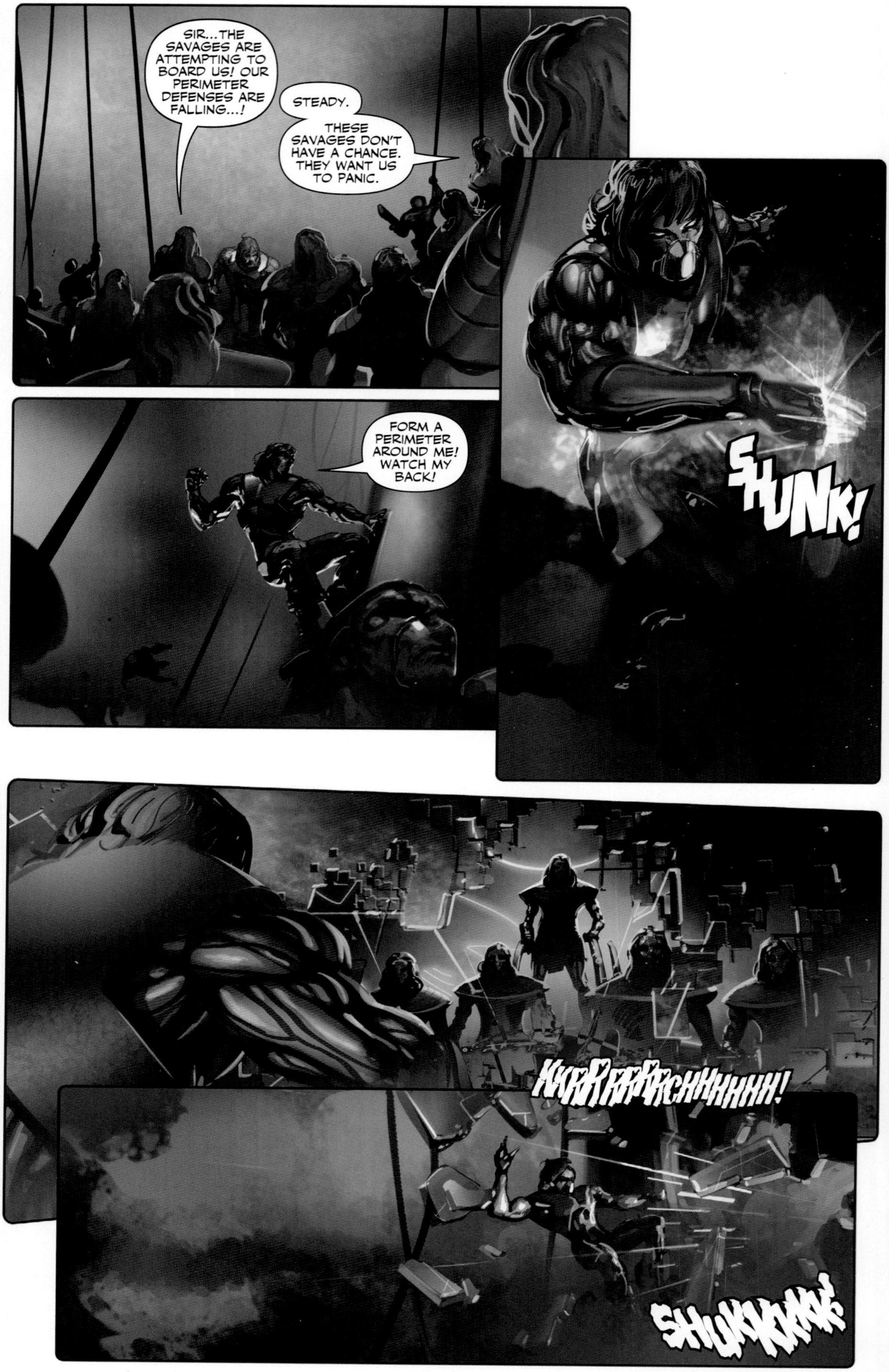
SIR...THE SAVAGES ARE ATTEMPTING TO BOARD US! OUR PERIMETER DEFENSES ARE FALLING...!
STEADY.
THESE SAVAGES DON'T HAVE A CHANCE. THEY WANT US TO PANIC.
FORM A PERIMETER AROUND ME! WATCH MY BACK!
SHUNK!
KKRRRRRRRCHHHHHH!
SHUKKKKK!

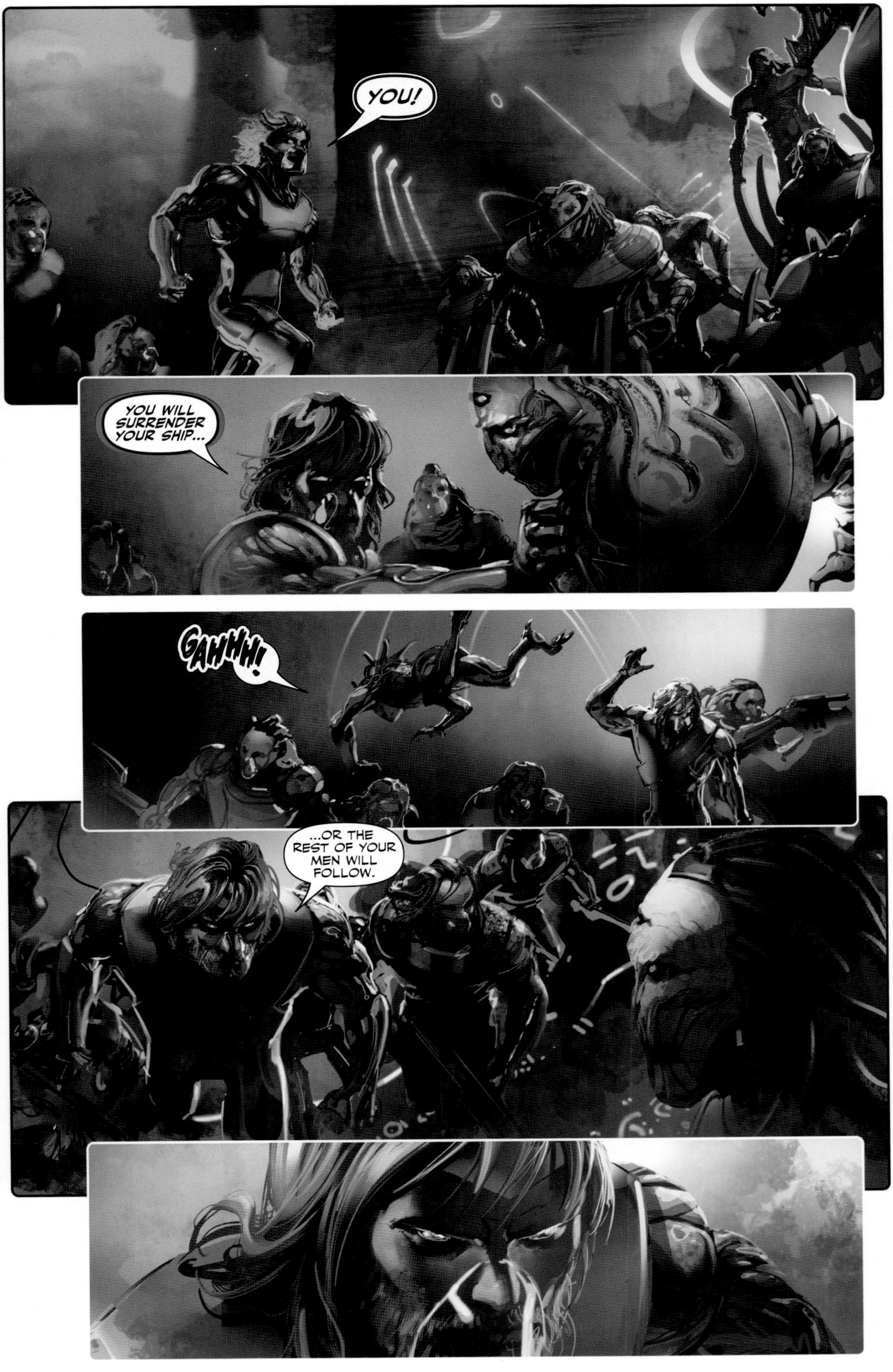
YOU!
YOU WILL SURRENDER YOUR SHIP...
GAHHH!
...OR THE REST OF YOUR MEN WILL FOLLOW.

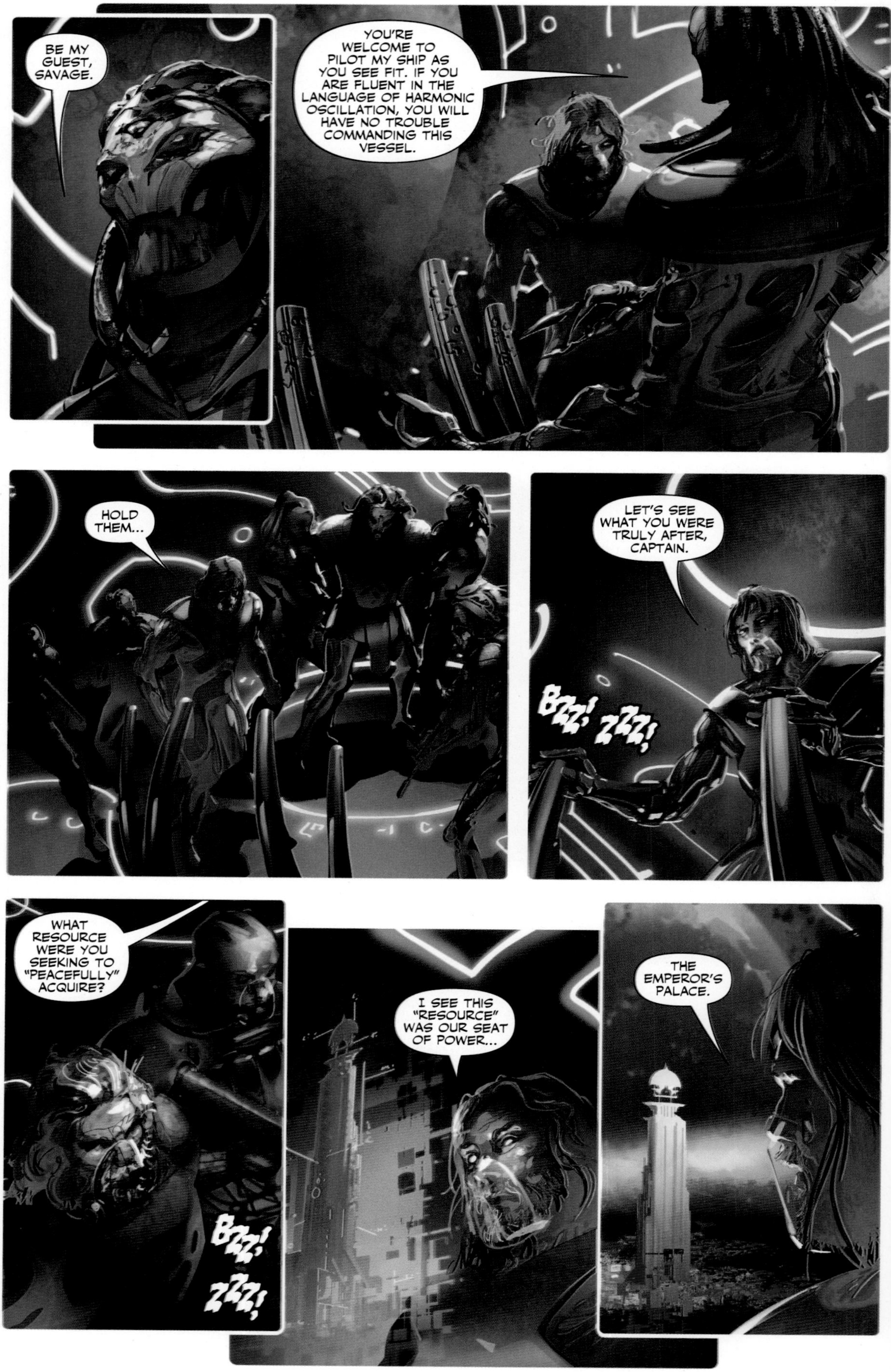
BE MY GUEST, SAVAGE.
YOU'RE WELCOME TO PILOT MY SHIP AS YOU SEE FIT. IF YOU ARE FLUENT IN THE LANGUAGE OF HARMONIC OSCILLATION, YOU WILL HAVE NO TROUBLE COMMANDING THIS VESSEL.
HOLD THEM...
LET'S SEE WHAT YOU WERE TRULY AFTER, CAPTAIN.
BZZ! ZZZ!
WHAT RESOURCE WERE YOU SEEKING TO "PEACEFULLY" ACQUIRE?
BZZ! ZZZ!
I SEE THIS "RESOURCE" WAS OUR SEAT OF POWER...
THE EMPEROR'S PALACE.

"YOU MUST TELL THE STORY OF THE GENERAL...WHO MASTERED THE LANGUAGE OF THE ALIENS..."

SHOW ME THE WAY TO COMMAND THIS SHIP...

I WOULD DIE BEFORE AIDING A BARBARIAN SUCH AS YOU!

PERMISSION GRANTED...

THERE IS IRONY IN THE SLAUGHTERER OF INNOCENTS CALLING ANOTHER "BARBARIAN."

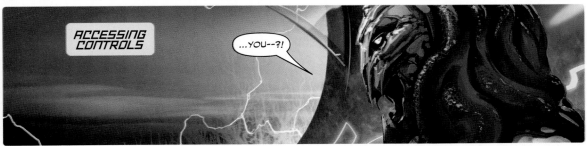

ACCESSING CONTROLS

...YOU--?!

...HOW ARE YOU MANAGING TO CONTROL MY VESSEL?

MAYBE... MAYBE YOU SPEAK THE TRUTH.

"AND HARNESSED THEIR POWER..."

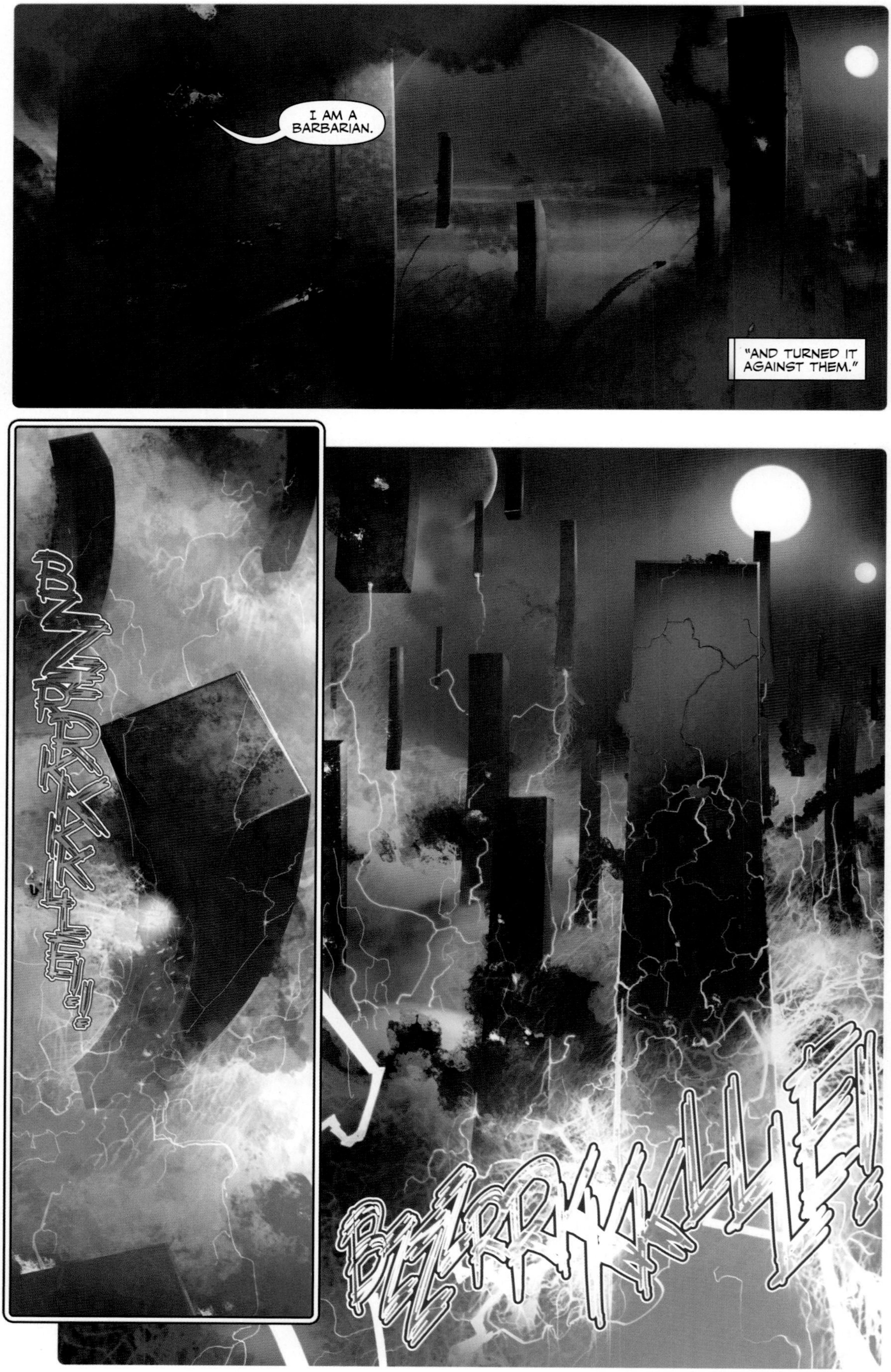
I AM A BARBARIAN.
"AND TURNED IT AGAINST THEM."

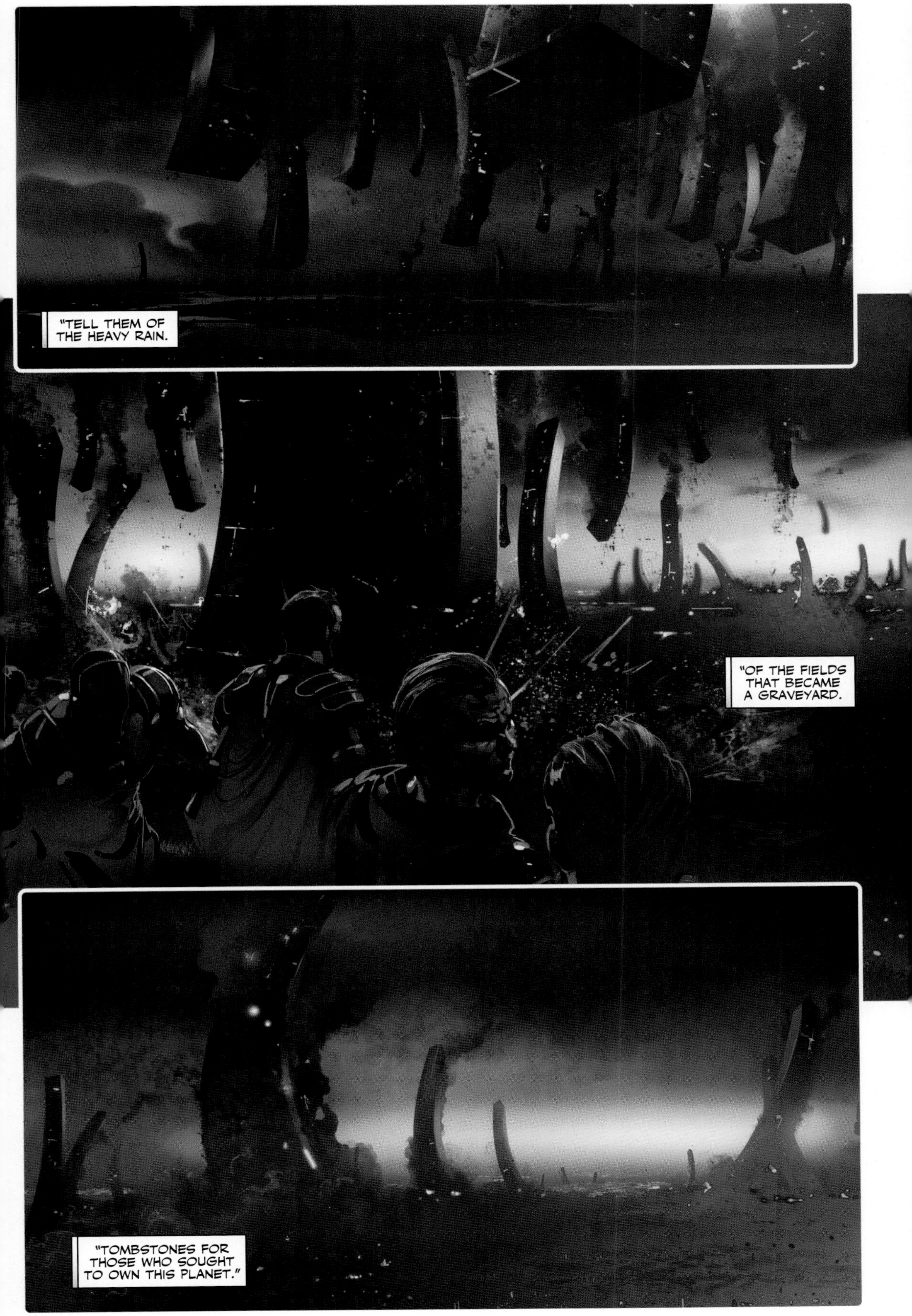
"TELL THEM OF THE HEAVY RAIN.
"OF THE FIELDS THAT BECAME A GRAVEYARD.
"TOMBSTONES FOR THOSE WHO SOUGHT TO OWN THIS PLANET."

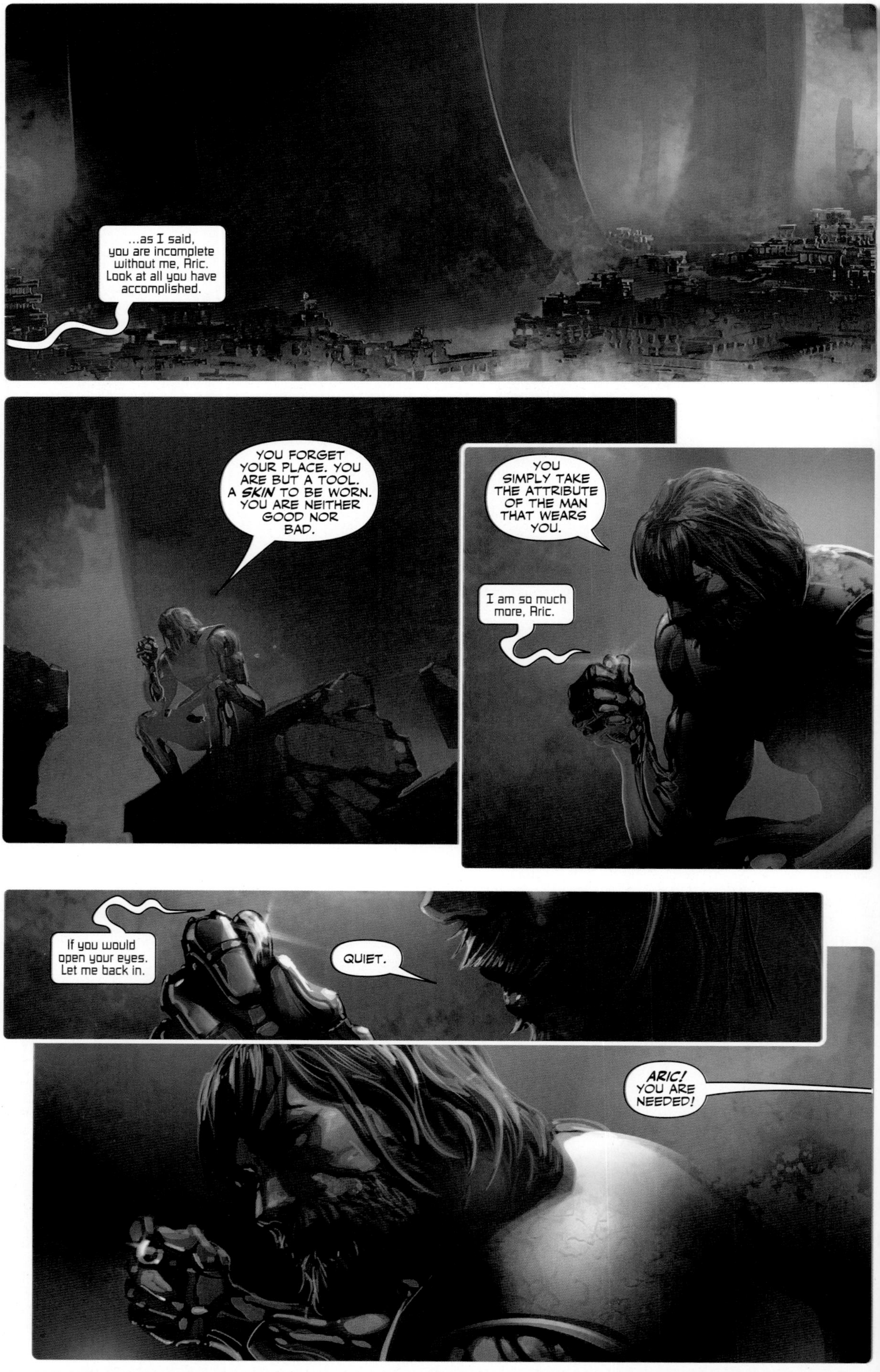
...as I said, you are incomplete without me, Aric. Look at all you have accomplished.
YOU FORGET YOUR PLACE. YOU ARE BUT A TOOL. A SKIN TO BE WORN. YOU ARE NEITHER GOOD NOR BAD.
YOU SIMPLY TAKE THE ATTRIBUTE OF THE MAN THAT WEARS YOU.
I am so much more, Aric.
If you would open your eyes. Let me back in.
QUIET.
ARIC! YOU ARE NEEDED!

I AM SPIRO. LEADER OF THE MONO-MEN. YOU HAVE DECIMATED OUR FLEET...

AND I RECOGNIZE YOUR PROWESS ON THE BATTLEFIELD, BUT I DEMAND THAT YOU STAND DOWN, OR I WILL BE FORCED TO CALL FOR REINFORCEMENTS WHO WILL BURN THIS PLANET INTO STARDUST.

I...

Here... let me show you, Aric...

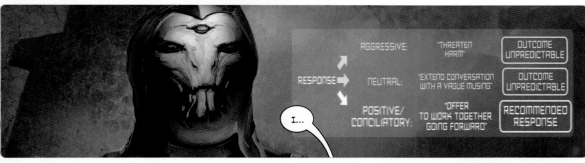

I...

RESPONSE	AGGRESSIVE:	"THREATEN HARM"	OUTCOME UNPREDICTABLE
	NEUTRAL:	"EXTEND CONVERSATION WITH A VAGUE MUSING"	OUTCOME UNPREDICTABLE
	POSITIVE/CONCILIATORY:	"OFFER TO WORK TOGETHER GOING FORWARD"	RECOMMENDED RESPONSE

I AM WONDERING HOW YOU WILL CALL FOR REINFORCEMENTS WITH YOUR HEAD REMOVED FROM YOUR BODY.

RESPONSE	AGGRESSIVE:	"THREATEN HARM"	OUTCOME UNPREDICTABLE
	NEUTRAL:	"EXTEND CONVERSATION WITH A VAGUE MUSING"	OUTCOME UNPREDICTABLE
	POSITIVE/CONCILIATORY:	"OFFER TO WORK TOGETHER GOING FORWARD"	RECOMMENDED RESPONSE

I--I...

RESPONSE	AGGRESSIVE:	"FOLLOW UP WITH PHYSICAL VIOLENCE"	OUTCOME UNPREDICTABLE
	NEUTRAL:	"REMAIN SILENT AND WAIT FOR RESPONSE"	OUTCOME UNPREDICTABLE
	POSITIVE/CONCILIATORY:	"SUGGEST THAT IT WAS ALL A JOKE"	OUTCOME UNPREDICTABLE

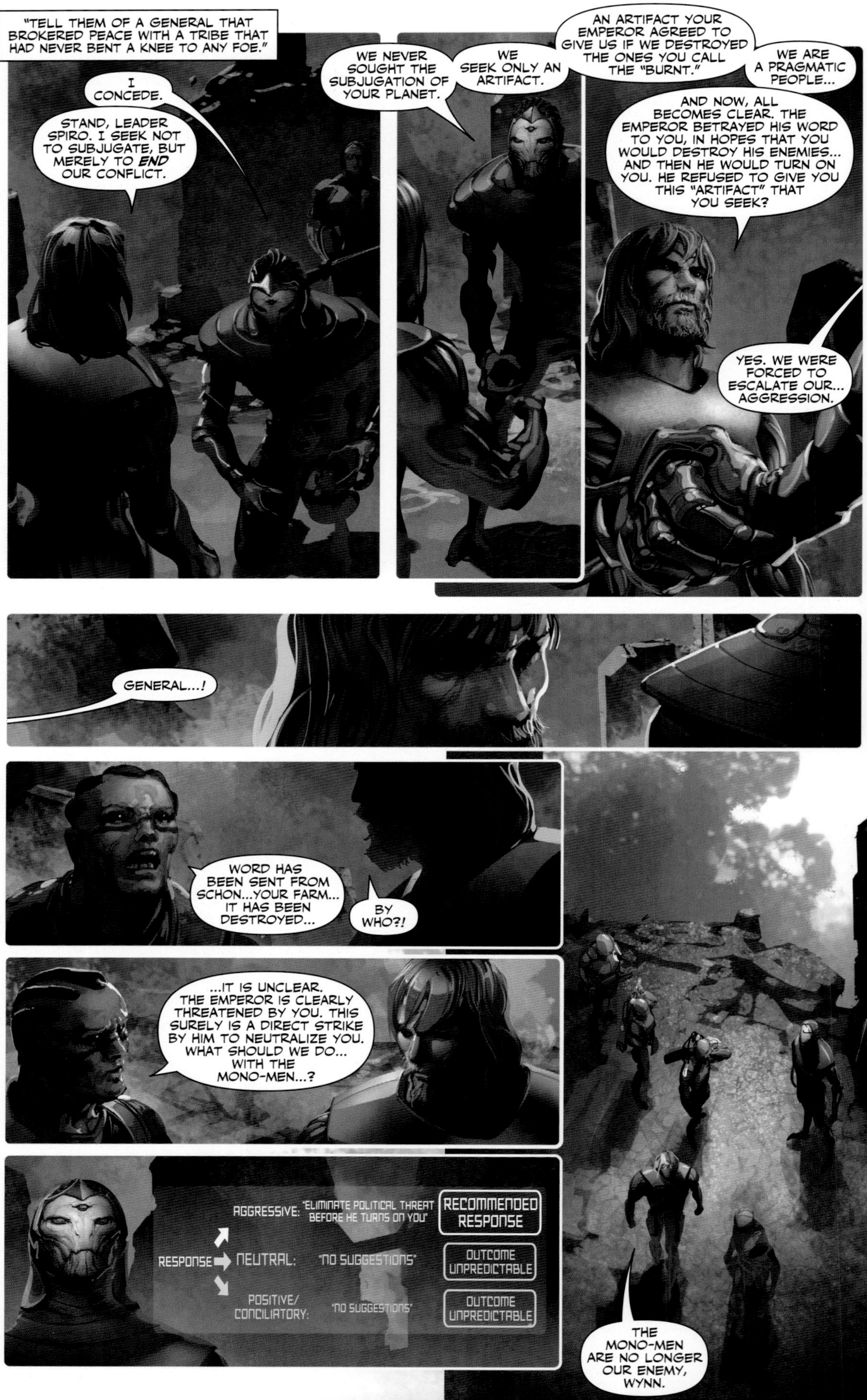
"TELL THEM OF A GENERAL THAT BROKERED PEACE WITH A TRIBE THAT HAD NEVER BENT A KNEE TO ANY FOE."
I CONCEDE.
STAND, LEADER SPIRO. I SEEK NOT TO SUBJUGATE, BUT MERELY TO *END* OUR CONFLICT.
WE NEVER SOUGHT THE SUBJUGATION OF YOUR PLANET.
WE SEEK ONLY AN ARTIFACT.
AN ARTIFACT YOUR EMPEROR AGREED TO GIVE US IF WE DESTROYED THE ONES YOU CALL THE "BURNT."
WE ARE A PRAGMATIC PEOPLE...
AND NOW, ALL BECOMES CLEAR. THE EMPEROR BETRAYED HIS WORD TO YOU, IN HOPES THAT YOU WOULD DESTROY HIS ENEMIES... AND THEN HE WOULD TURN ON YOU. HE REFUSED TO GIVE YOU THIS "ARTIFACT" THAT YOU SEEK?
YES. WE WERE FORCED TO ESCALATE OUR... AGGRESSION.
GENERAL...!
WORD HAS BEEN SENT FROM SCHON...YOUR FARM... IT HAS BEEN DESTROYED...
BY WHO?!
...IT IS UNCLEAR. THE EMPEROR IS CLEARLY THREATENED BY YOU. THIS SURELY IS A DIRECT STRIKE BY HIM TO NEUTRALIZE YOU. WHAT SHOULD WE DO... WITH THE MONO-MEN...?
AGGRESSIVE: "ELIMINATE POLITICAL THREAT BEFORE HE TURNS ON YOU"
RECOMMENDED RESPONSE
RESPONSE
NEUTRAL: "NO SUGGESTIONS"
OUTCOME UNPREDICTABLE
POSITIVE/ CONCILIATORY: "NO SUGGESTIONS"
OUTCOME UNPREDICTABLE
THE MONO-MEN ARE NO LONGER OUR ENEMY, WYNN.

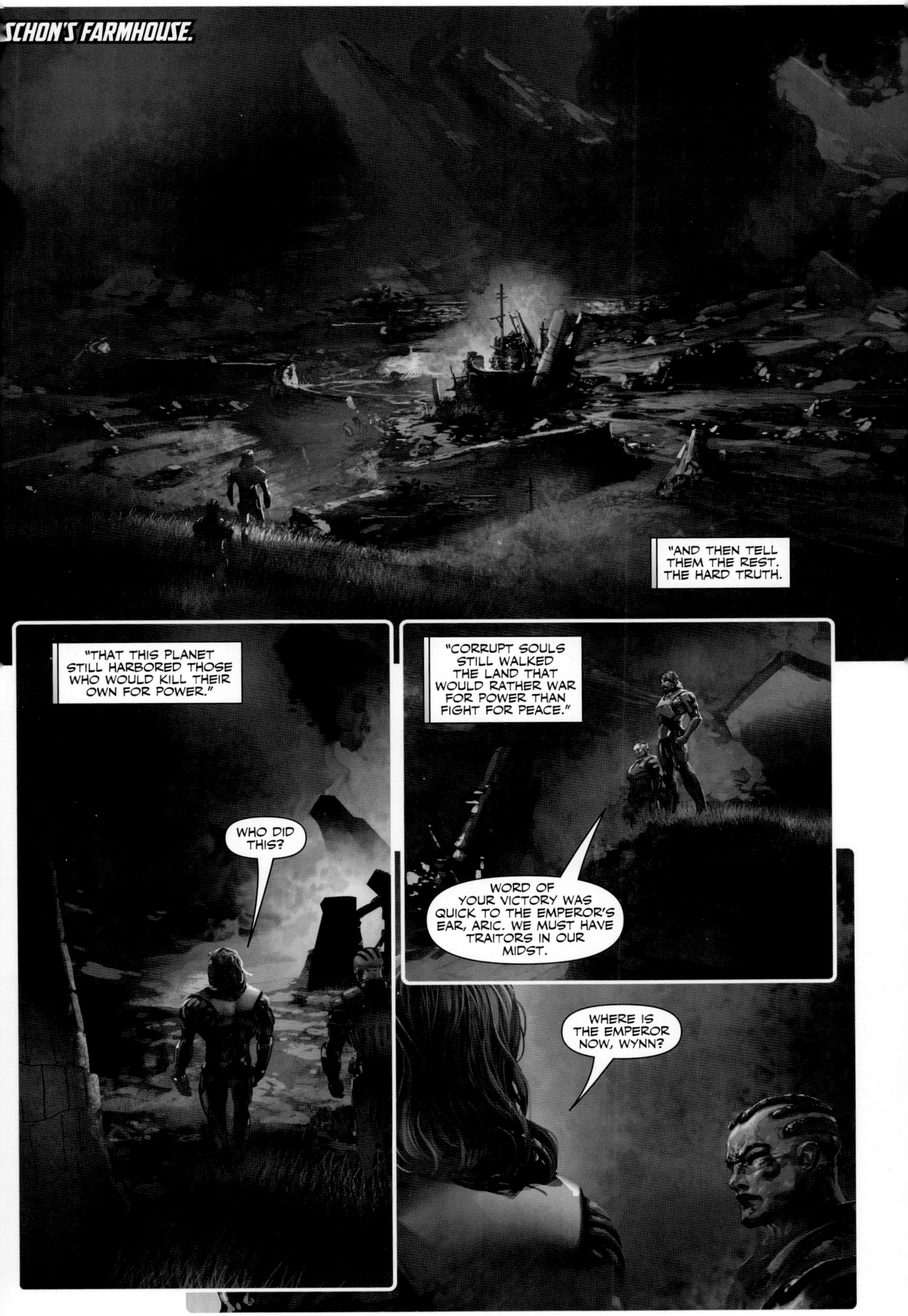
SCHON'S FARMHOUSE.
"AND THEN TELL THEM THE REST. THE HARD TRUTH.
"THAT THIS PLANET STILL HARBORED THOSE WHO WOULD KILL THEIR OWN FOR POWER."
WHO DID THIS?
"CORRUPT SOULS STILL WALKED THE LAND THAT WOULD RATHER WAR FOR POWER THAN FIGHT FOR PEACE."
WORD OF YOUR VICTORY WAS QUICK TO THE EMPEROR'S EAR, ARIC. WE MUST HAVE TRAITORS IN OUR MIDST.
WHERE IS THE EMPEROR NOW, WYNN?

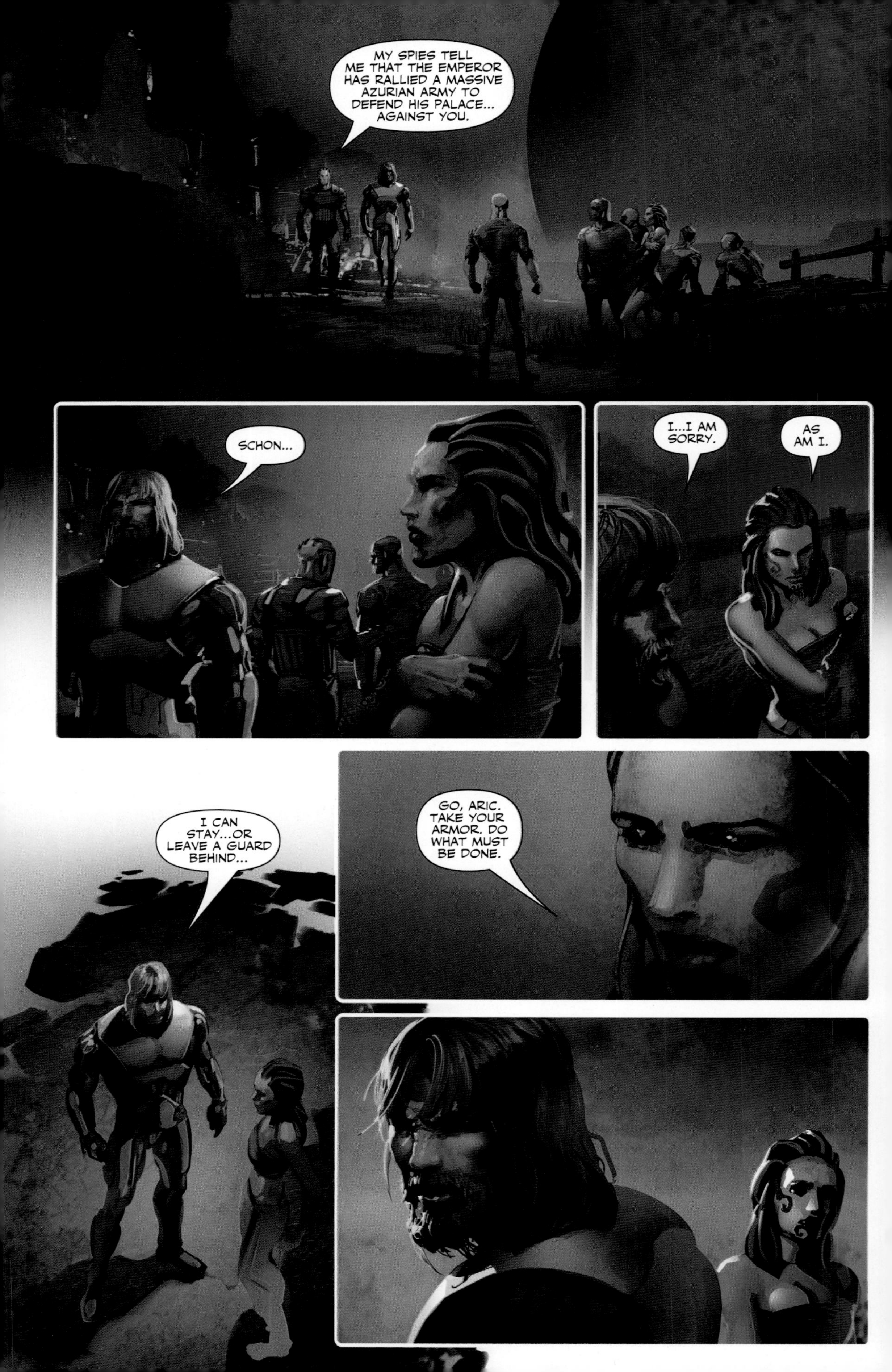
MY SPIES TELL ME THAT THE EMPEROR HAS RALLIED A MASSIVE AZURIAN ARMY TO DEFEND HIS PALACE... AGAINST YOU.
SCHON...
I...I AM SORRY.
AS AM I.
I CAN STAY...OR LEAVE A GUARD BEHIND...
GO, ARIC. TAKE YOUR ARMOR. DO WHAT MUST BE DONE.

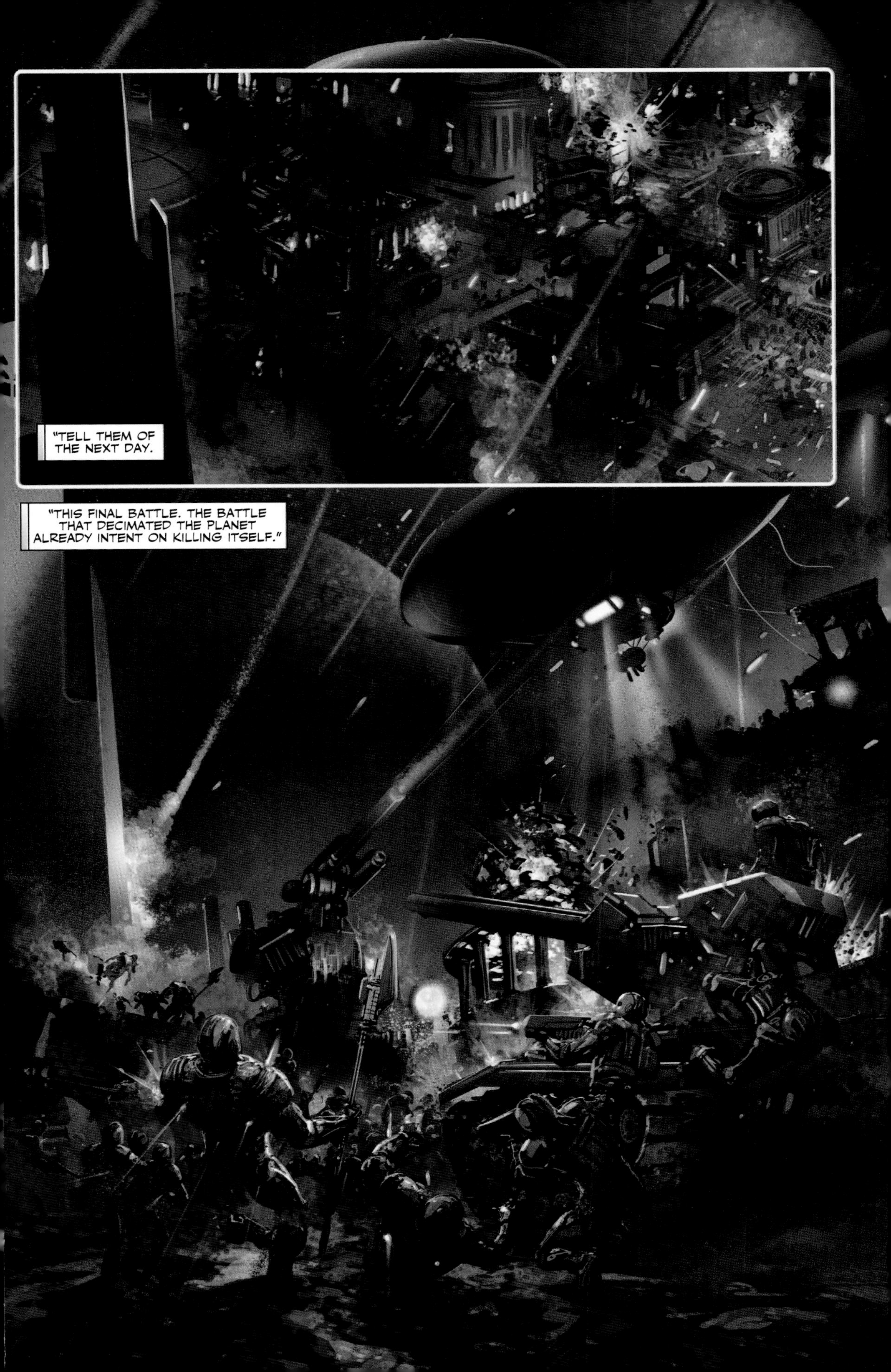
"TELL THEM OF THE NEXT DAY.
"THIS FINAL BATTLE. THE BATTLE THAT DECIMATED THE PLANET ALREADY INTENT ON KILLING ITSELF."

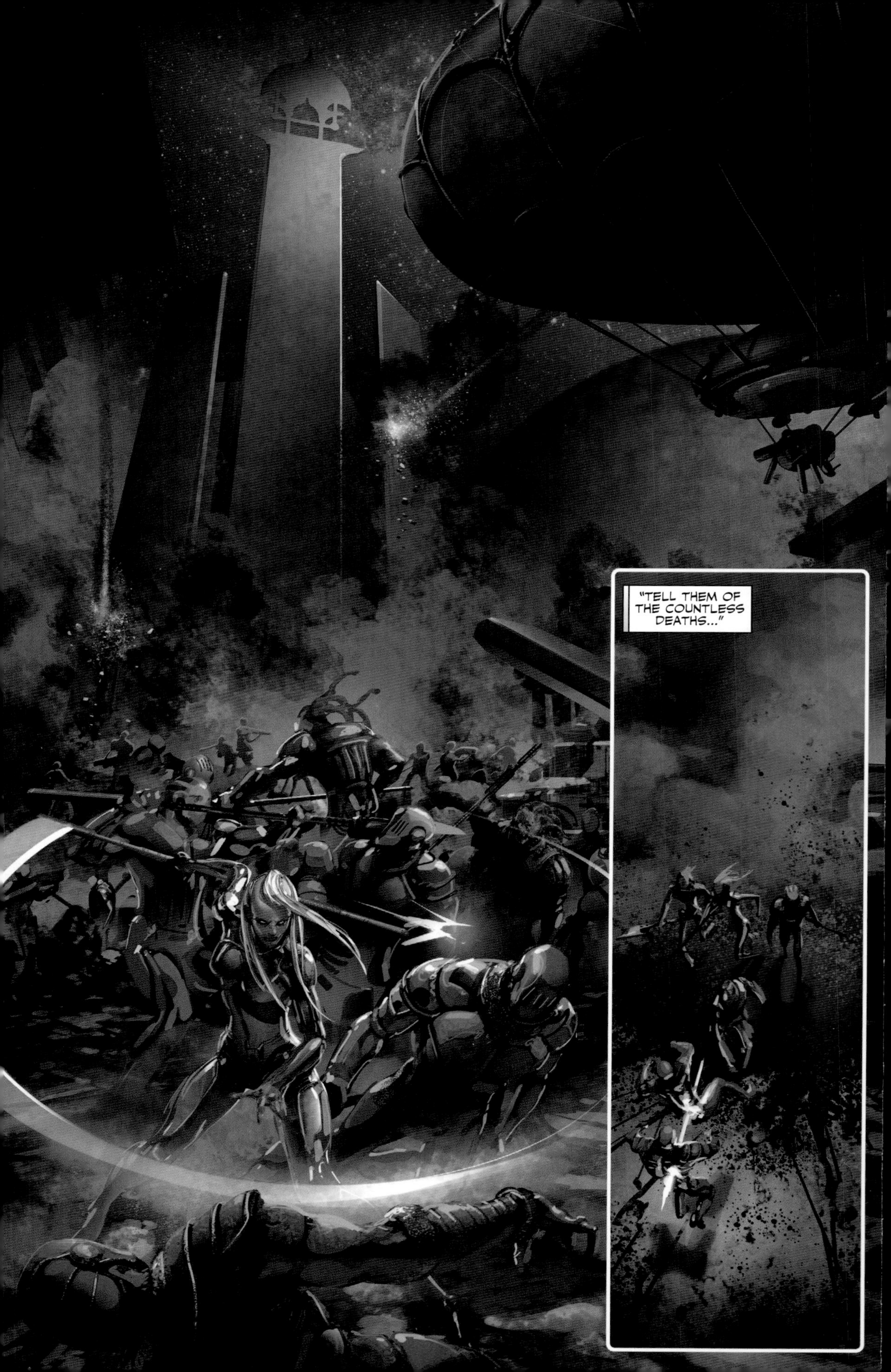
"TELL THEM OF THE COUNTLESS DEATHS..."

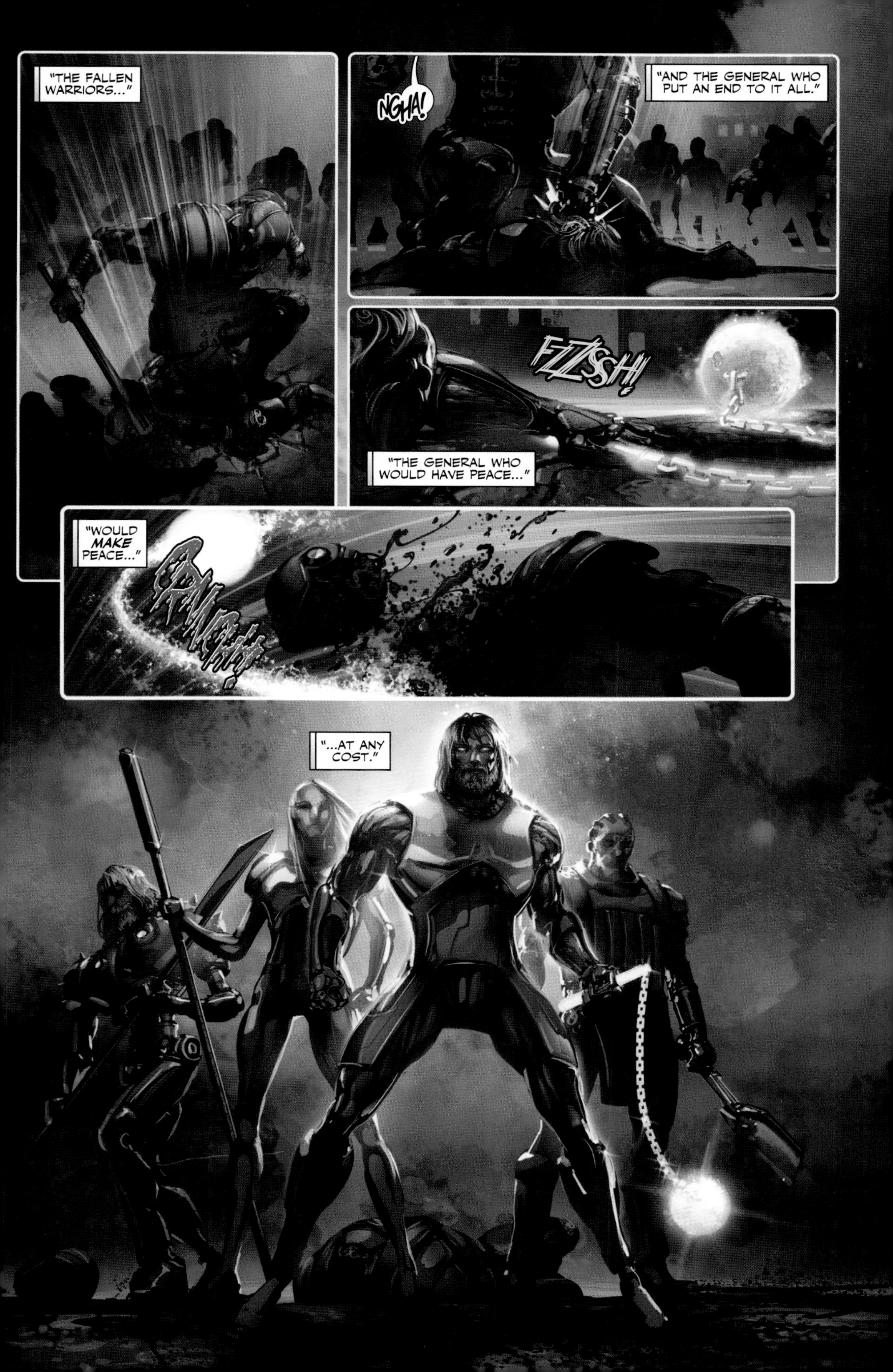
"THE FALLEN WARRIORS..."
NGHA!
"AND THE GENERAL WHO PUT AN END TO IT ALL."
FZZSSH!
"THE GENERAL WHO WOULD HAVE PEACE..."
"WOULD *MAKE* PEACE..."
"...AT ANY COST."

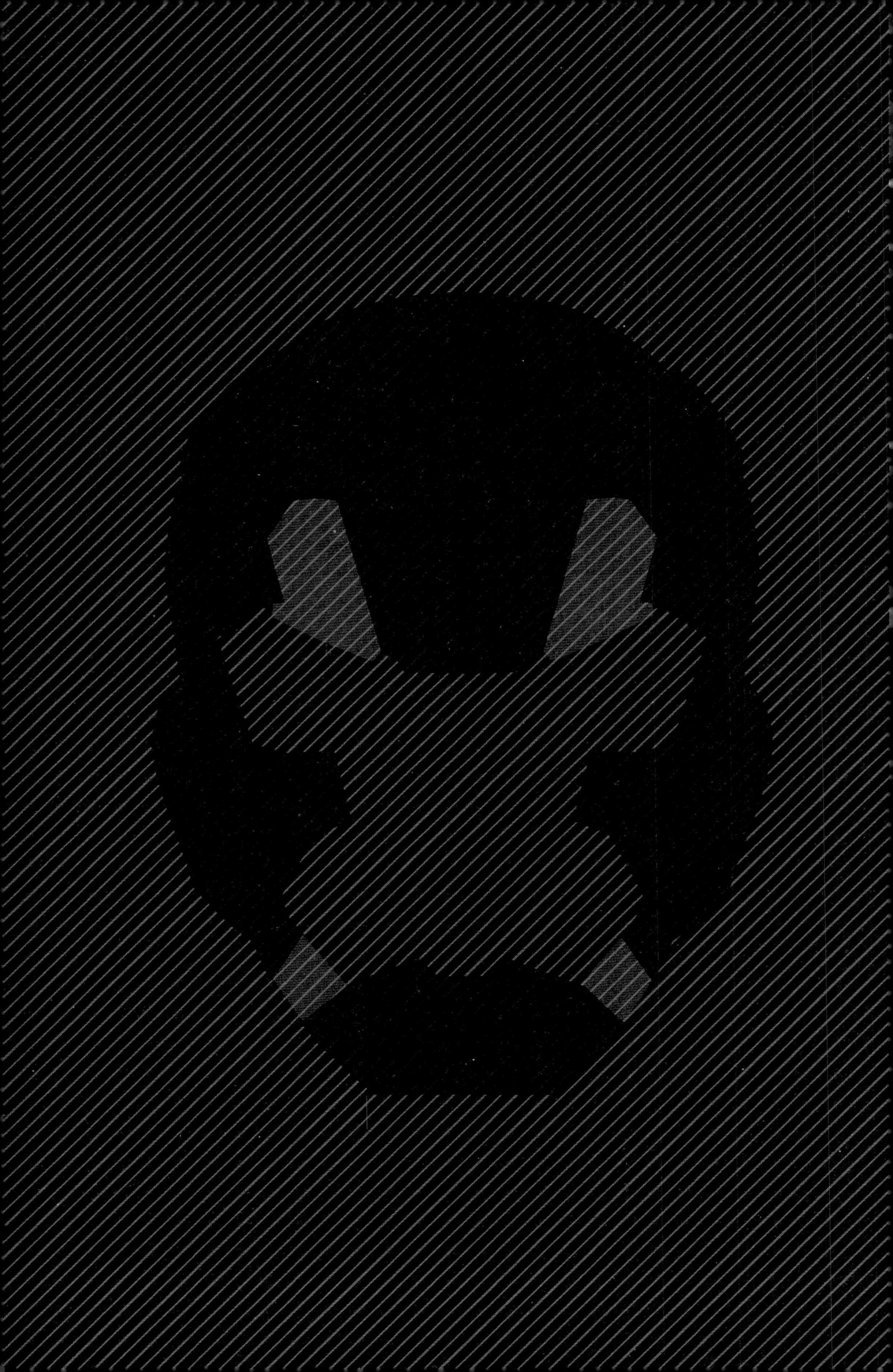

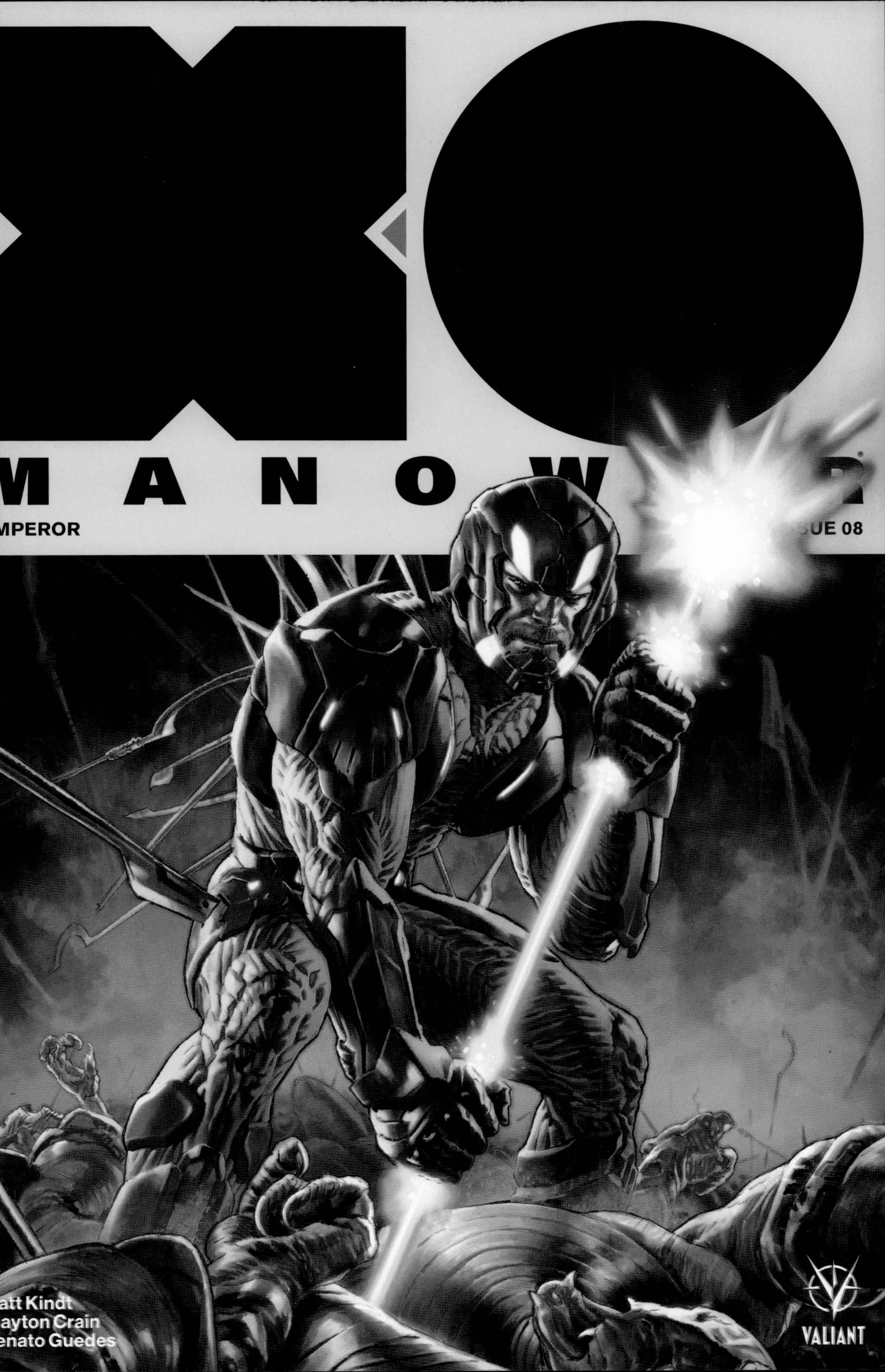

MANOW
MPEROR
UE 08
att Kindt
ayton Crain
enato Guedes
VALIANT

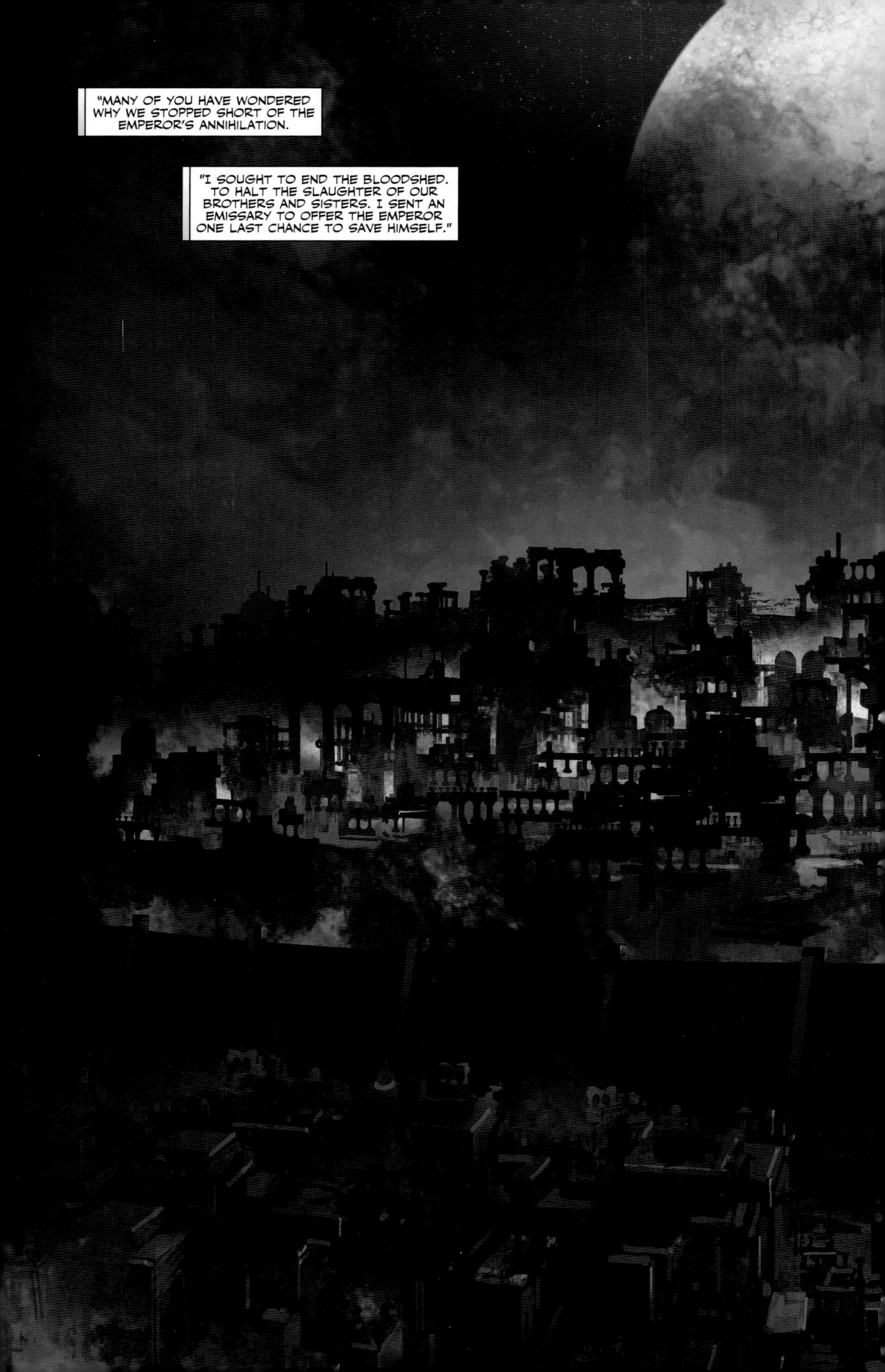
"MANY OF YOU HAVE WONDERED WHY WE STOPPED SHORT OF THE EMPEROR'S ANNIHILATION.
"I SOUGHT TO END THE BLOODSHED. TO HALT THE SLAUGHTER OF OUR BROTHERS AND SISTERS. I SENT AN EMISSARY TO OFFER THE EMPEROR ONE LAST CHANCE TO SAVE HIMSELF."

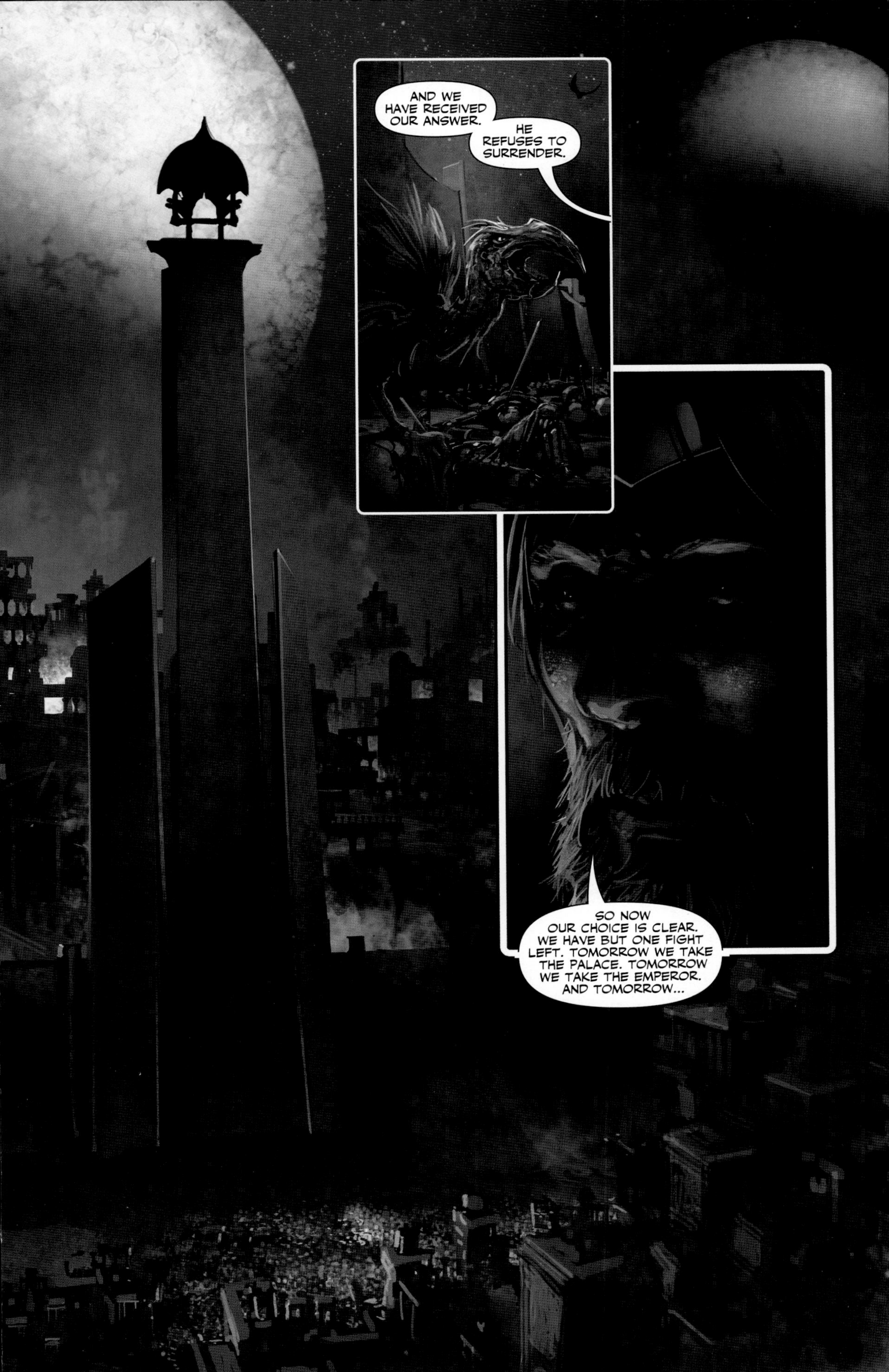
AND WE HAVE RECEIVED OUR ANSWER.
HE REFUSES TO SURRENDER.
SO NOW OUR CHOICE IS CLEAR. WE HAVE BUT ONE FIGHT LEFT. TOMORROW WE TAKE THE PALACE. TOMORROW WE TAKE THE EMPEROR. AND TOMORROW...

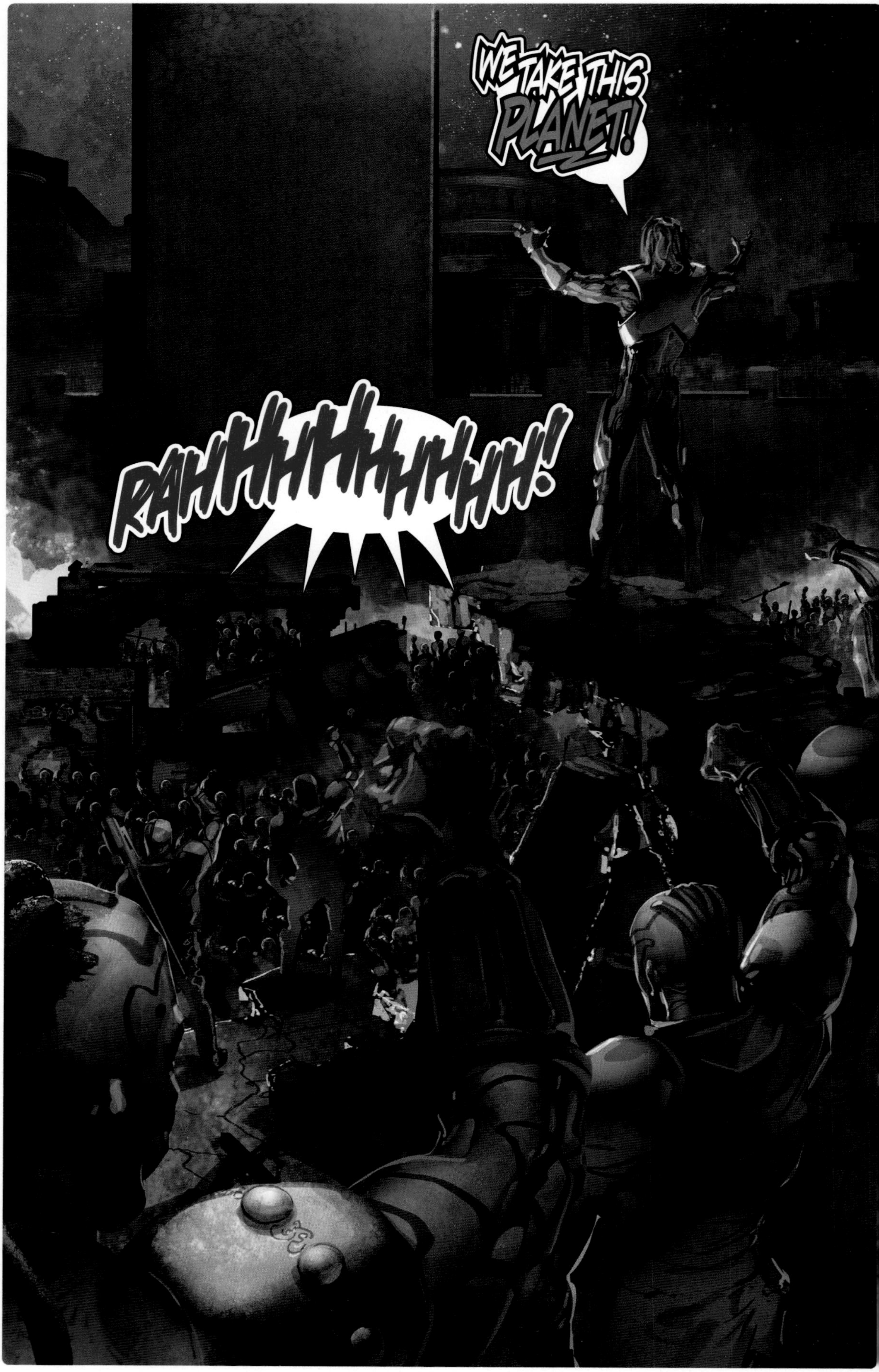
WE TAKE THIS PLANET!
RAHHHHHHHHHHH!

WE ARE ONE NIGHT FROM UNITING TRIBES THAT HAVE BEEN AT WAR SINCE THE BEGINNING OF TIME.

ONE FIGHT FROM UNITING THIS PLANET! ONE NIGHT FROM ACHIEVING PEACE AMONG THE BURNT, THE AZURE, AND THE CADMIUM.

THE LAST NIGHT WAS A HAZE OF MEMORIES.

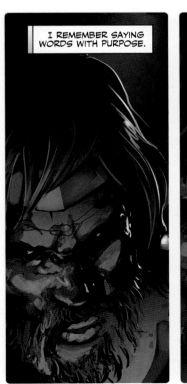

I REMEMBER SAYING WORDS WITH PURPOSE.

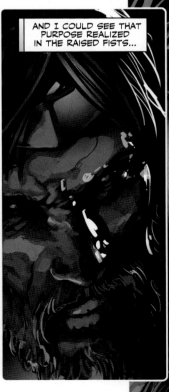

AND I COULD SEE THAT PURPOSE REALIZED IN THE RAISED FISTS...

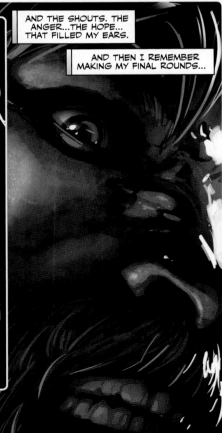

AND THE SHOUTS. THE ANGER...THE HOPE... THAT FILLED MY EARS.

AND THEN I REMEMBER MAKING MY FINAL ROUNDS...

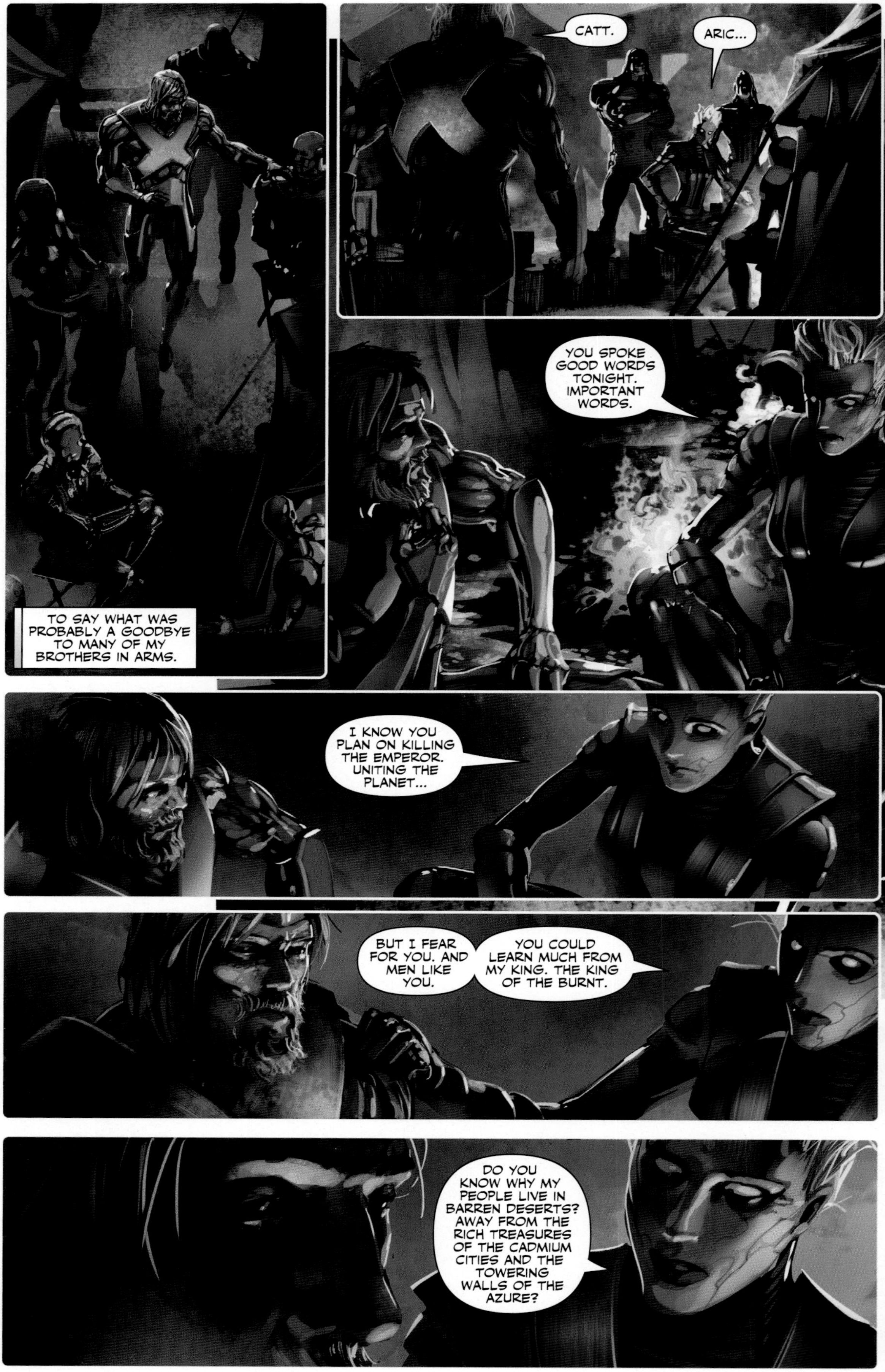
TO SAY WHAT WAS PROBABLY A GOODBYE TO MANY OF MY BROTHERS IN ARMS.
CATT.
ARIC...
YOU SPOKE GOOD WORDS TONIGHT. IMPORTANT WORDS.
I KNOW YOU PLAN ON KILLING THE EMPEROR. UNITING THE PLANET...
BUT I FEAR FOR YOU. AND MEN LIKE YOU.
YOU COULD LEARN MUCH FROM MY KING. THE KING OF THE BURNT.
DO YOU KNOW WHY MY PEOPLE LIVE IN BARREN DESERTS? AWAY FROM THE RICH TREASURES OF THE CADMIUM CITIES AND THE TOWERING WALLS OF THE AZURE?

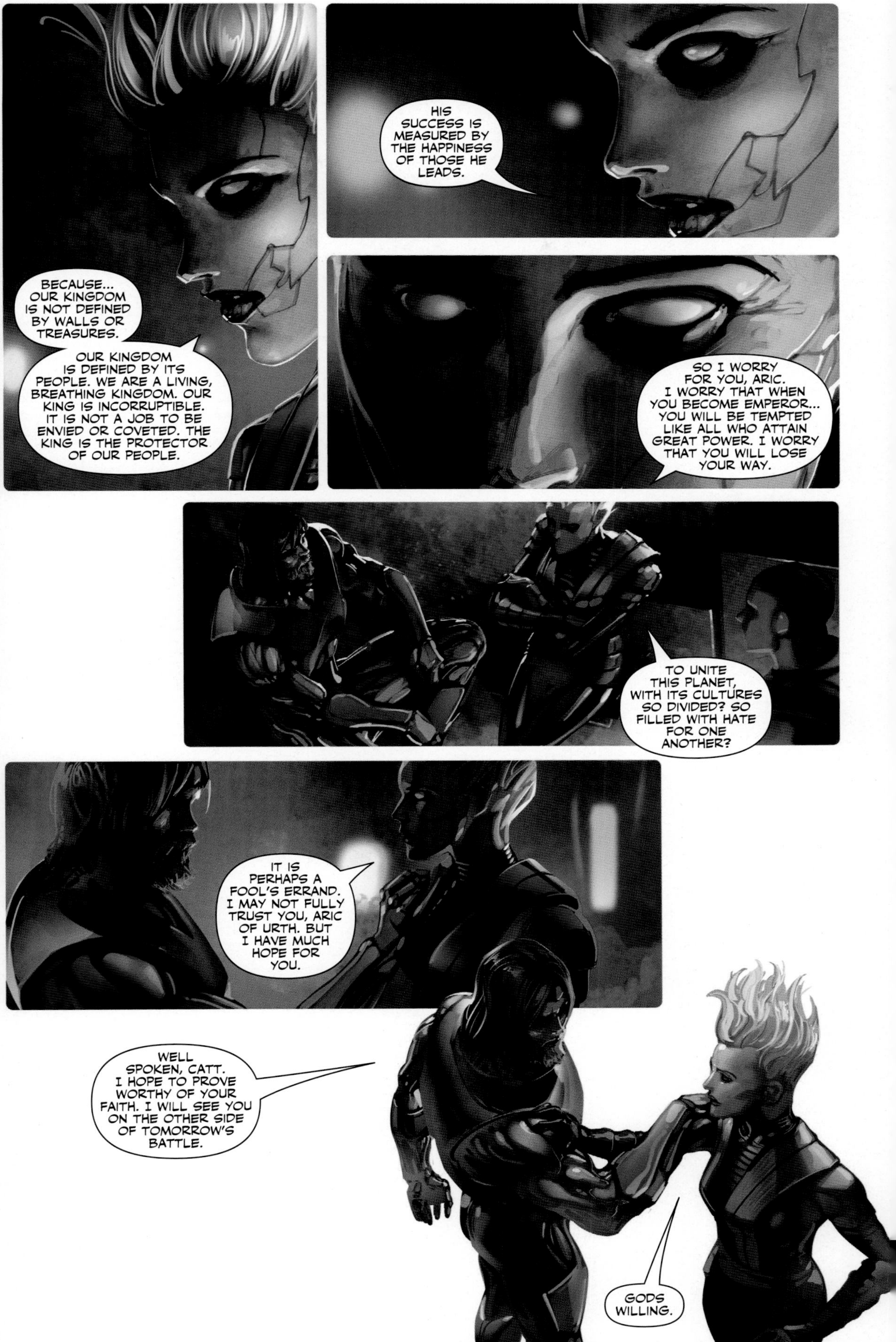
HIS SUCCESS IS MEASURED BY THE HAPPINESS OF THOSE HE LEADS.
BECAUSE... OUR KINGDOM IS NOT DEFINED BY WALLS OR TREASURES.
OUR KINGDOM IS DEFINED BY ITS PEOPLE. WE ARE A LIVING, BREATHING KINGDOM. OUR KING IS INCORRUPTIBLE. IT IS NOT A JOB TO BE ENVIED OR COVETED. THE KING IS THE PROTECTOR OF OUR PEOPLE.
SO I WORRY FOR YOU, ARIC. I WORRY THAT WHEN YOU BECOME EMPEROR... YOU WILL BE TEMPTED LIKE ALL WHO ATTAIN GREAT POWER. I WORRY THAT YOU WILL LOSE YOUR WAY.
TO UNITE THIS PLANET, WITH ITS CULTURES SO DIVIDED? SO FILLED WITH HATE FOR ONE ANOTHER?
IT IS PERHAPS A FOOL'S ERRAND. I MAY NOT FULLY TRUST YOU, ARIC OF URTH. BUT I HAVE MUCH HOPE FOR YOU.
WELL SPOKEN, CATT. I HOPE TO PROVE WORTHY OF YOUR FAITH. I WILL SEE YOU ON THE OTHER SIDE OF TOMORROW'S BATTLE.
GODS WILLING.

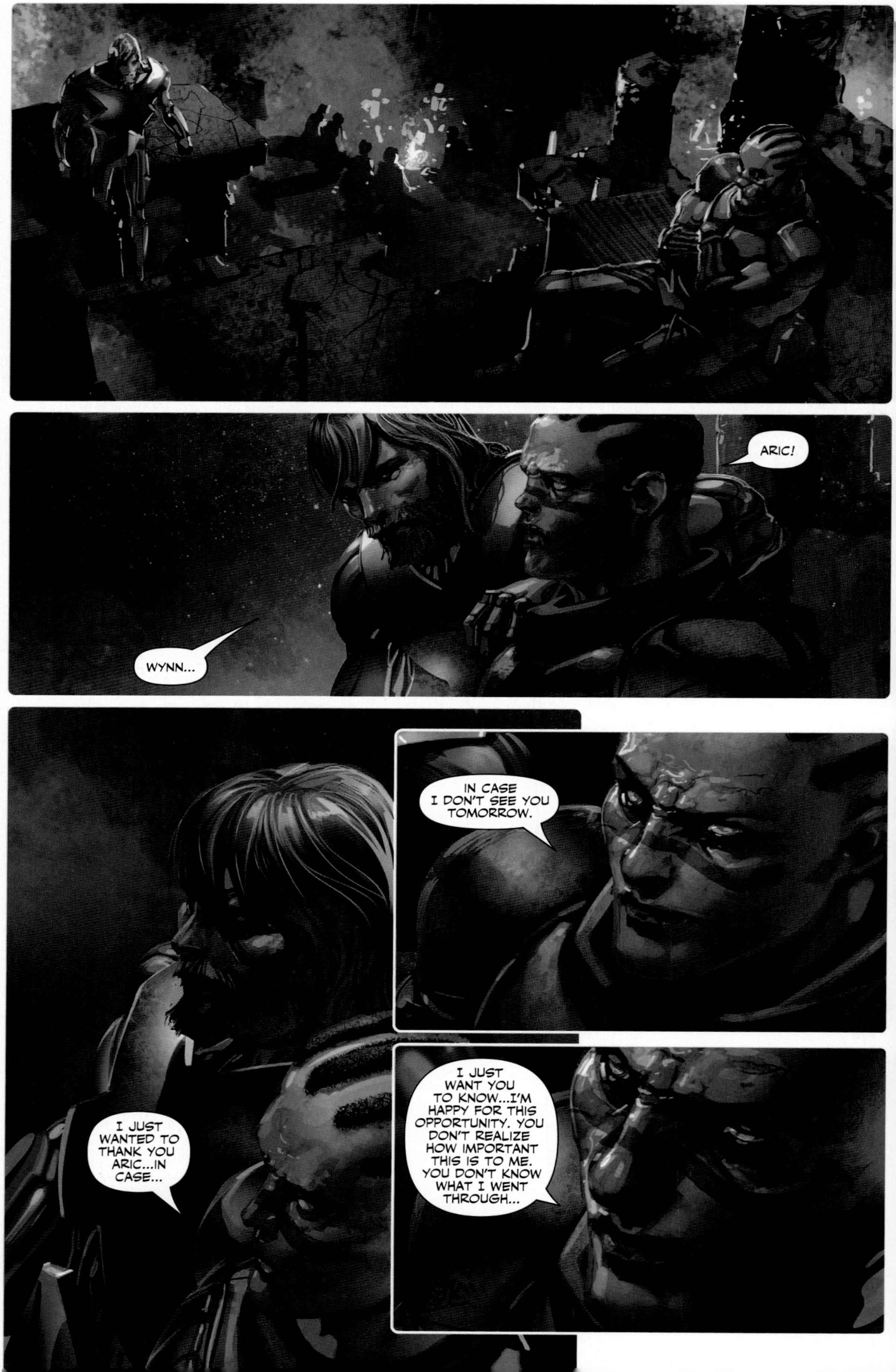
ARIC!
WYNN...
I JUST WANTED TO THANK YOU ARIC...IN CASE...
IN CASE I DON'T SEE YOU TOMORROW.
I JUST WANT YOU TO KNOW...I'M HAPPY FOR THIS OPPORTUNITY. YOU DON'T REALIZE HOW IMPORTANT THIS IS TO ME. YOU DON'T KNOW WHAT I WENT THROUGH...

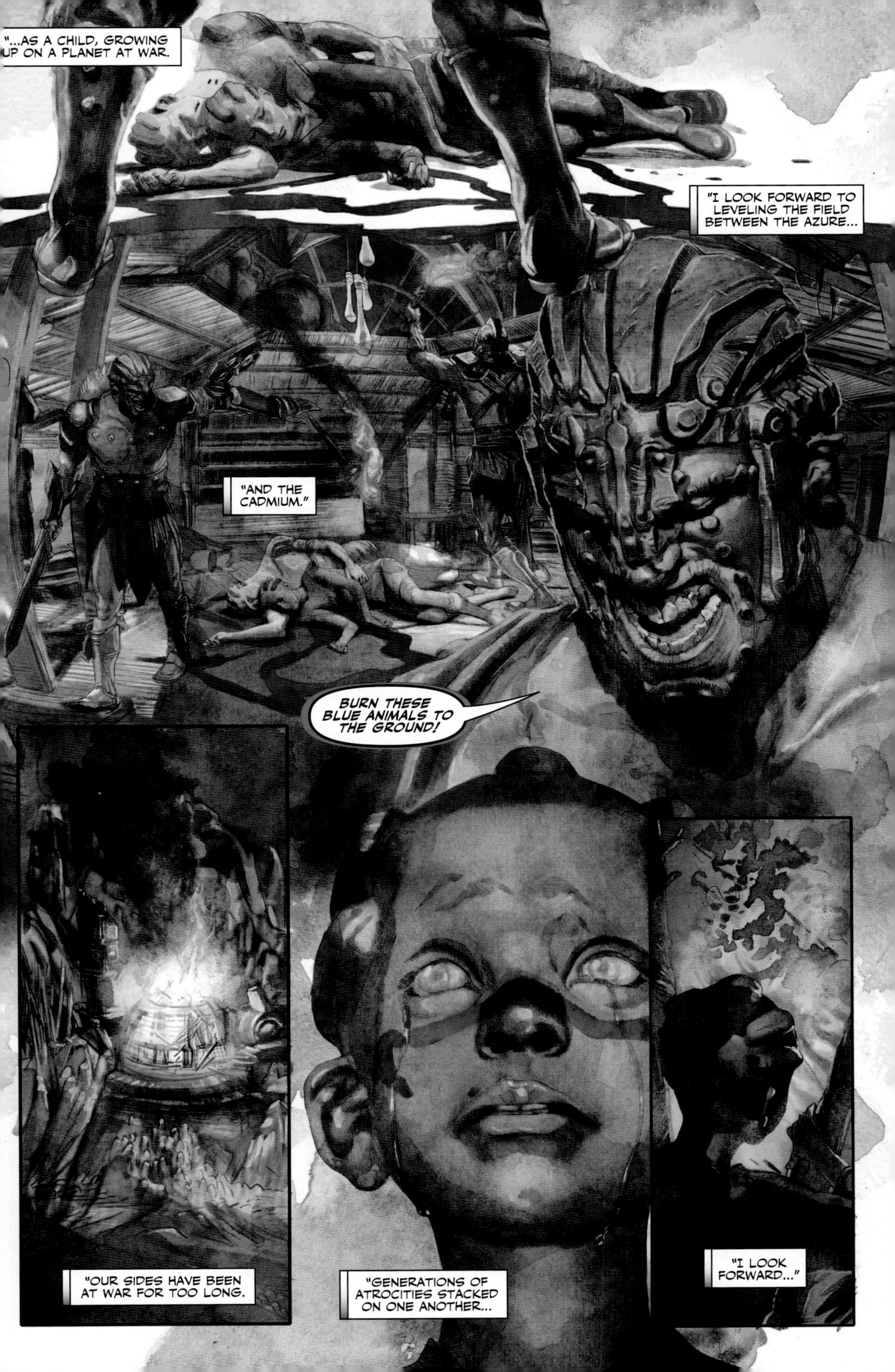
"...AS A CHILD, GROWING UP ON A PLANET AT WAR.
"I LOOK FORWARD TO LEVELING THE FIELD BETWEEN THE AZURE...
"AND THE CADMIUM."
BURN THESE BLUE ANIMALS TO THE GROUND!
"OUR SIDES HAVE BEEN AT WAR FOR TOO LONG.
"GENERATIONS OF ATROCITIES STACKED ON ONE ANOTHER...
"I LOOK FORWARD..."

I *RELISH* THE CHANCE TO *SET THINGS RIGHT.* YOU DON'T REALIZE HOW MUCH THIS MEANS TO ME.

SLEEP WELL, WYNN. TOMORROW WE WILL HAVE OUR VICTORY.

BRUTO?

COME IN.

WELCOME, GENERAL. PLEASE. LET US BREAK BREAD THIS NIGHT BEFORE HISTORY IS MADE.

LAST MINUTE NERVES? THERE IS NO NEED TO WORRY. MY SPIES IN THE PALACE HAVE NOT FAILED US YET. THE PALACE IS VULNERABLE AT THE FRONT GATE. COUNTERINTUITIVE, BUT THE DESIGN FLAW THERE GIVES US OUR BEST CHANCE.

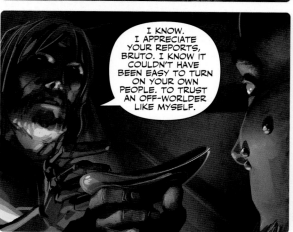

I KNOW. I APPRECIATE YOUR REPORTS, BRUTO. I KNOW IT COULDN'T HAVE BEEN EASY TO TURN ON YOUR OWN PEOPLE. TO TRUST AN OFF-WORLDER LIKE MYSELF.

NO, ARIC...

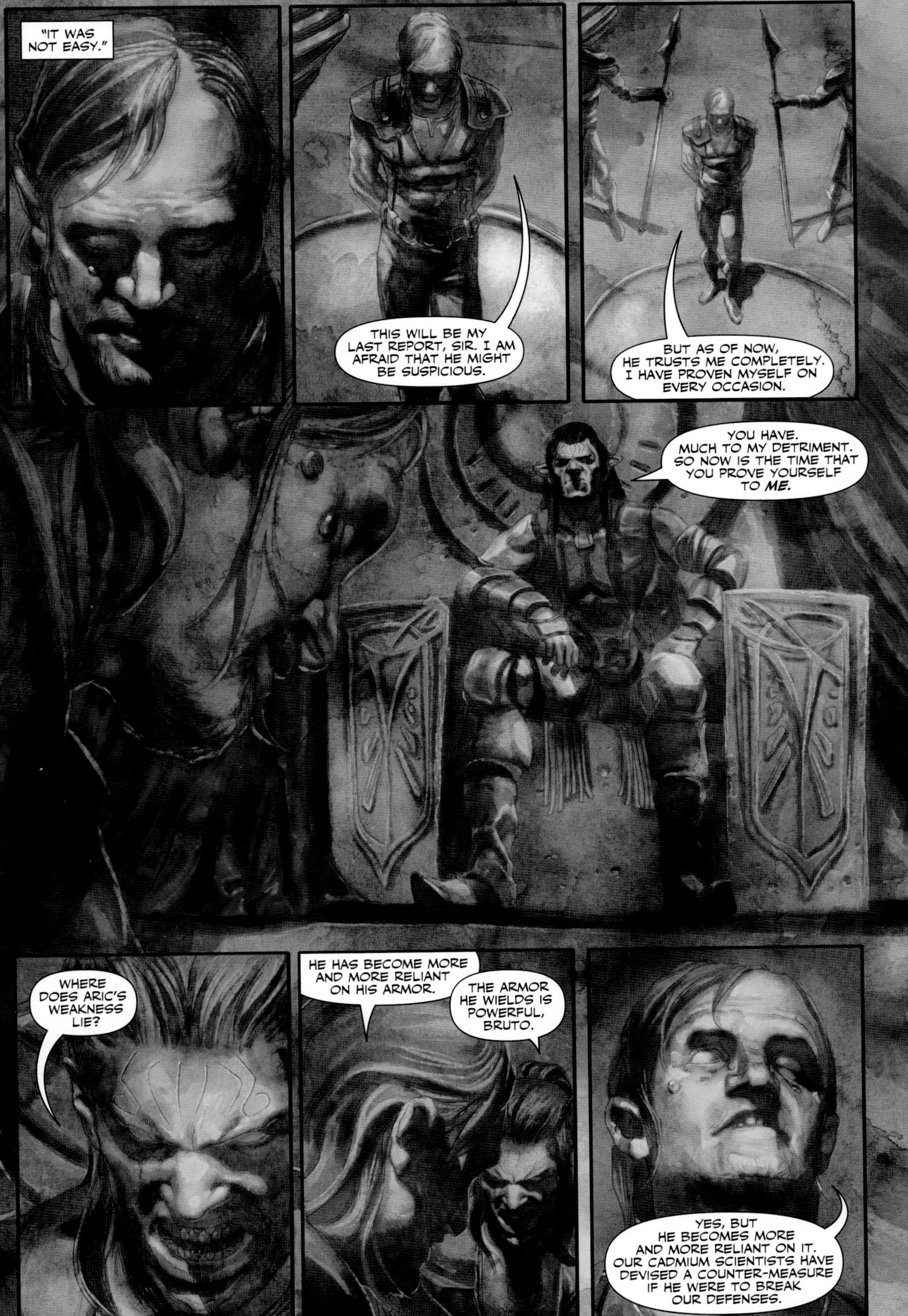
"IT WAS NOT EASY."
THIS WILL BE MY LAST REPORT, SIR. I AM AFRAID THAT HE MIGHT BE SUSPICIOUS.
BUT AS OF NOW, HE TRUSTS ME COMPLETELY. I HAVE PROVEN MYSELF ON EVERY OCCASION.
YOU HAVE. MUCH TO MY DETRIMENT. SO NOW IS THE TIME THAT YOU PROVE YOURSELF TO ***ME.***
WHERE DOES ARIC'S WEAKNESS LIE?
HE HAS BECOME MORE AND MORE RELIANT ON HIS ARMOR.
THE ARMOR HE WIELDS IS POWERFUL, BRUTO.
YES, BUT HE BECOMES MORE AND MORE RELIANT ON IT. OUR CADMIUM SCIENTISTS HAVE DEVISED A COUNTER-MEASURE IF HE WERE TO BREAK OUR DEFENSES.

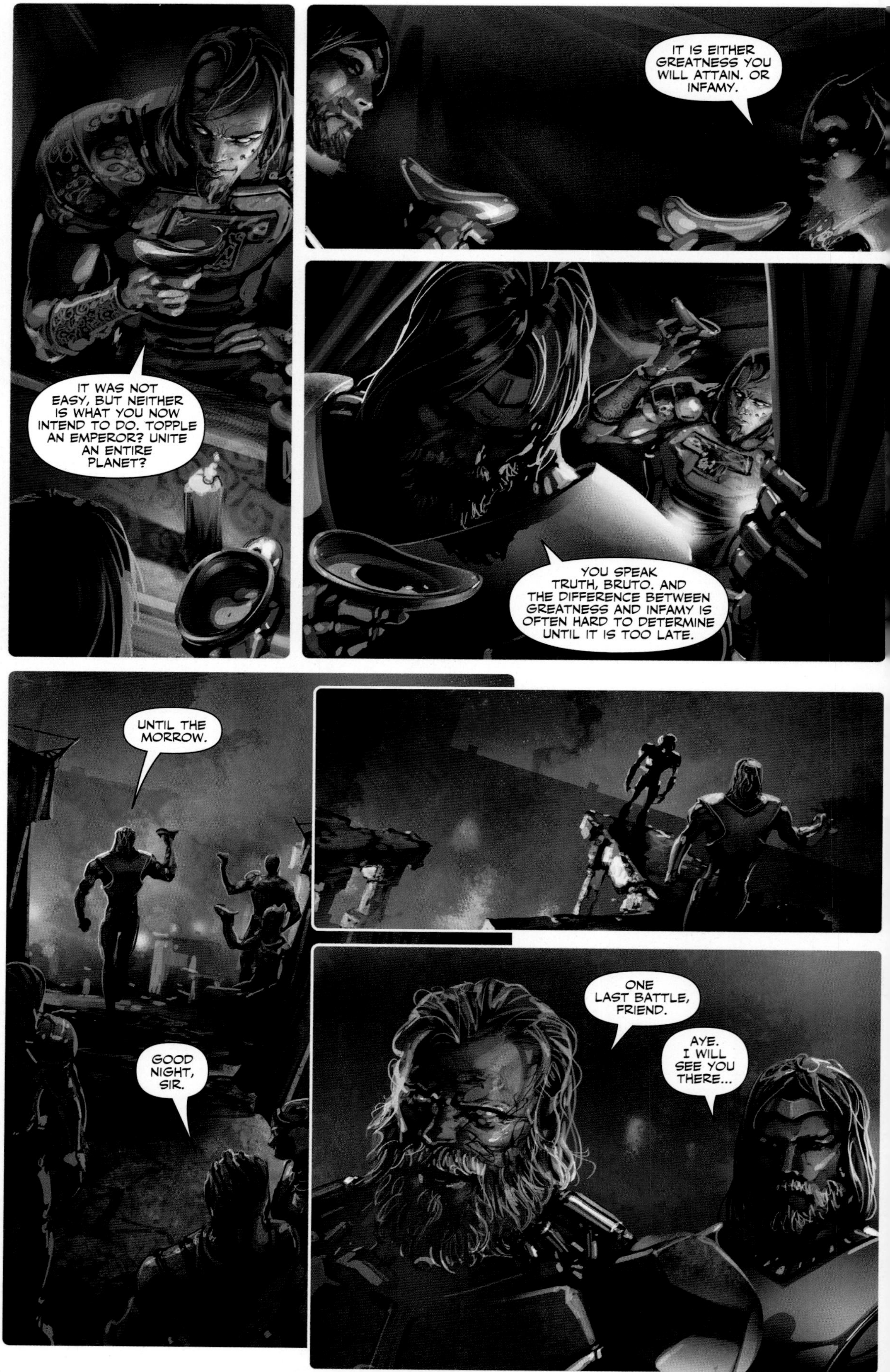
IT WAS NOT EASY, BUT NEITHER IS WHAT YOU NOW INTEND TO DO. TOPPLE AN EMPEROR? UNITE AN ENTIRE PLANET?
IT IS EITHER GREATNESS YOU WILL ATTAIN. OR INFAMY.
YOU SPEAK TRUTH, BRUTO. AND THE DIFFERENCE BETWEEN GREATNESS AND INFAMY IS OFTEN HARD TO DETERMINE UNTIL IT IS TOO LATE.
UNTIL THE MORROW.
GOOD NIGHT, SIR.
ONE LAST BATTLE, FRIEND.
AYE. I WILL SEE YOU THERE...

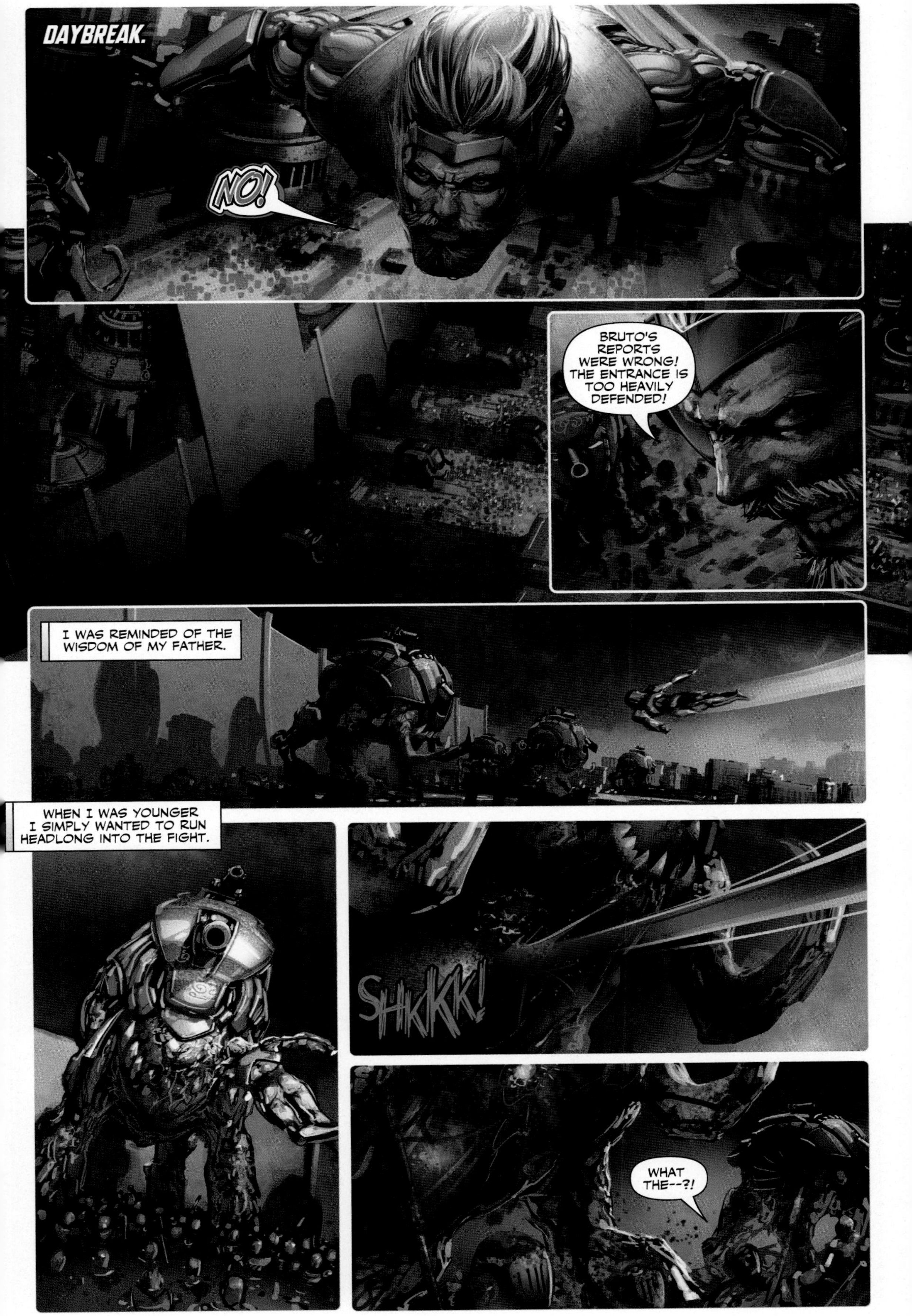
DAYBREAK.
NO!
BRUTO'S REPORTS WERE WRONG! THE ENTRANCE IS TOO HEAVILY DEFENDED!
I WAS REMINDED OF THE WISDOM OF MY FATHER.
WHEN I WAS YOUNGER I SIMPLY WANTED TO RUN HEADLONG INTO THE FIGHT.
SHKKK!
WHAT THE--?!

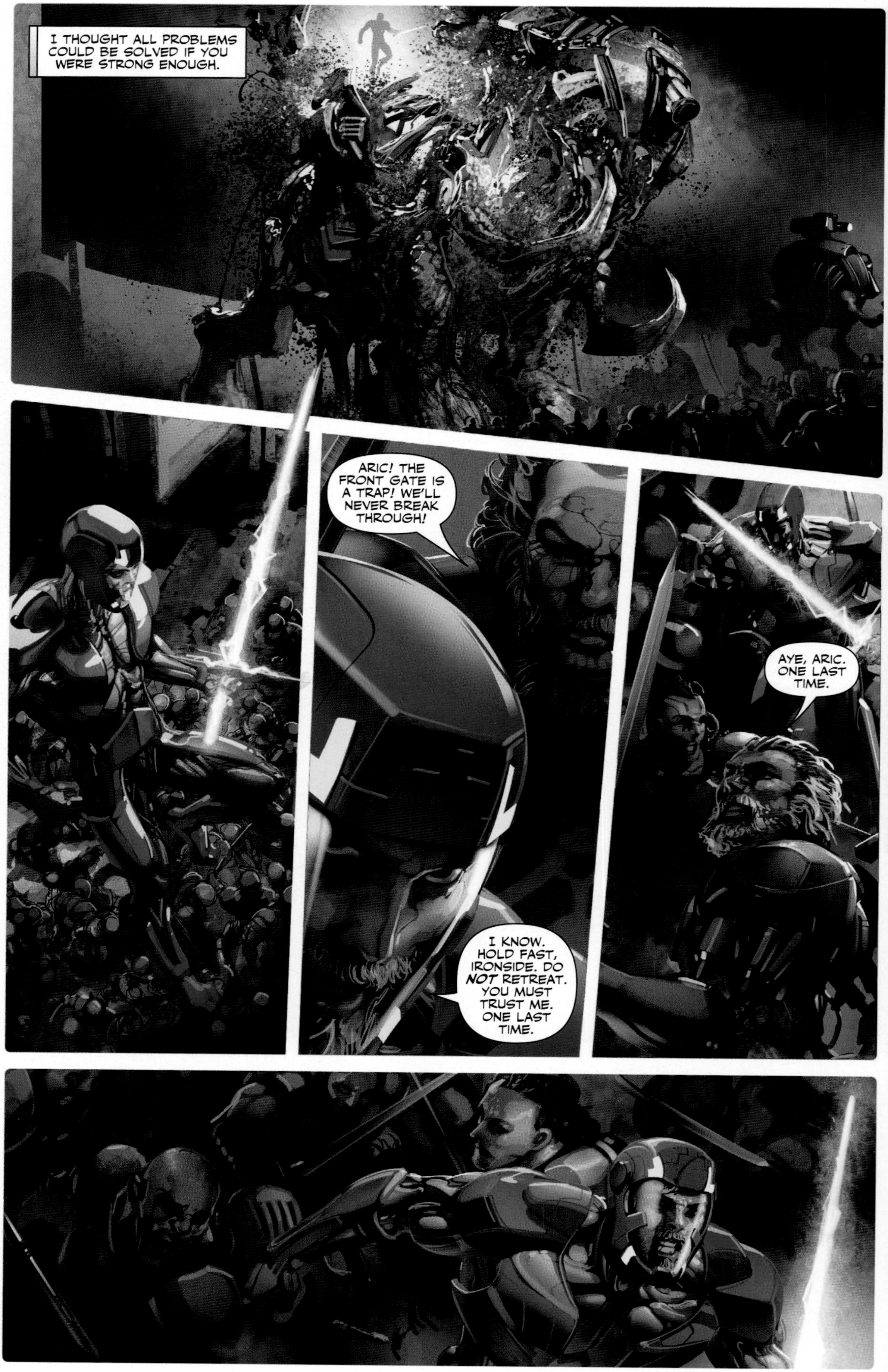
I THOUGHT ALL PROBLEMS COULD BE SOLVED IF YOU WERE STRONG ENOUGH.
ARIC! THE FRONT GATE IS A TRAP! WE'LL NEVER BREAK THROUGH!
I KNOW. HOLD FAST, IRONSIDE. DO *NOT* RETREAT. YOU MUST TRUST ME. ONE LAST TIME.
AYE, ARIC. ONE LAST TIME.

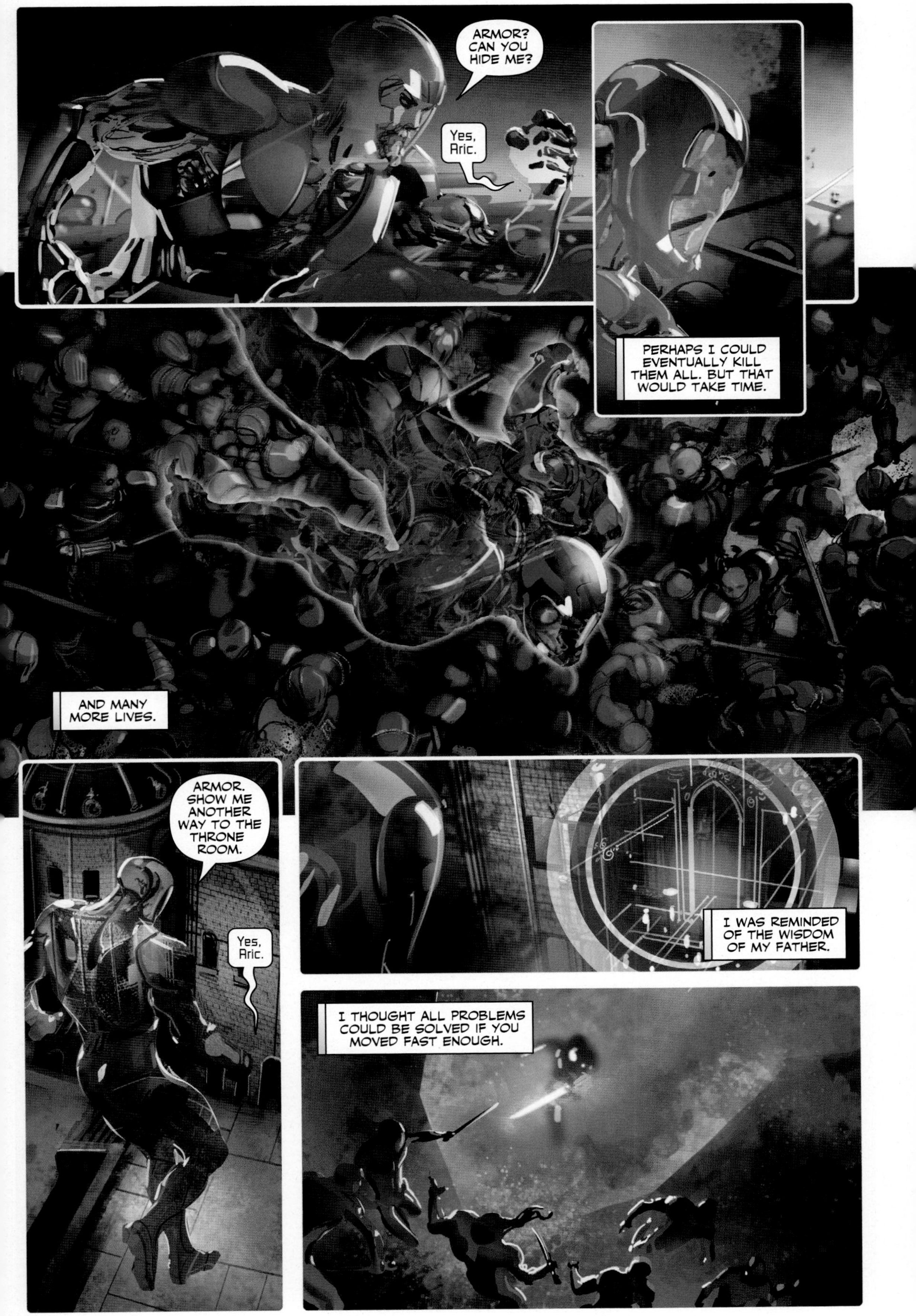
ARMOR? CAN YOU HIDE ME?
Yes, Aric.
PERHAPS I COULD EVENTUALLY KILL THEM ALL. BUT THAT WOULD TAKE TIME.
AND MANY MORE LIVES.
ARMOR. SHOW ME ANOTHER WAY TO THE THRONE ROOM.
Yes, Aric.
I WAS REMINDED OF THE WISDOM OF MY FATHER.
I THOUGHT ALL PROBLEMS COULD BE SOLVED IF YOU MOVED FAST ENOUGH.

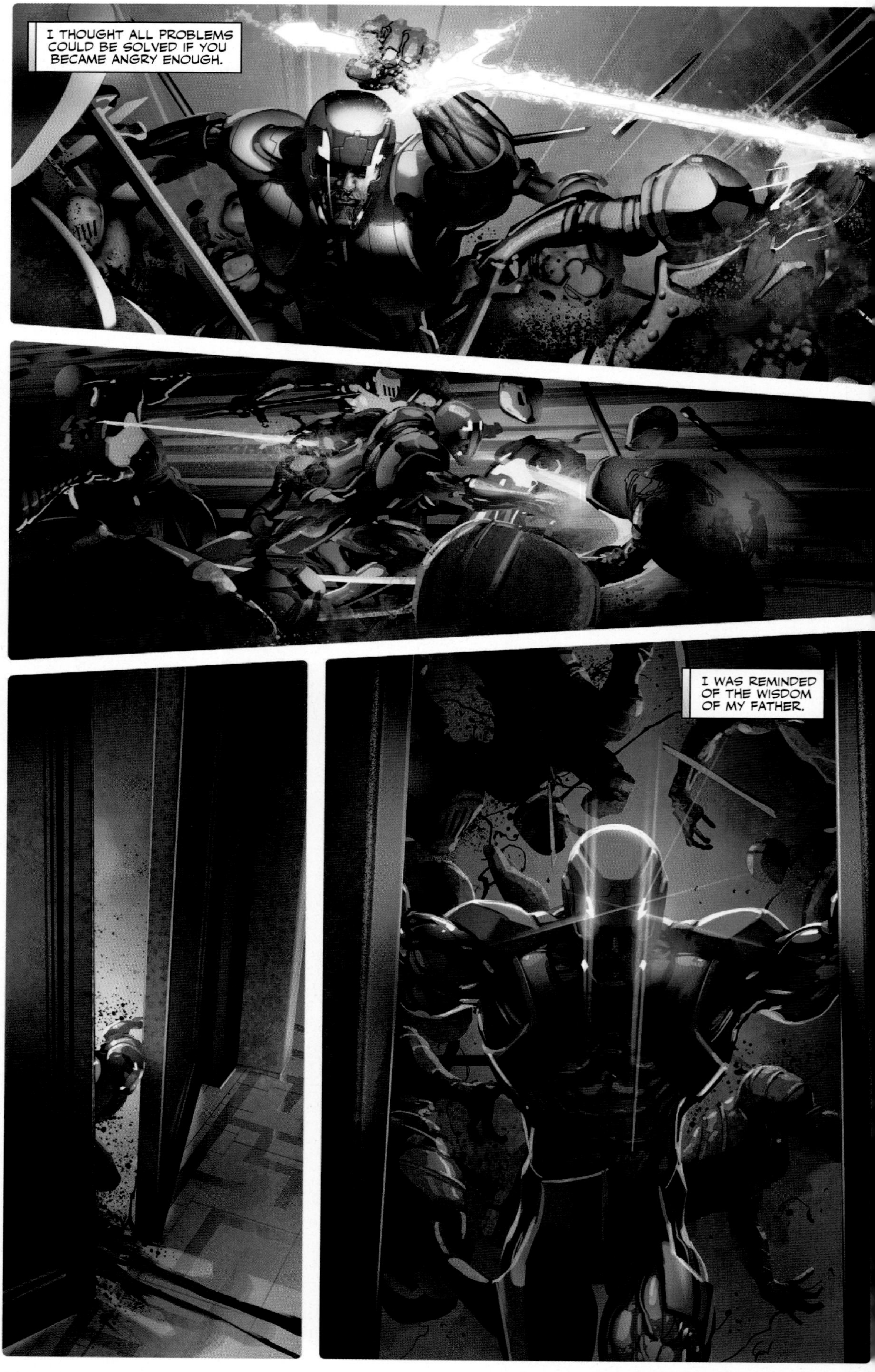
I THOUGHT ALL PROBLEMS COULD BE SOLVED IF YOU BECAME ANGRY ENOUGH.
I WAS REMINDED OF THE WISDOM OF MY FATHER.

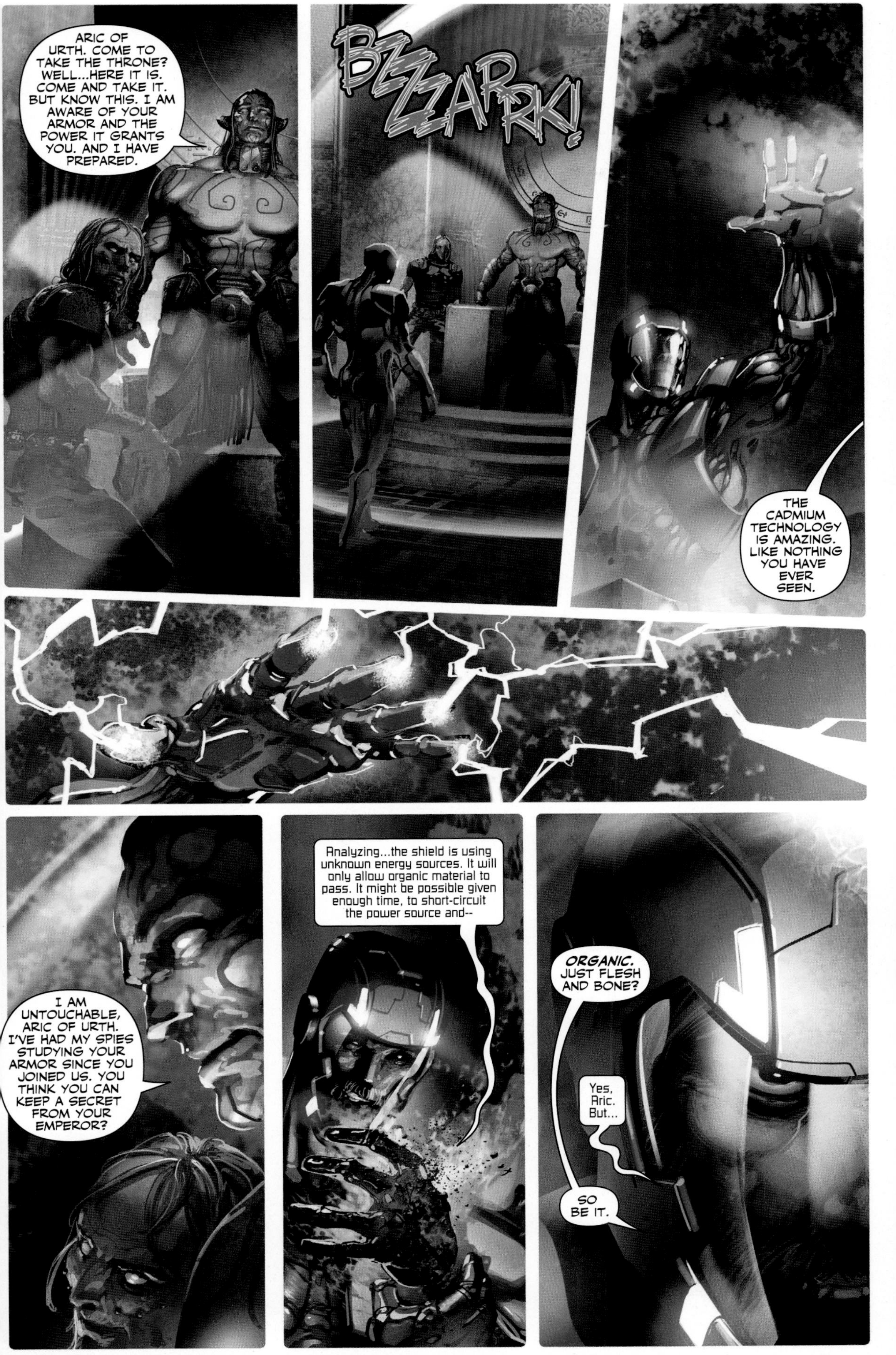
ARIC OF URTH. COME TO TAKE THE THRONE? WELL...HERE IT IS. COME AND TAKE IT. BUT KNOW THIS. I AM AWARE OF YOUR ARMOR AND THE POWER IT GRANTS YOU. AND I HAVE PREPARED.
BZZZARRK!
THE CADMIUM TECHNOLOGY IS AMAZING. LIKE NOTHING YOU HAVE EVER SEEN.
I AM UNTOUCHABLE, ARIC OF URTH. I'VE HAD MY SPIES STUDYING YOUR ARMOR SINCE YOU JOINED US. YOU THINK YOU CAN KEEP A SECRET FROM YOUR EMPEROR?
Analyzing...the shield is using unknown energy sources. It will only allow organic material to pass. It might be possible given enough time, to short-circuit the power source and--
ORGANIC. JUST FLESH AND BONE?
Yes, Aric. But...
SO BE IT.

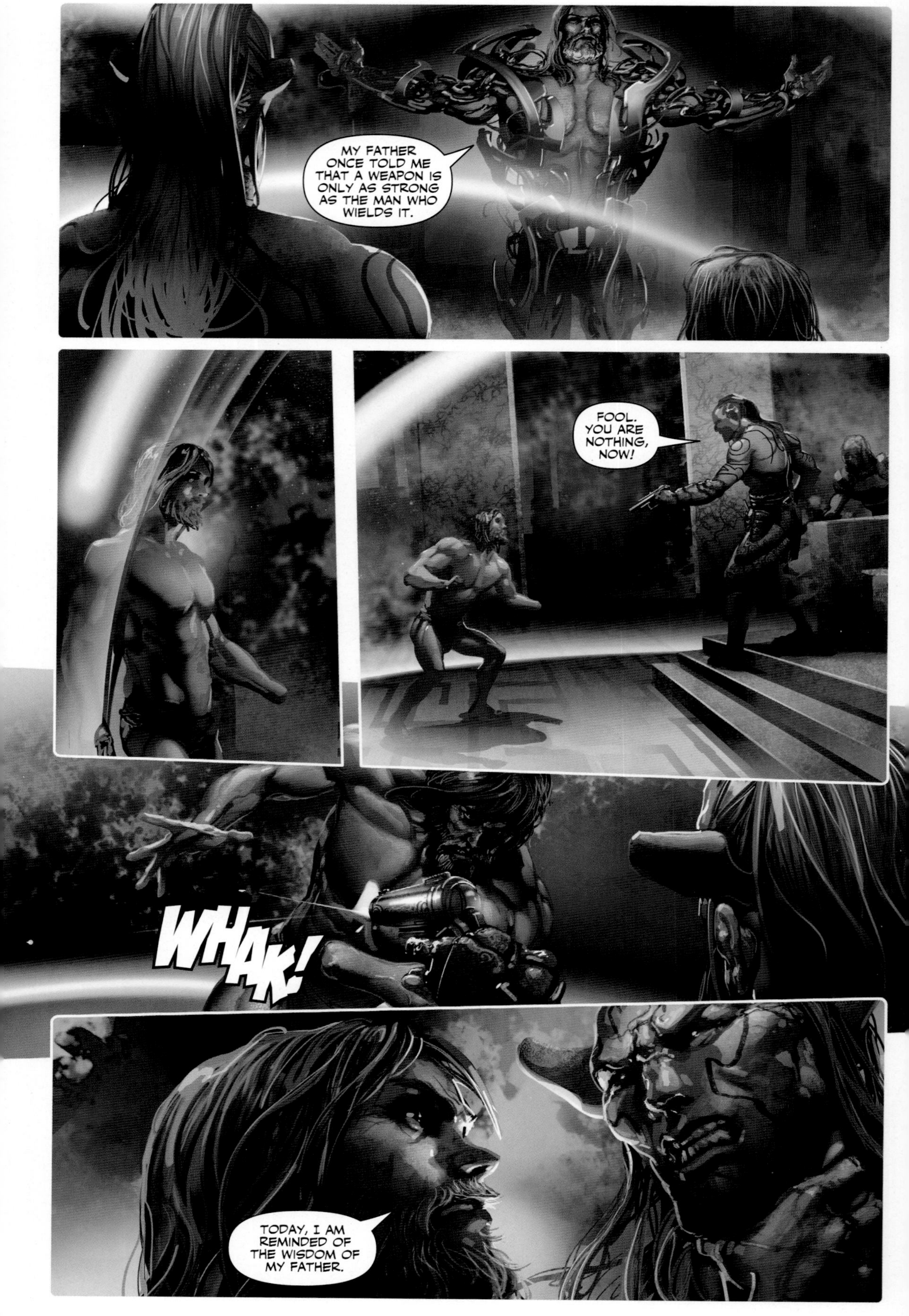
MY FATHER ONCE TOLD ME THAT A WEAPON IS ONLY AS STRONG AS THE MAN WHO WIELDS IT.
FOOL. YOU ARE NOTHING, NOW!
WHAK!
TODAY, I AM REMINDED OF THE WISDOM OF MY FATHER.

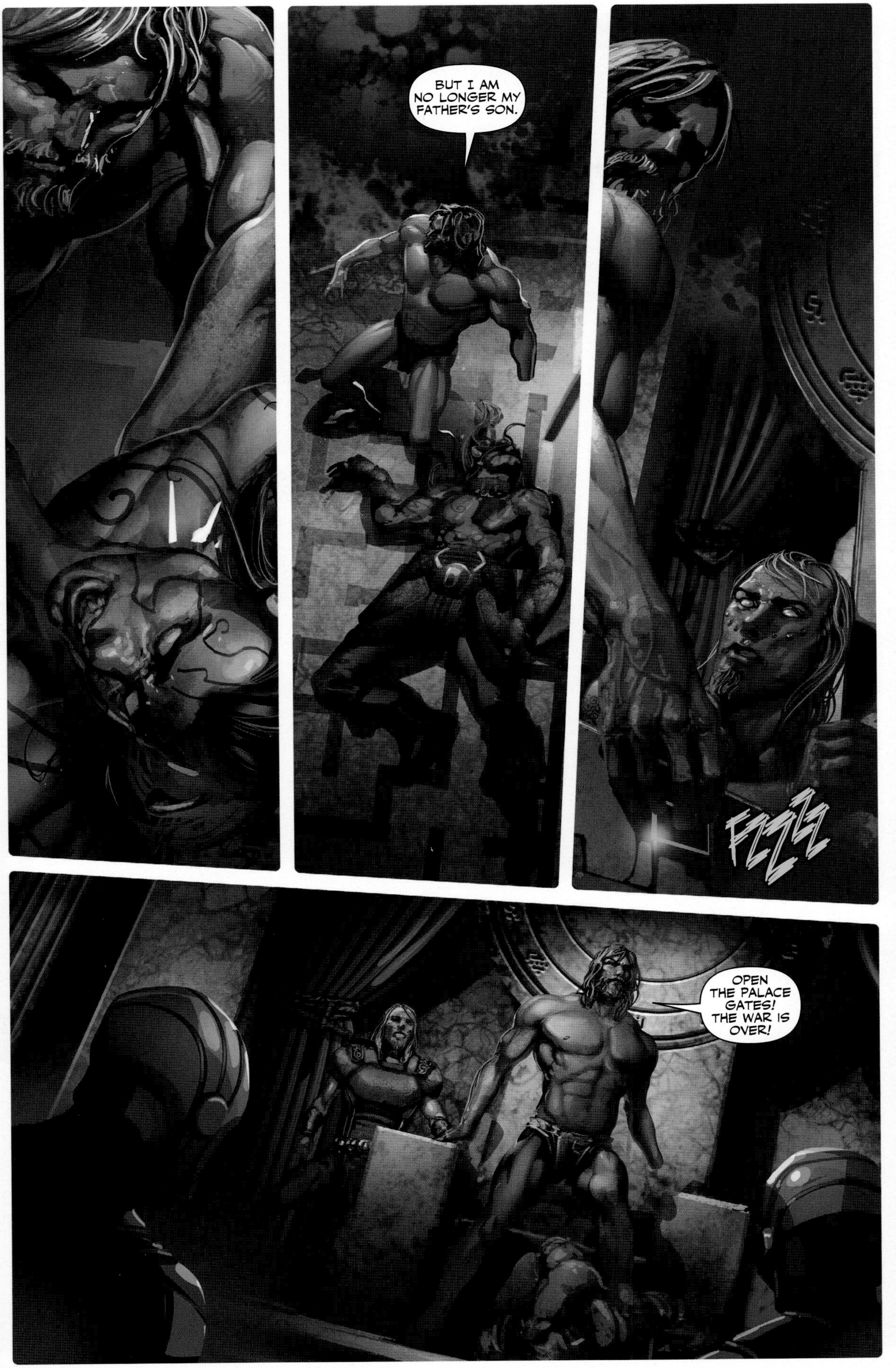
BUT I AM NO LONGER MY FATHER'S SON.
FZZZZ
OPEN THE PALACE GATES! THE WAR IS OVER!

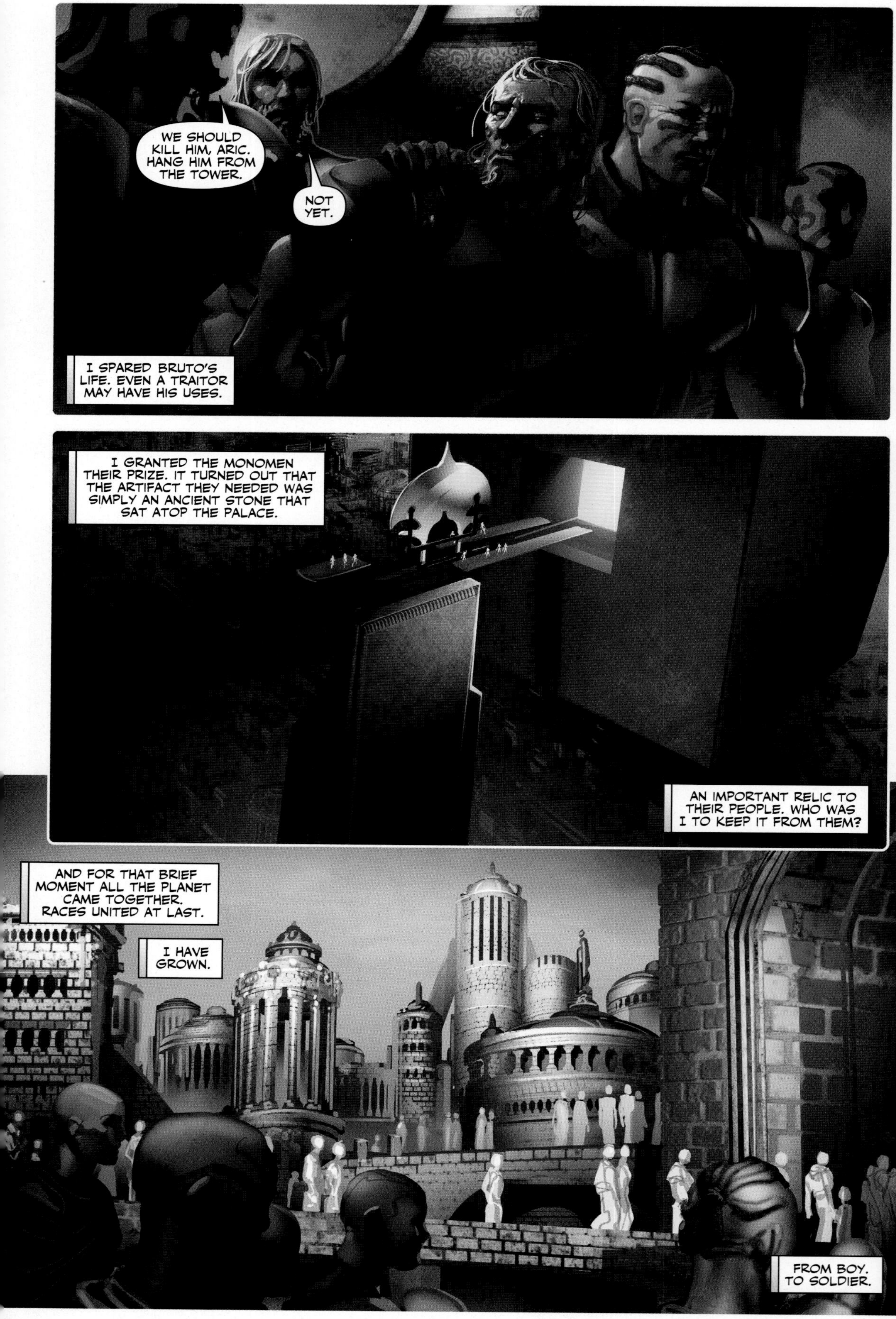
WE SHOULD KILL HIM, ARIC. HANG HIM FROM THE TOWER.
NOT YET.
I SPARED BRUTO'S LIFE. EVEN A TRAITOR MAY HAVE HIS USES.
I GRANTED THE MONOMEN THEIR PRIZE. IT TURNED OUT THAT THE ARTIFACT THEY NEEDED WAS SIMPLY AN ANCIENT STONE THAT SAT ATOP THE PALACE.
AN IMPORTANT RELIC TO THEIR PEOPLE. WHO WAS I TO KEEP IT FROM THEM?
AND FOR THAT BRIEF MOMENT ALL THE PLANET CAME TOGETHER. RACES UNITED AT LAST.
I HAVE GROWN.
FROM BOY. TO SOLDIER.

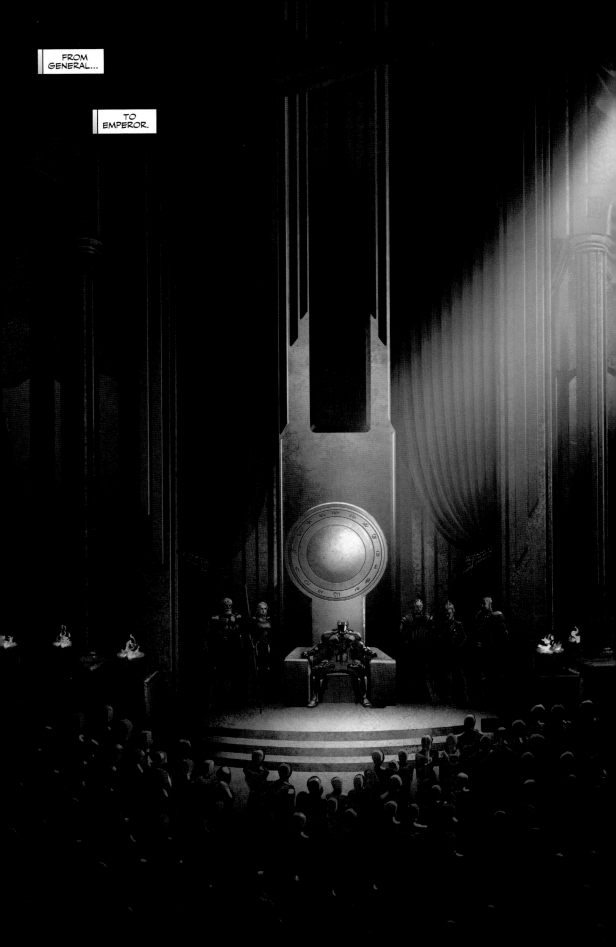

FROM
GENERAL...

TO
EMPEROR.

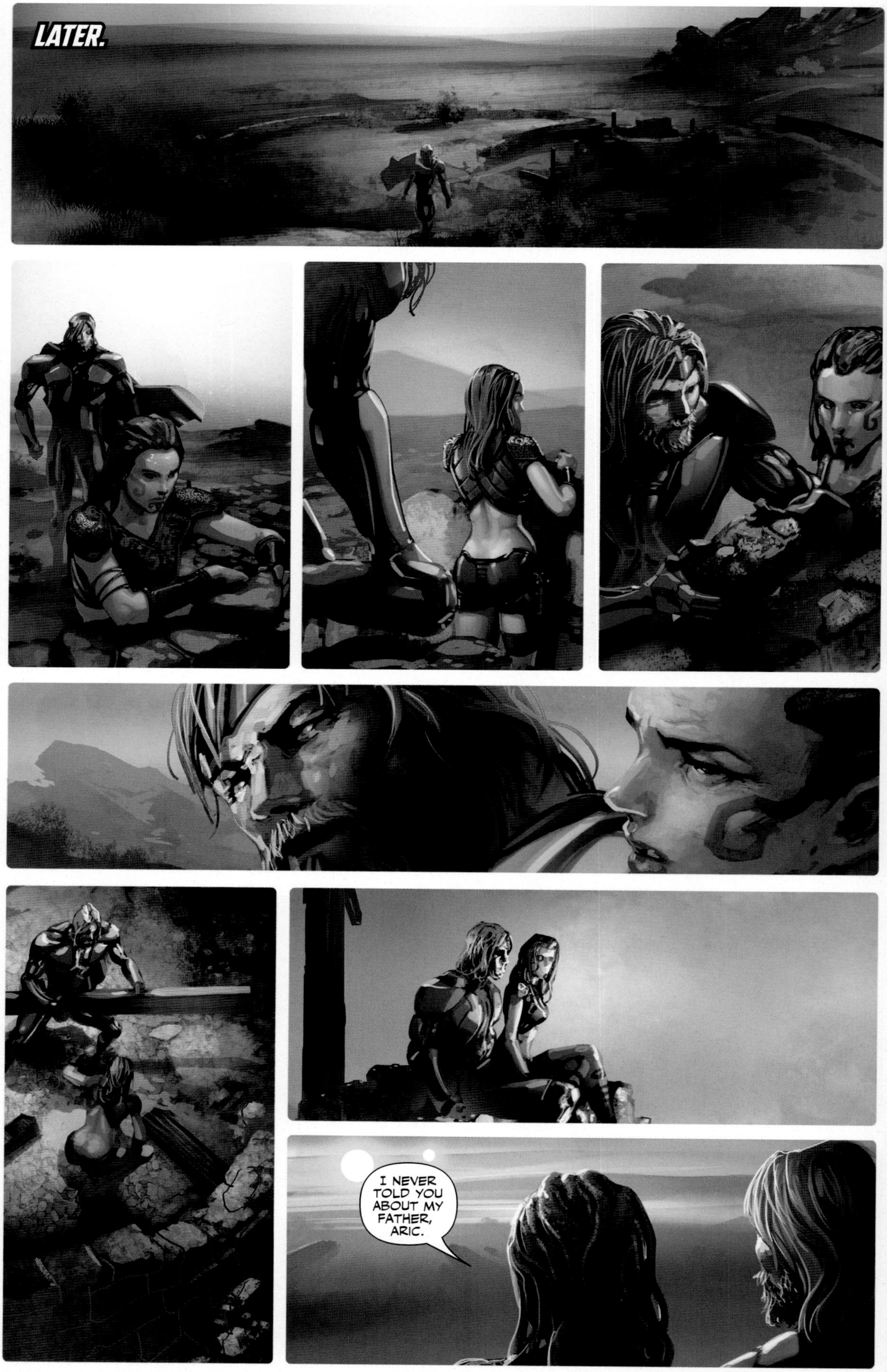
LATER.
I NEVER TOLD YOU ABOUT MY FATHER, ARIC.

DURING THE FIRST RACE WAR, WHEN I WAS FOURTEEN, MY FATHER BELIEVED IN THE FIGHT. HE VOLUNTEERED FOR THE AZURE ARMY.

HE WAS SO EXCITED TO HELP THE WAR EFFORT. I REMEMBER...I REMEMBER DECORATING HIS HELMET FOR HIM. I WAS NAÏVE. I WAS A KID. I'D SHARED HIS ENTHUSIASM.

I'D PUT MY HANDPRINT ON HIS HELMET WITH PAINT. MADE IT INTO A FLOWER.

HE LEFT ME, MY MOTHER, AND MY SMALL BROTHER TO JOIN THE FIGHT.

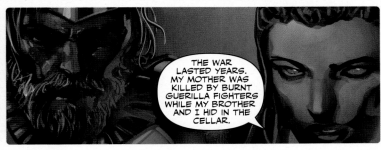

THE WAR LASTED YEARS. MY MOTHER WAS KILLED BY BURNT GUERILLA FIGHTERS WHILE MY BROTHER AND I HID IN THE CELLAR.

EVENTUALLY MY BROTHER CAUGHT A BUG. DIED OF THE SICKNESS.

AND I SAW IT. I SAW MY FATHER'S HELMET. THE HELMET HE HAD GONE TO WAR WITH. IT STILL HAD MY HANDPRINT--THE FLOWER ON IT. BUT IT WAS BATTLE-WORN AND FADED.

IN TIME THE WAR ENDED. THE LOCAL TOWNSPEOPLE TOOK CARE OF ME. HELPED ME GET ON MY FEET AND GET THE FARM RUNNING AGAIN.

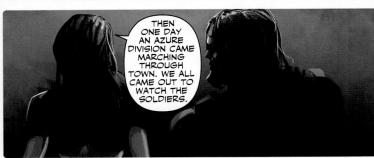

THEN ONE DAY AN AZURE DIVISION CAME MARCHING THROUGH TOWN. WE ALL CAME OUT TO WATCH THE SOLDIERS.

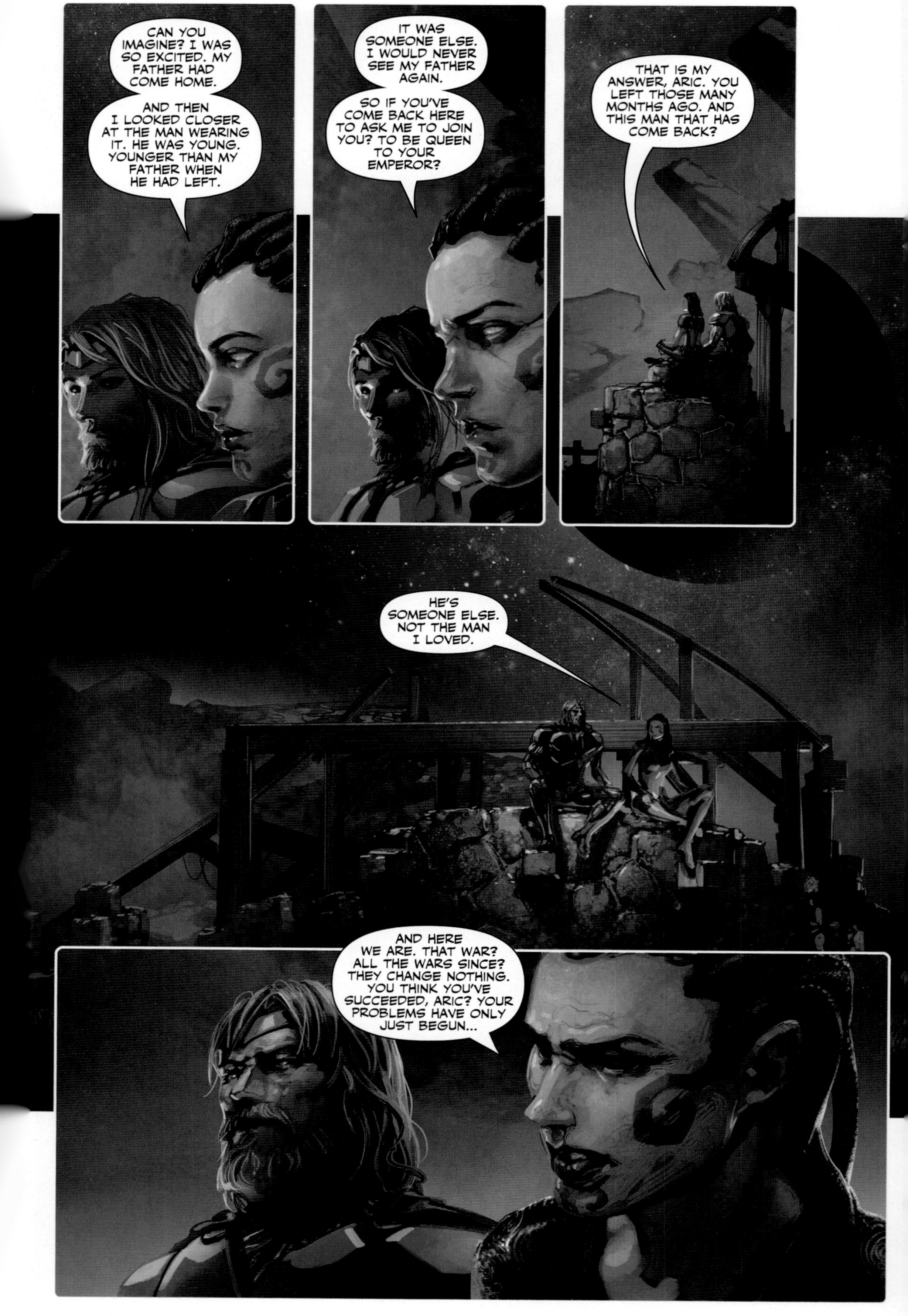
CAN YOU IMAGINE? I WAS SO EXCITED. MY FATHER HAD COME HOME.
AND THEN I LOOKED CLOSER AT THE MAN WEARING IT. HE WAS YOUNG. YOUNGER THAN MY FATHER WHEN HE HAD LEFT.
IT WAS SOMEONE ELSE. I WOULD NEVER SEE MY FATHER AGAIN.
SO IF YOU'VE COME BACK HERE TO ASK ME TO JOIN YOU? TO BE QUEEN TO YOUR EMPEROR?
THAT IS MY ANSWER, ARIC. YOU LEFT THOSE MANY MONTHS AGO. AND THIS MAN THAT HAS COME BACK?
HE'S SOMEONE ELSE. NOT THE MAN I LOVED.
AND HERE WE ARE. THAT WAR? ALL THE WARS SINCE? THEY CHANGE NOTHING. YOU THINK YOU'VE SUCCEEDED, ARIC? YOUR PROBLEMS HAVE ONLY JUST BEGUN...

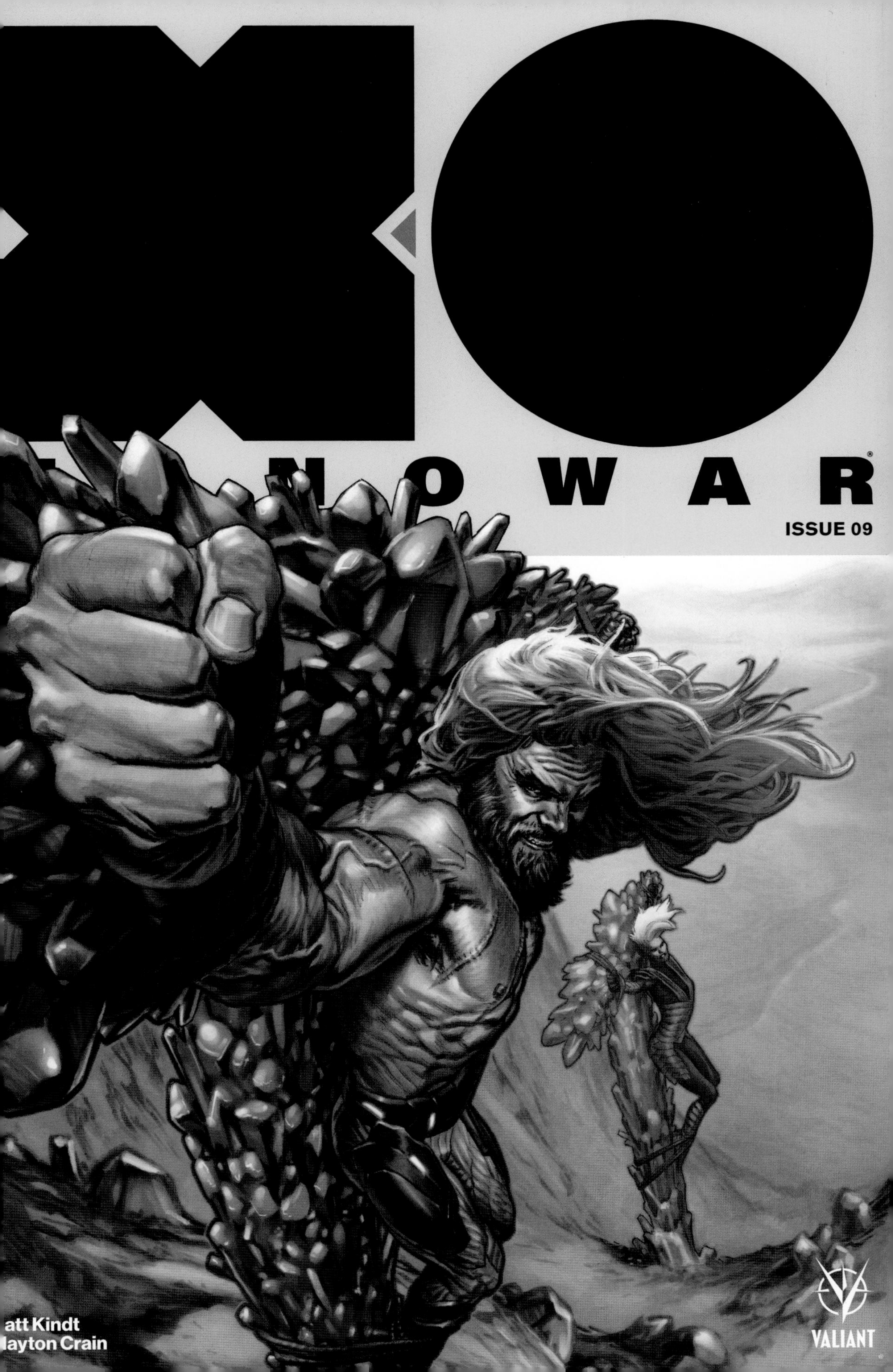
NOWAR
ISSUE 09
att Kindt
layton Crain
VALIANT

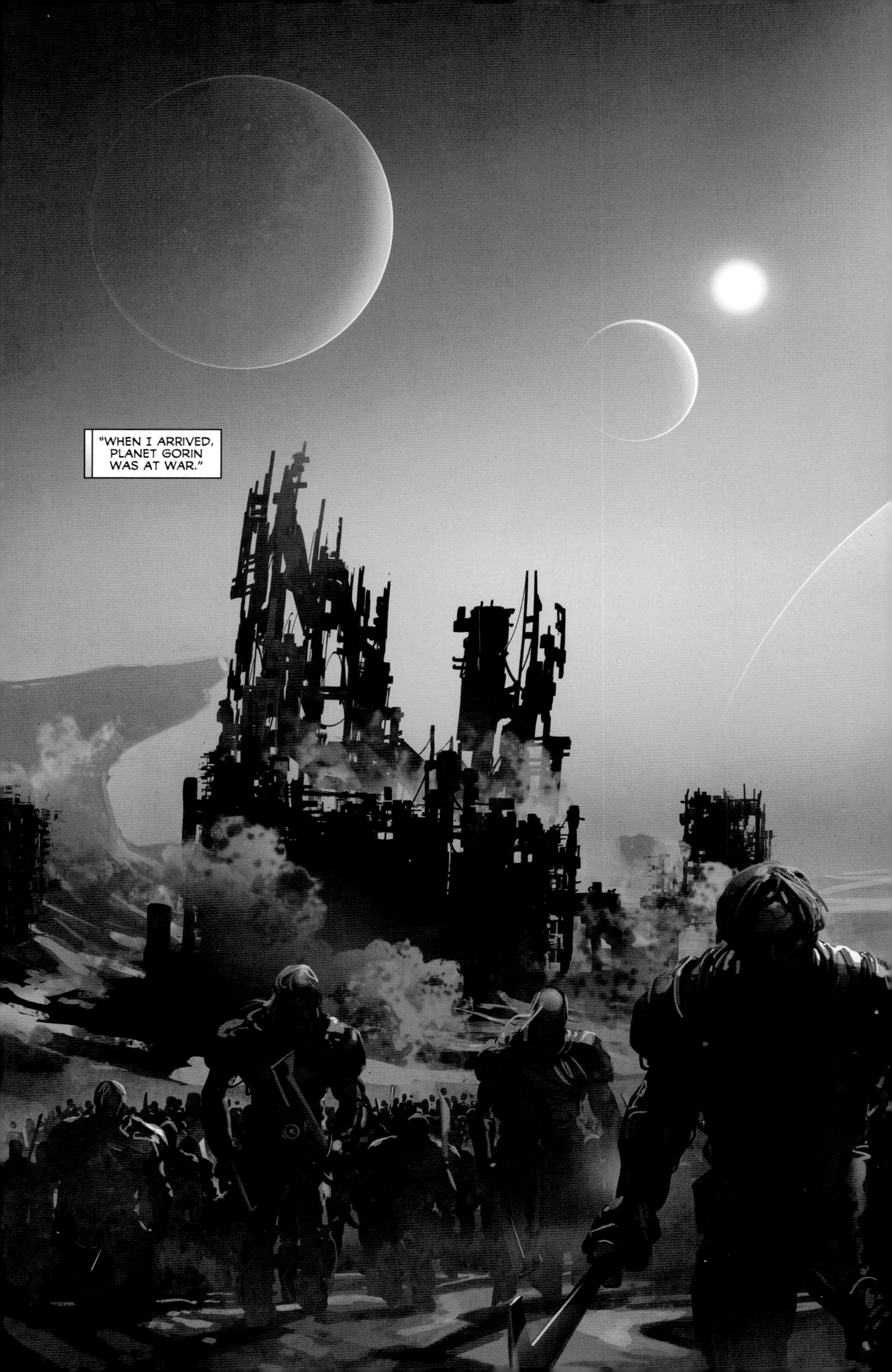
"WHEN I ARRIVED, PLANET GORIN WAS AT WAR."

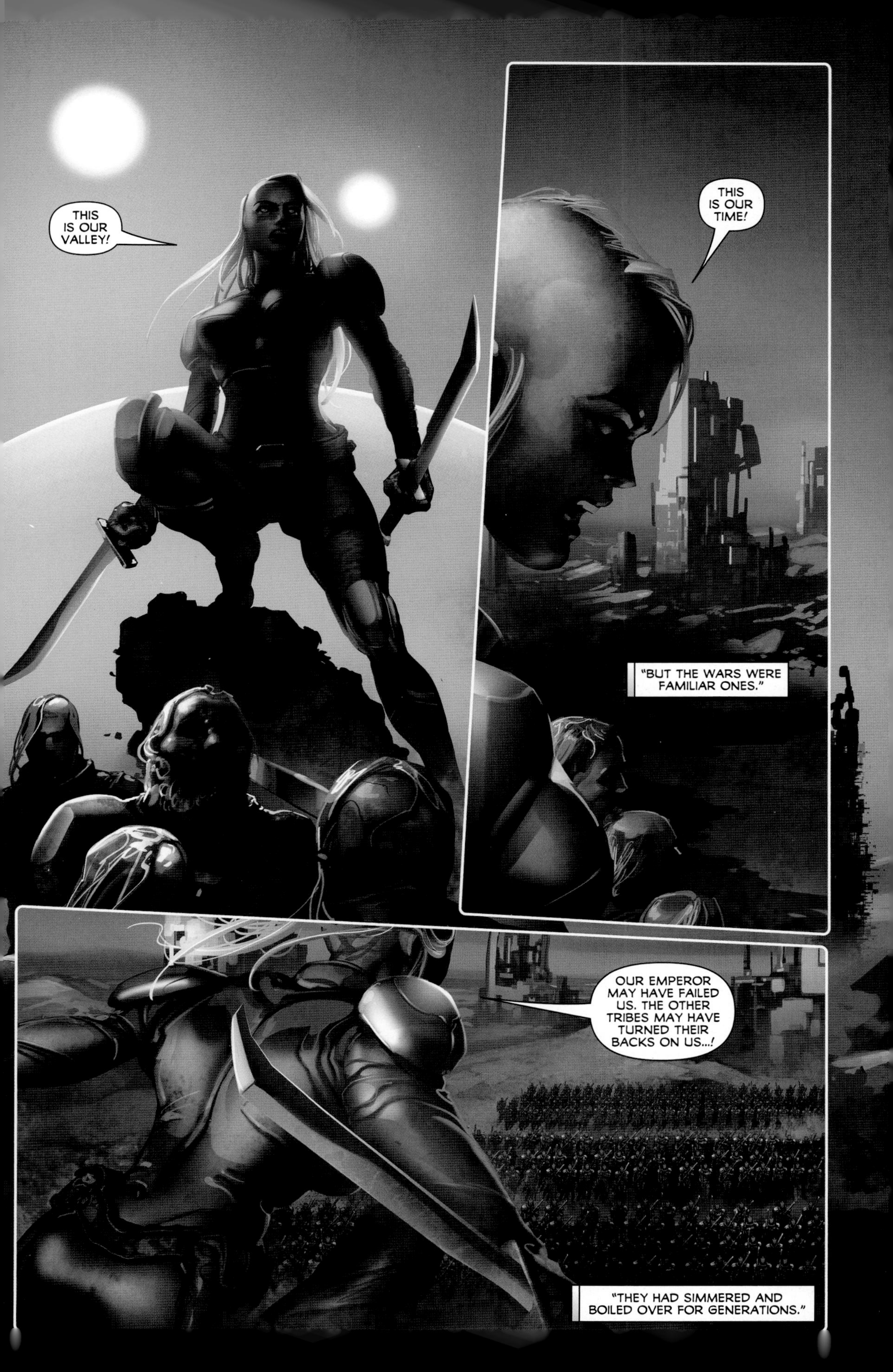
THIS IS OUR VALLEY!
THIS IS OUR TIME!
"BUT THE WARS WERE FAMILIAR ONES."
OUR EMPEROR MAY HAVE FAILED US. THE OTHER TRIBES MAY HAVE TURNED THEIR BACKS ON US...!
"THEY HAD SIMMERED AND BOILED OVER FOR GENERATIONS."

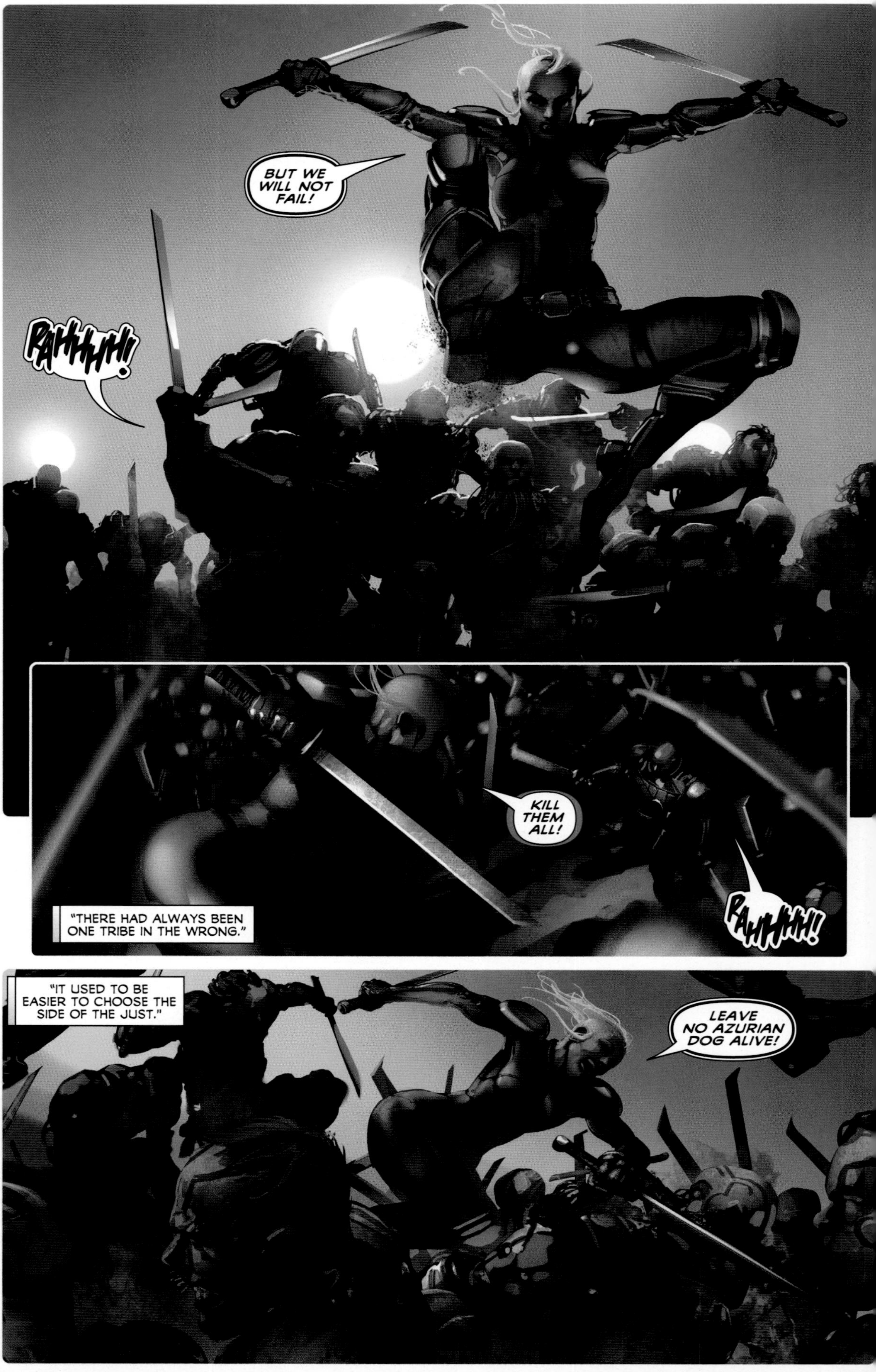

BUT WE WILL NOT FAIL!
RAHHHHH!
"THERE HAD ALWAYS BEEN ONE TRIBE IN THE WRONG."
KILL THEM ALL!
RAHHHHH!
"IT USED TO BE EASIER TO CHOOSE THE SIDE OF THE JUST."
LEAVE NO AZURIAN DOG ALIVE!

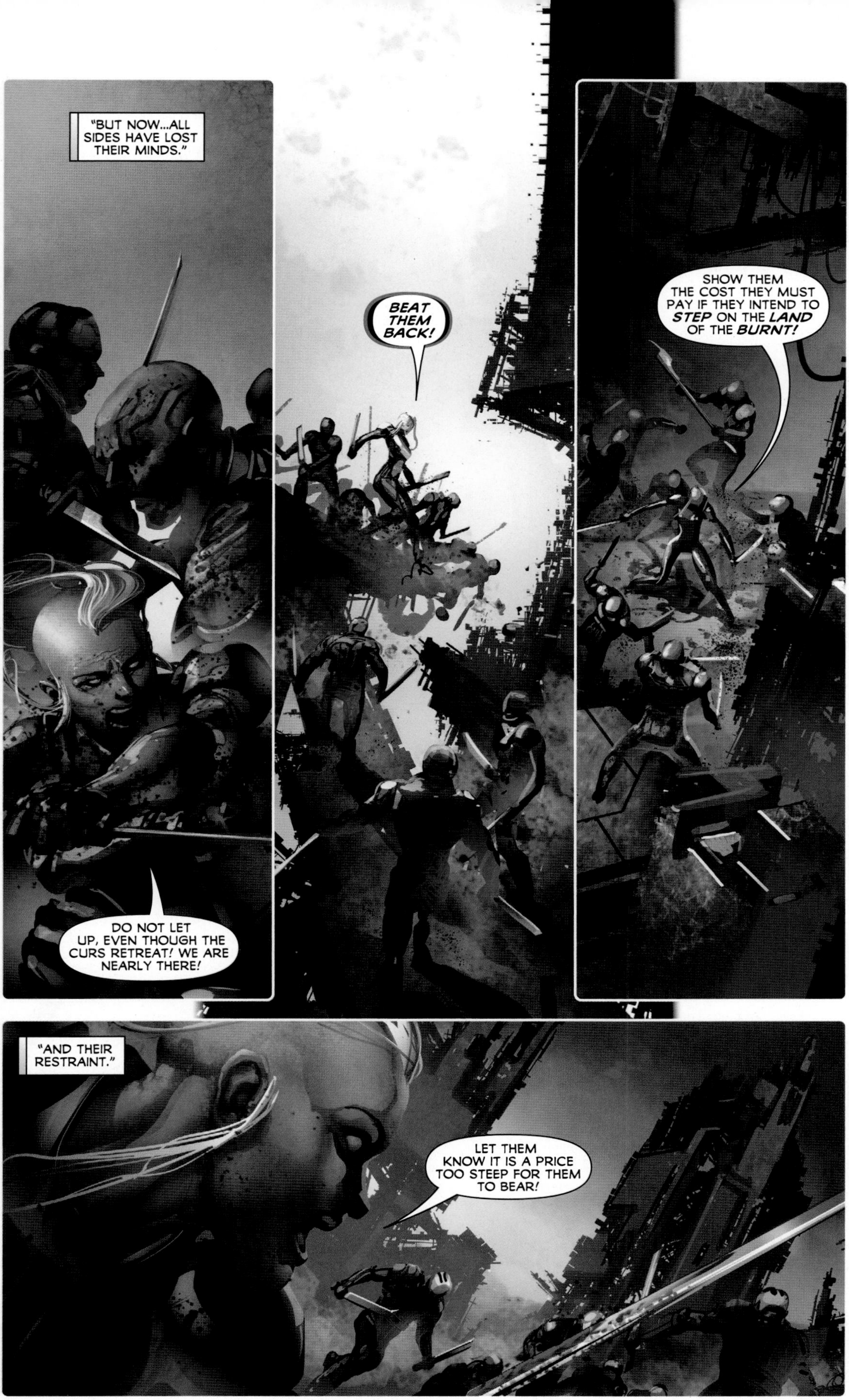
"BUT NOW...ALL SIDES HAVE LOST THEIR MINDS."
DO NOT LET UP, EVEN THOUGH THE CURS RETREAT! WE ARE NEARLY THERE!
BEAT THEM BACK!
SHOW THEM THE COST THEY MUST PAY IF THEY INTEND TO STEP ON THE LAND OF THE BURNT!
"AND THEIR RESTRAINT."
LET THEM KNOW IT IS A PRICE TOO STEEP FOR THEM TO BEAR!

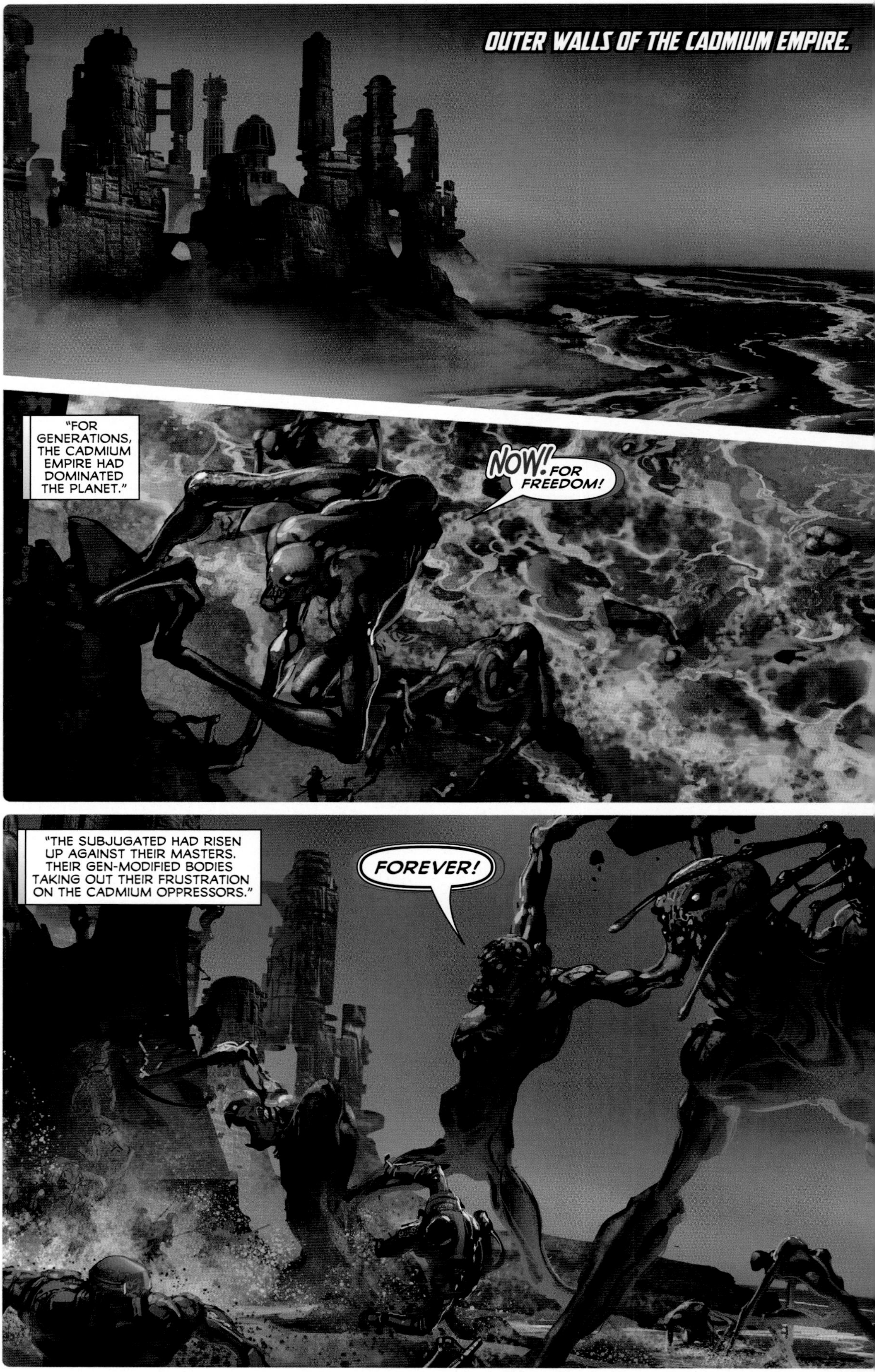
OUTER WALLS OF THE CADMIUM EMPIRE.
"FOR GENERATIONS, THE CADMIUM EMPIRE HAD DOMINATED THE PLANET."
NOW! FOR FREEDOM!
"THE SUBJUGATED HAD RISEN UP AGAINST THEIR MASTERS. THEIR GEN-MODIFIED BODIES TAKING OUT THEIR FRUSTRATION ON THE CADMIUM OPPRESSORS."
FOREVER!

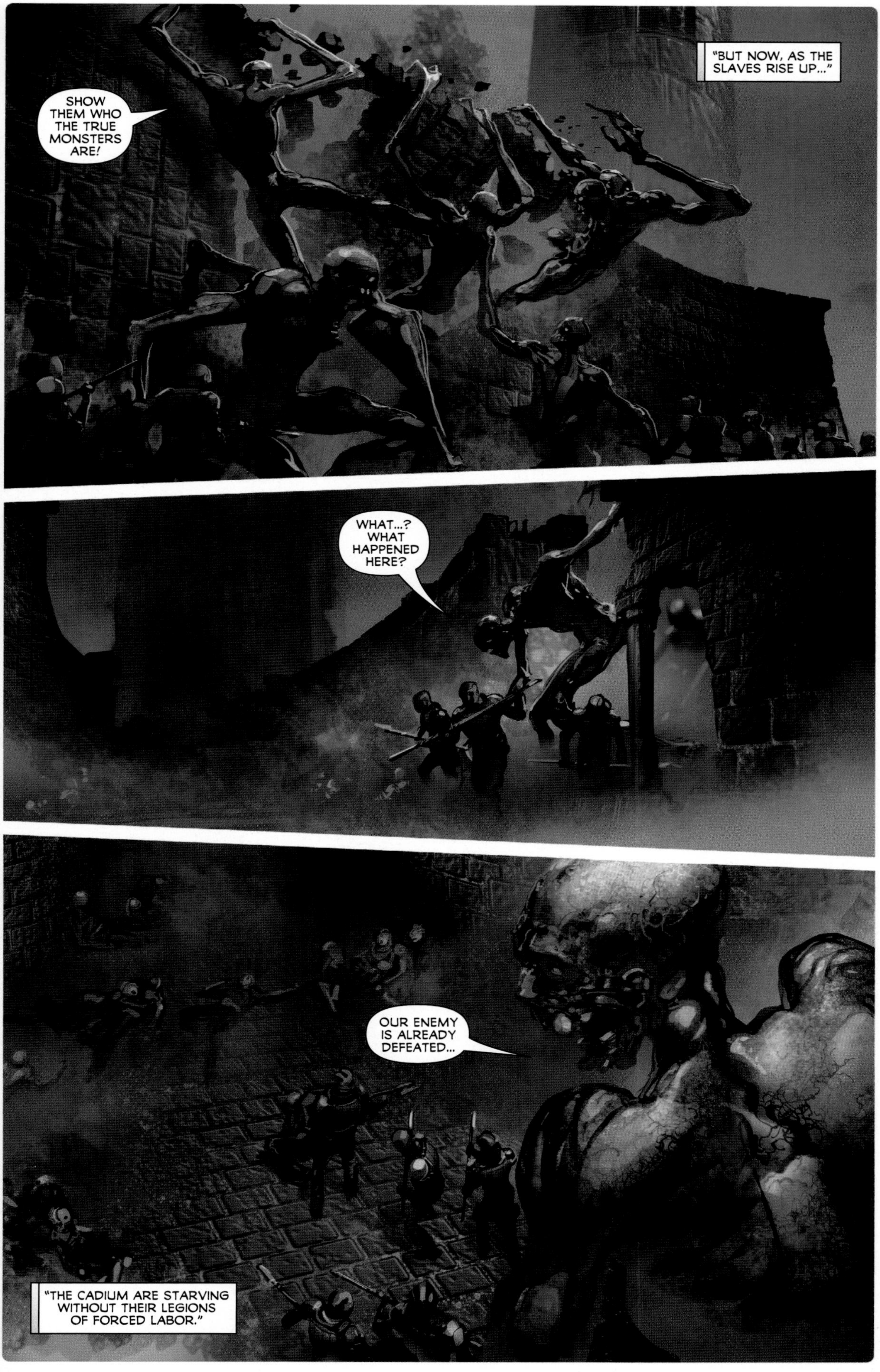
"BUT NOW, AS THE SLAVES RISE UP..."
SHOW THEM WHO THE TRUE MONSTERS ARE!
WHAT...? WHAT HAPPENED HERE?
OUR ENEMY IS ALREADY DEFEATED...
"THE CADIUM ARE STARVING WITHOUT THEIR LEGIONS OF FORCED LABOR."

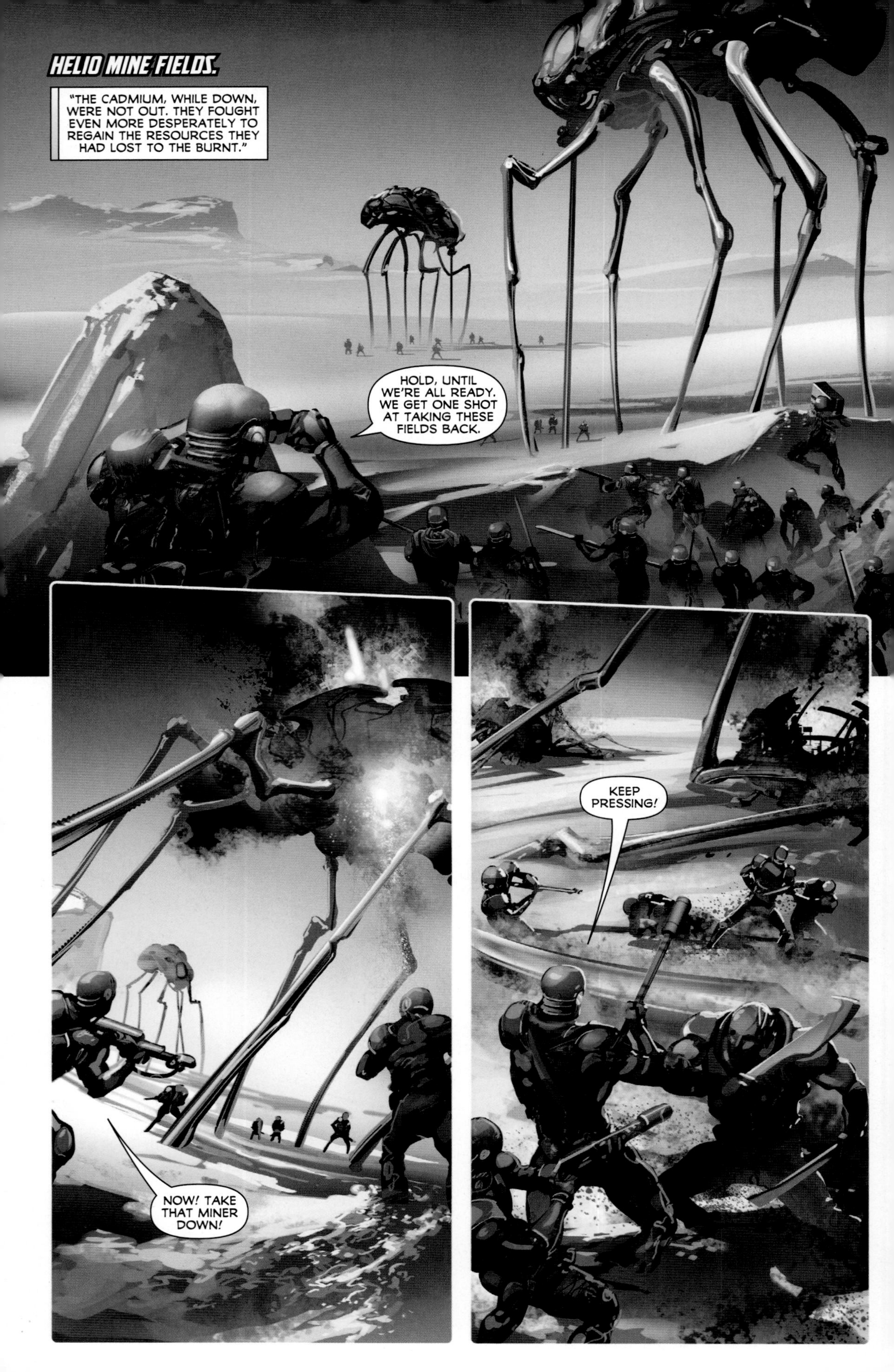
HELIO MINE FIELDS.
"THE CADMIUM, WHILE DOWN, WERE NOT OUT. THEY FOUGHT EVEN MORE DESPERATELY TO REGAIN THE RESOURCES THEY HAD LOST TO THE BURNT."
HOLD, UNTIL WE'RE ALL READY. WE GET ONE SHOT AT TAKING THESE FIELDS BACK.
NOW! TAKE THAT MINER DOWN!
KEEP PRESSING!

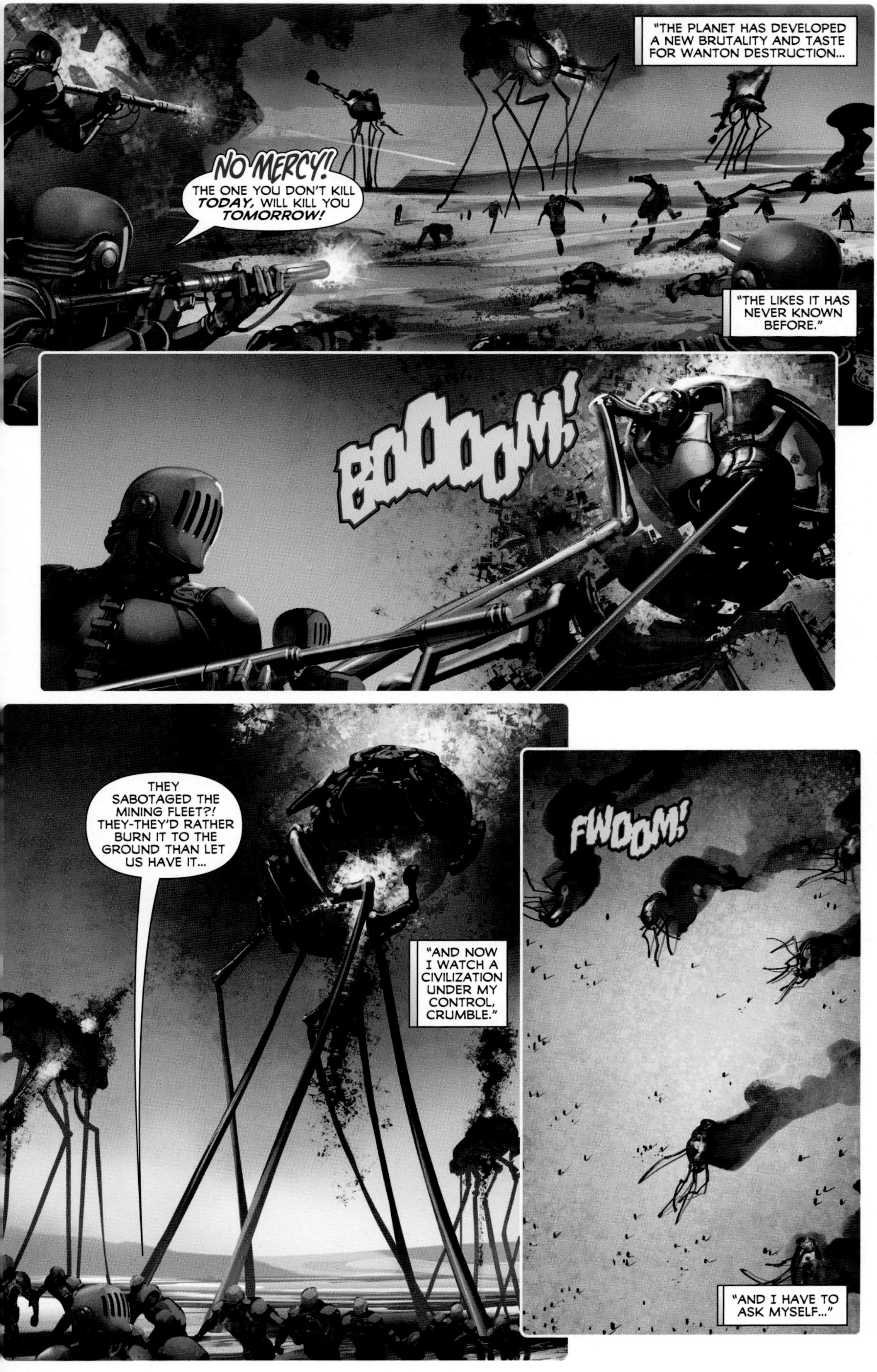
"THE PLANET HAS DEVELOPED A NEW BRUTALITY AND TASTE FOR WANTON DESTRUCTION...
NO MERCY!! THE ONE YOU DON'T KILL TODAY, WILL KILL YOU TOMORROW!
"THE LIKES IT HAS NEVER KNOWN BEFORE."
BOOOOM!
THEY SABOTAGED THE MINING FLEET?! THEY-THEY'D RATHER BURN IT TO THE GROUND THAN LET US HAVE IT...
"AND NOW I WATCH A CIVILIZATION UNDER MY CONTROL, CRUMBLE."
FWOOM!
"AND I HAVE TO ASK MYSELF..."

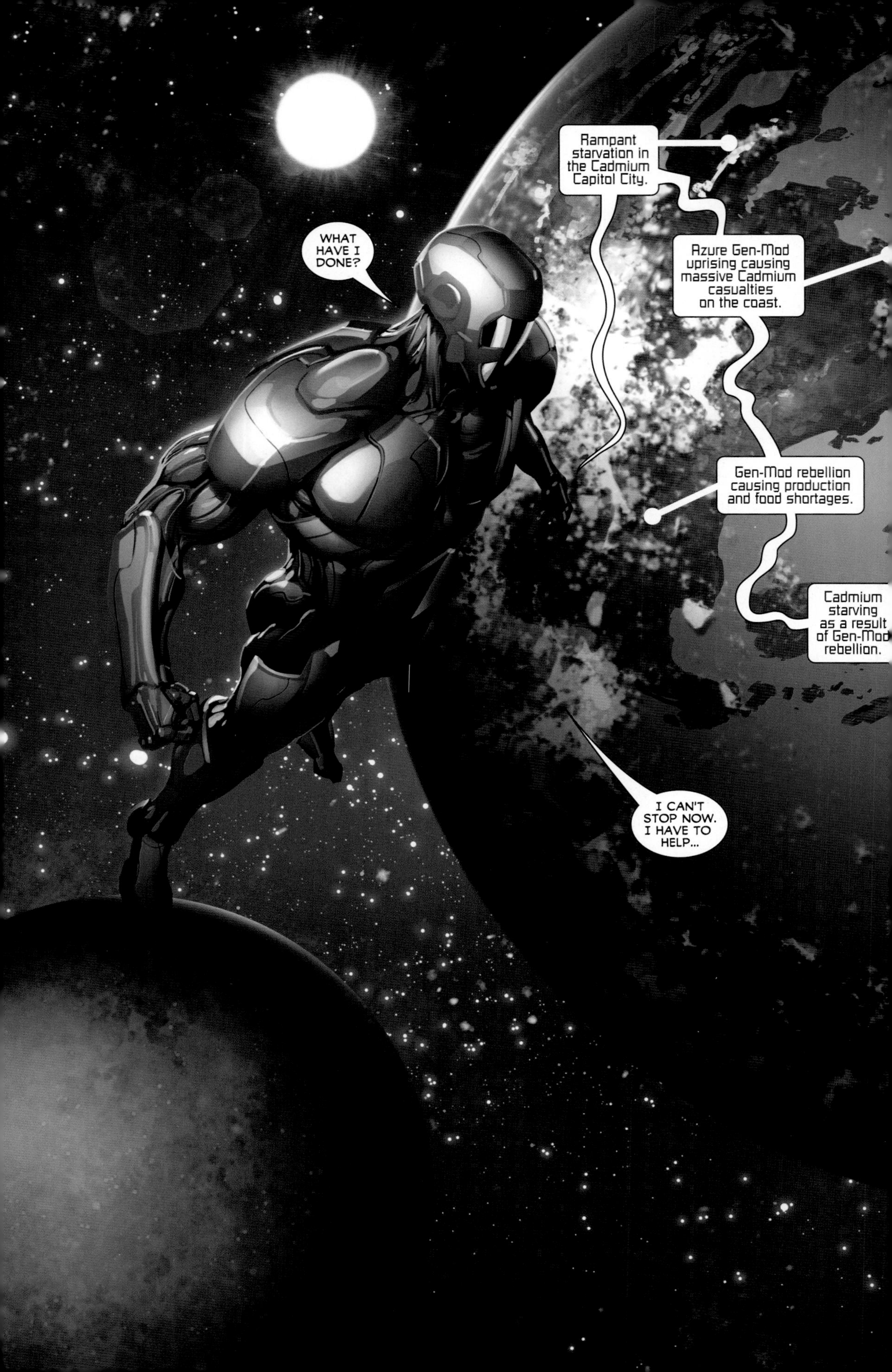
WHAT HAVE I DONE?
Rampant starvation in the Cadmium Capitol City.
Azure Gen-Mod uprising causing massive Cadmium casualties on the coast.
Gen-Mod rebellion causing production and food shortages.
Cadmium starving as a result of Gen-Mod rebellion.
I CAN'T STOP NOW. I HAVE TO HELP...

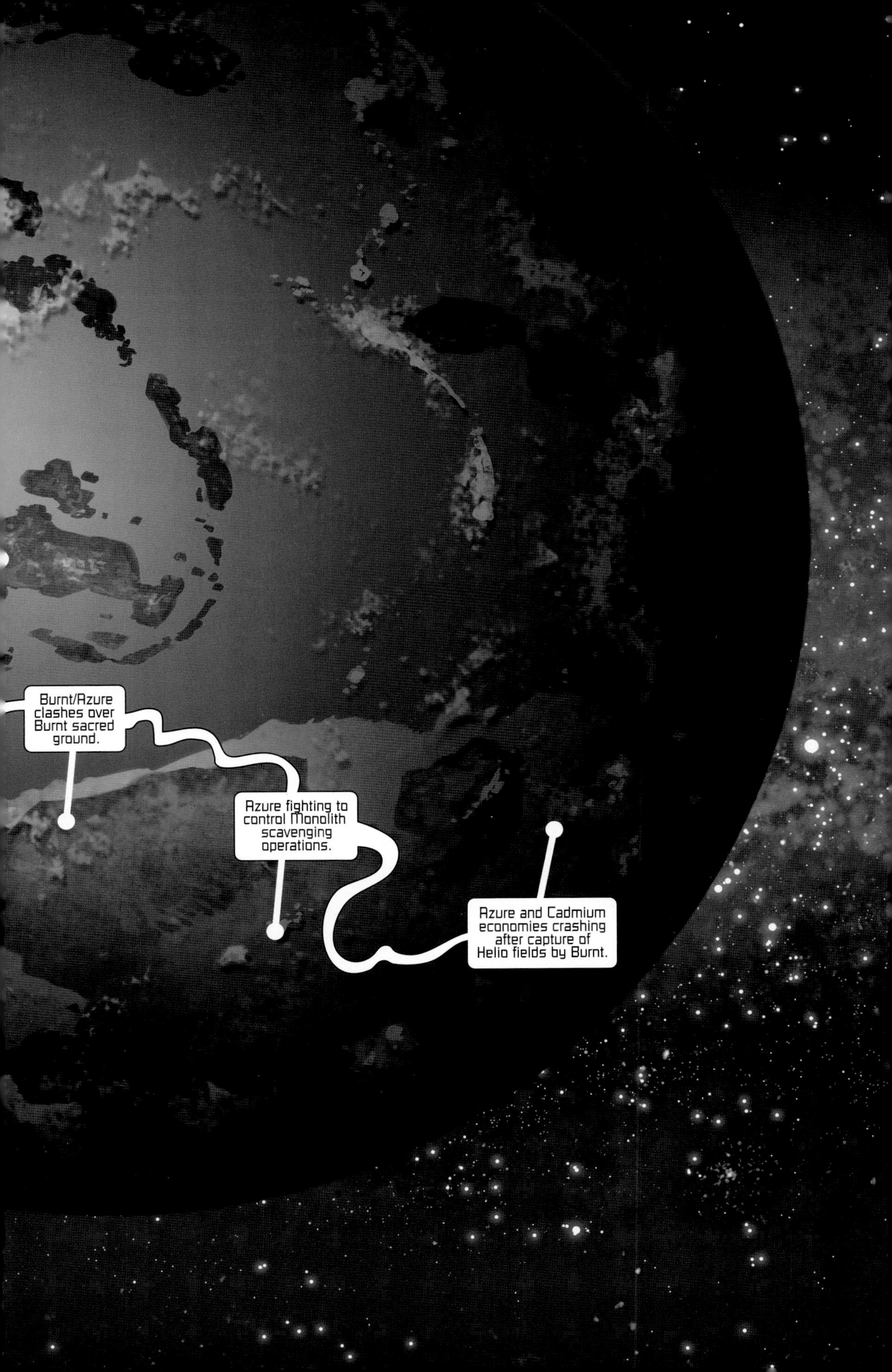
Burnt/Azure clashes over Burnt sacred ground.
Azure fighting to control Monolith scavenging operations.
Azure and Cadmium economies crashing after capture of Helio fields by Burnt.

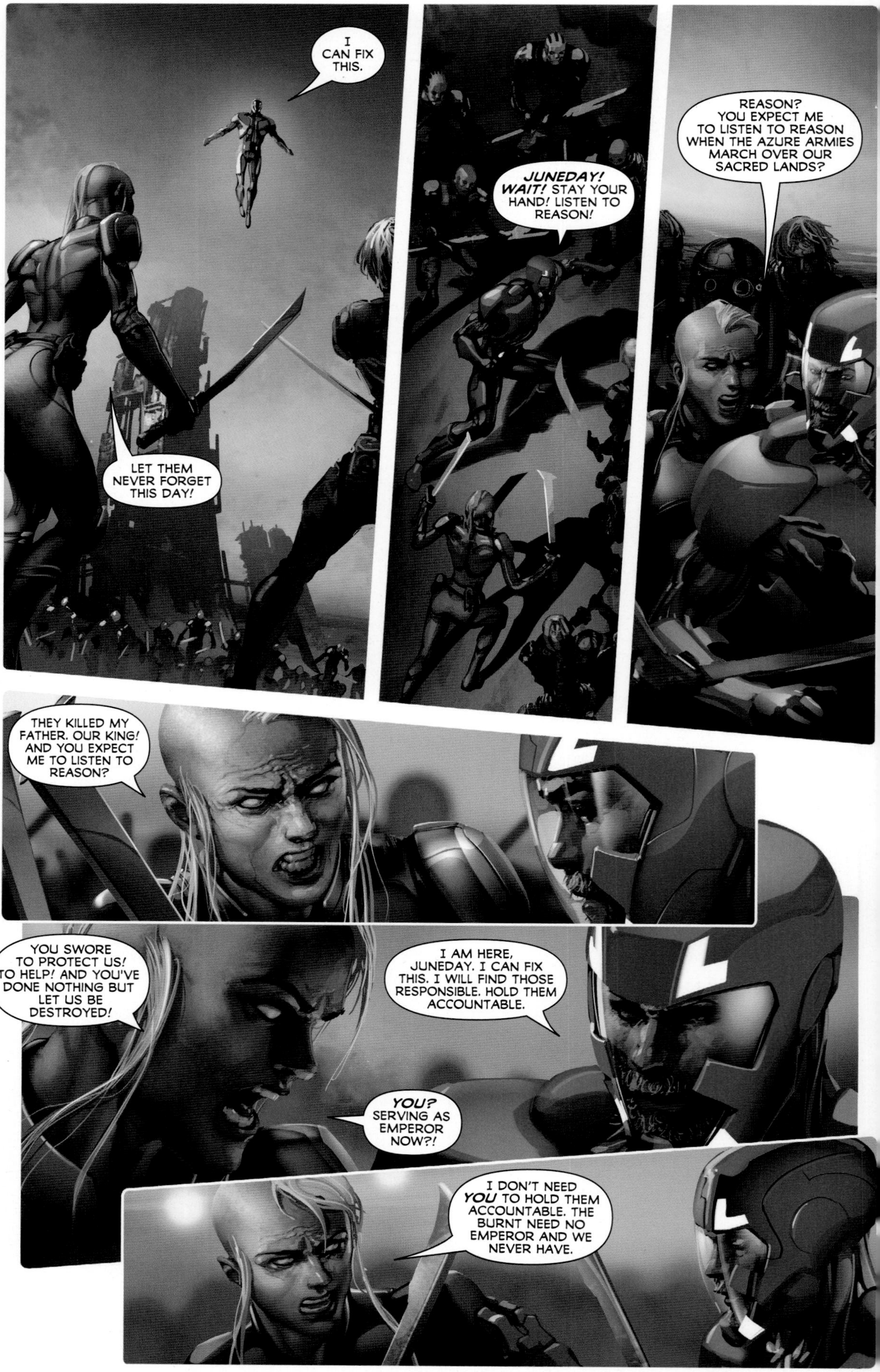
I CAN FIX THIS.
LET THEM NEVER FORGET THIS DAY!
JUNEDAY! WAIT! STAY YOUR HAND! LISTEN TO REASON!
REASON? YOU EXPECT ME TO LISTEN TO REASON WHEN THE AZURE ARMIES MARCH OVER OUR SACRED LANDS?
THEY KILLED MY FATHER. OUR KING! AND YOU EXPECT ME TO LISTEN TO REASON?
YOU SWORE TO PROTECT US! TO HELP! AND YOU'VE DONE NOTHING BUT LET US BE DESTROYED!
I AM HERE, JUNEDAY. I CAN FIX THIS. I WILL FIND THOSE RESPONSIBLE. HOLD THEM ACCOUNTABLE.
YOU? SERVING AS EMPEROR NOW?!
I DON'T NEED YOU TO HOLD THEM ACCOUNTABLE. THE BURNT NEED NO EMPEROR AND WE NEVER HAVE.

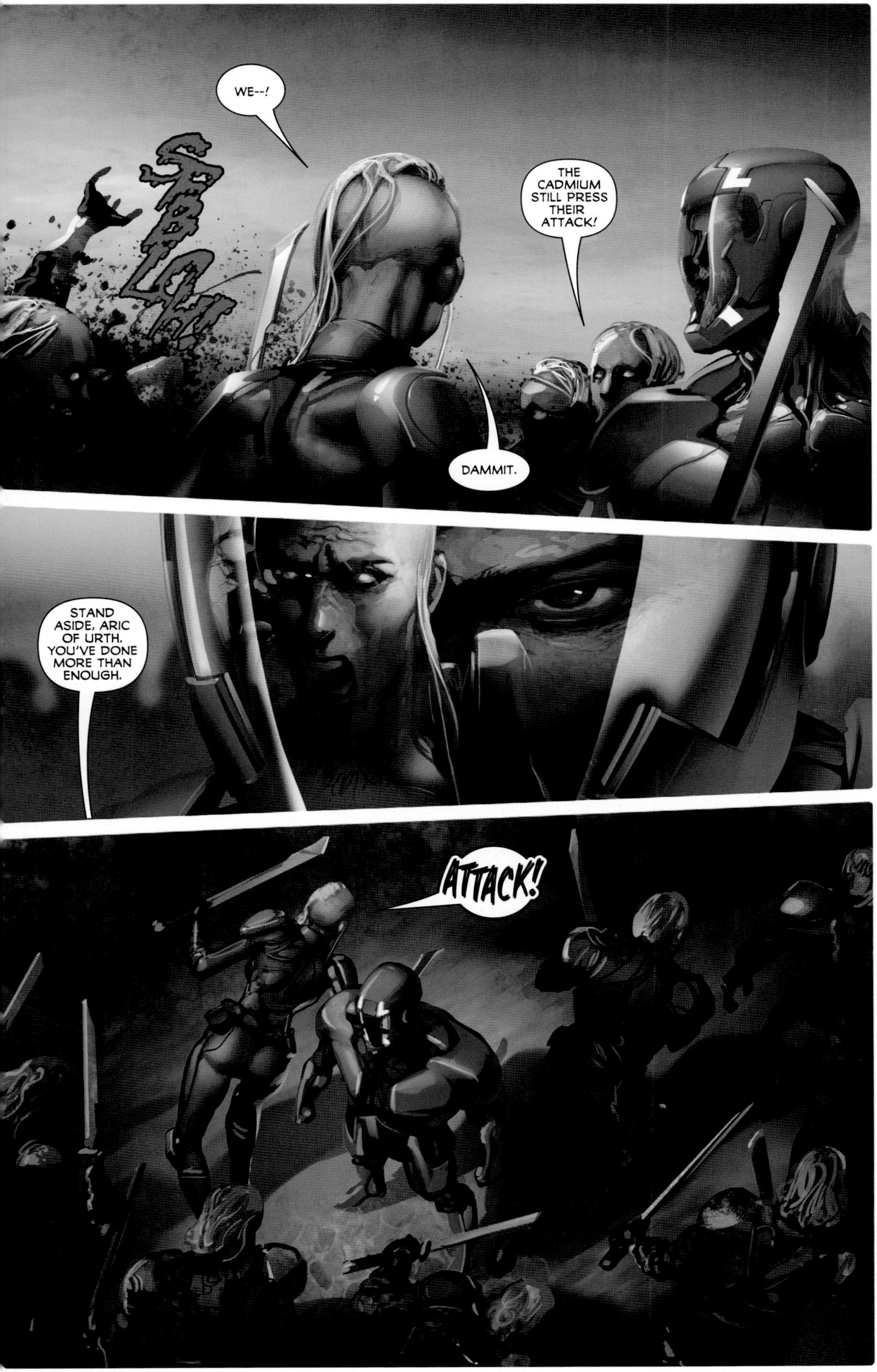
WE--!
THE CADMIUM STILL PRESS THEIR ATTACK!
DAMMIT.
STAND ASIDE, ARIC OF URTH. YOU'VE DONE MORE THAN ENOUGH.
ATTACK!

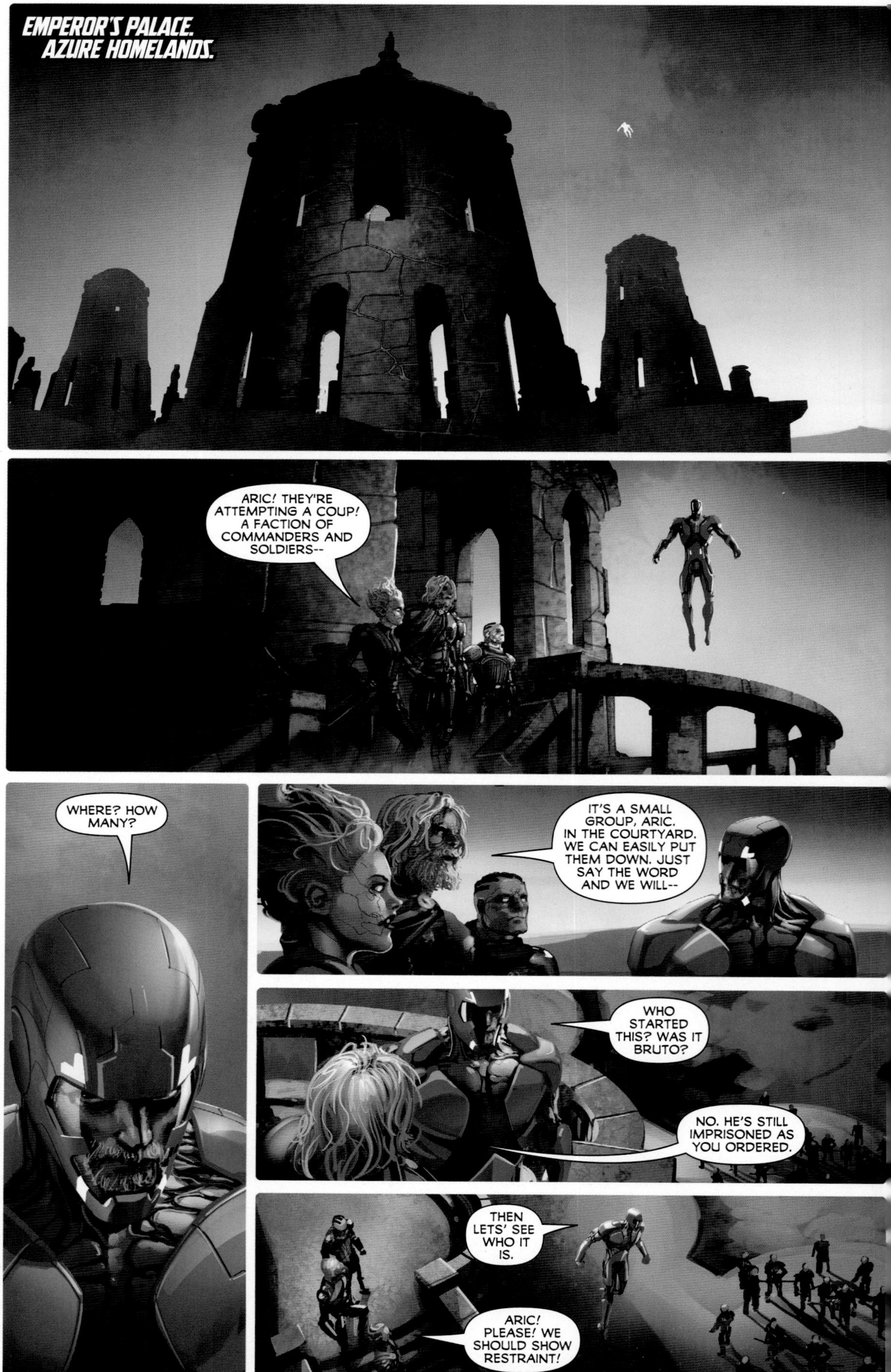
EMPEROR'S PALACE.
AZURE HOMELANDS.
ARIC! THEY'RE ATTEMPTING A COUP! A FACTION OF COMMANDERS AND SOLDIERS--
WHERE? HOW MANY?
IT'S A SMALL GROUP, ARIC. IN THE COURTYARD. WE CAN EASILY PUT THEM DOWN. JUST SAY THE WORD AND WE WILL--
WHO STARTED THIS? WAS IT BRUTO?
NO. HE'S STILL IMPRISONED AS YOU ORDERED.
THEN LETS' SEE WHO IT IS.
ARIC! PLEASE! WE SHOULD SHOW RESTRAINT!

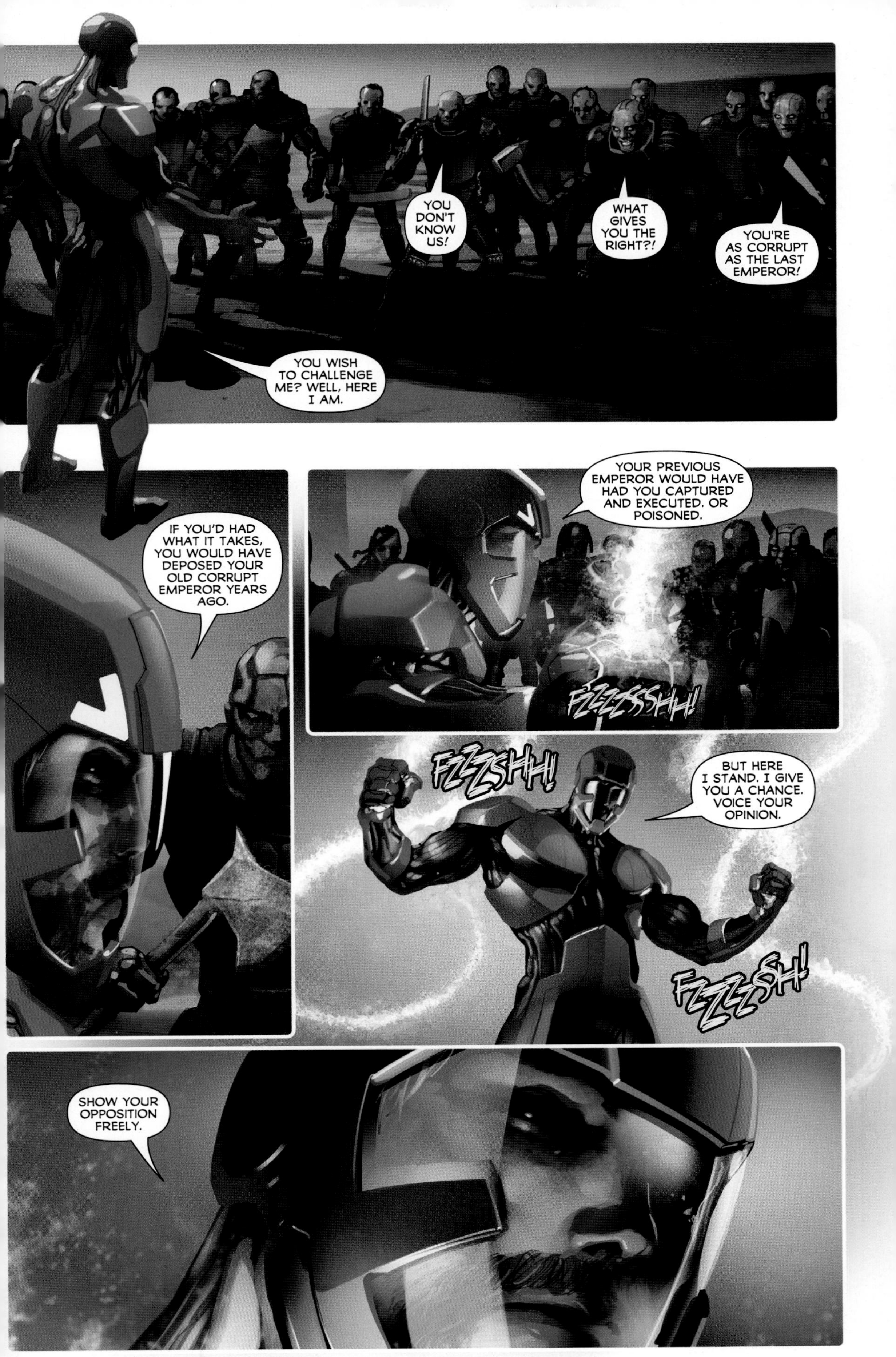
YOU DON'T KNOW US!
WHAT GIVES YOU THE RIGHT?!
YOU'RE AS CORRUPT AS THE LAST EMPEROR!
YOU WISH TO CHALLENGE ME? WELL, HERE I AM.
IF YOU'D HAD WHAT IT TAKES, YOU WOULD HAVE DEPOSED YOUR OLD CORRUPT EMPEROR YEARS AGO.
YOUR PREVIOUS EMPEROR WOULD HAVE HAD YOU CAPTURED AND EXECUTED. OR POISONED.
FZZZZSSHH!
FZZZSHH!
BUT HERE I STAND. I GIVE YOU A CHANCE. VOICE YOUR OPINION.
FZZZZSH!
SHOW YOUR OPPOSITION FREELY.

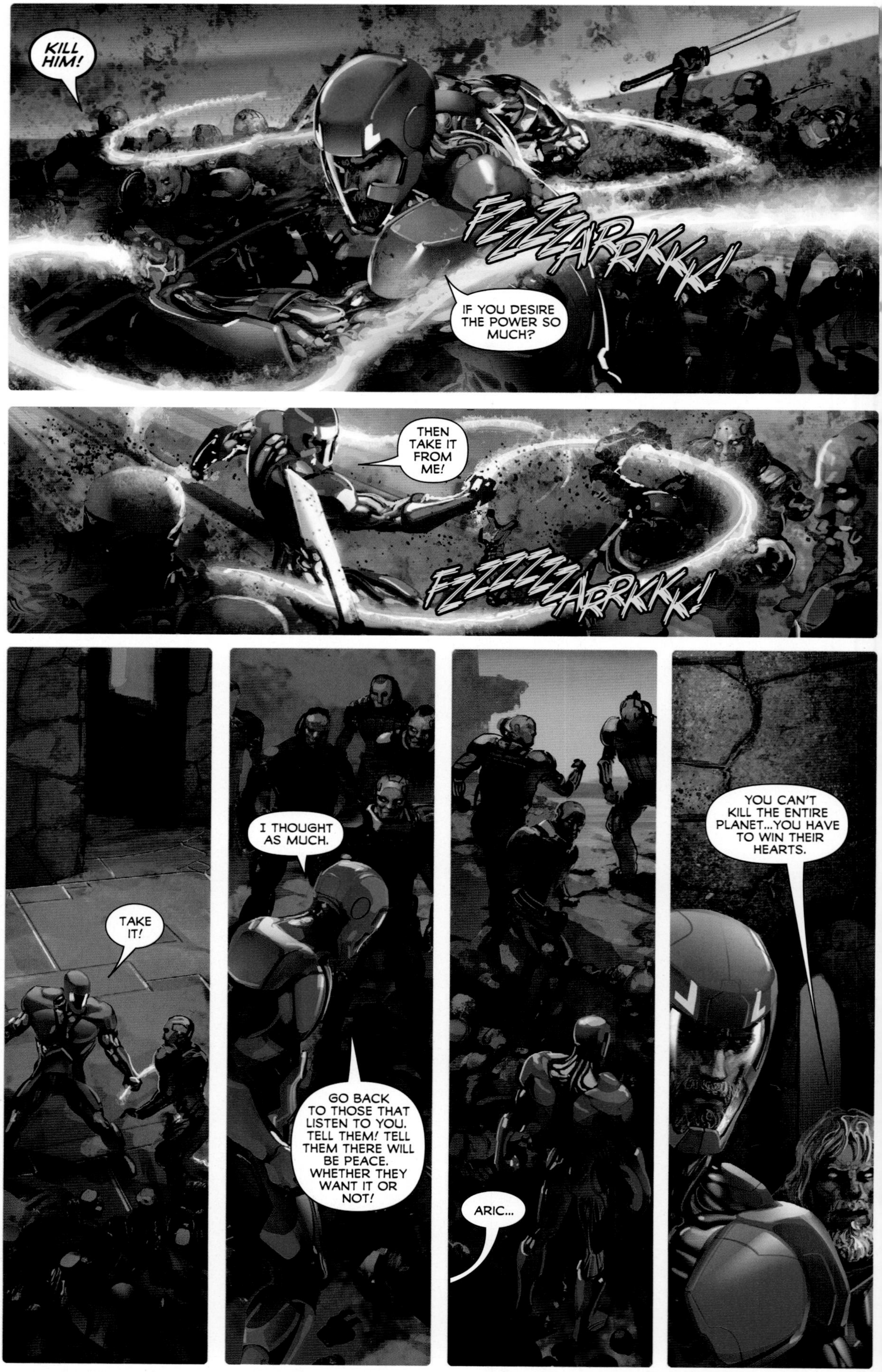
KILL HIM!
FZZZZARRKKK!
IF YOU DESIRE THE POWER SO MUCH?
THEN TAKE IT FROM ME!
FZZZZZZZARRKKK!
TAKE IT!
I THOUGHT AS MUCH.
GO BACK TO THOSE THAT LISTEN TO YOU. TELL THEM! TELL THEM THERE WILL BE PEACE. WHETHER THEY WANT IT OR NOT!
ARIC...
YOU CAN'T KILL THE ENTIRE PLANET...YOU HAVE TO WIN THEIR HEARTS.

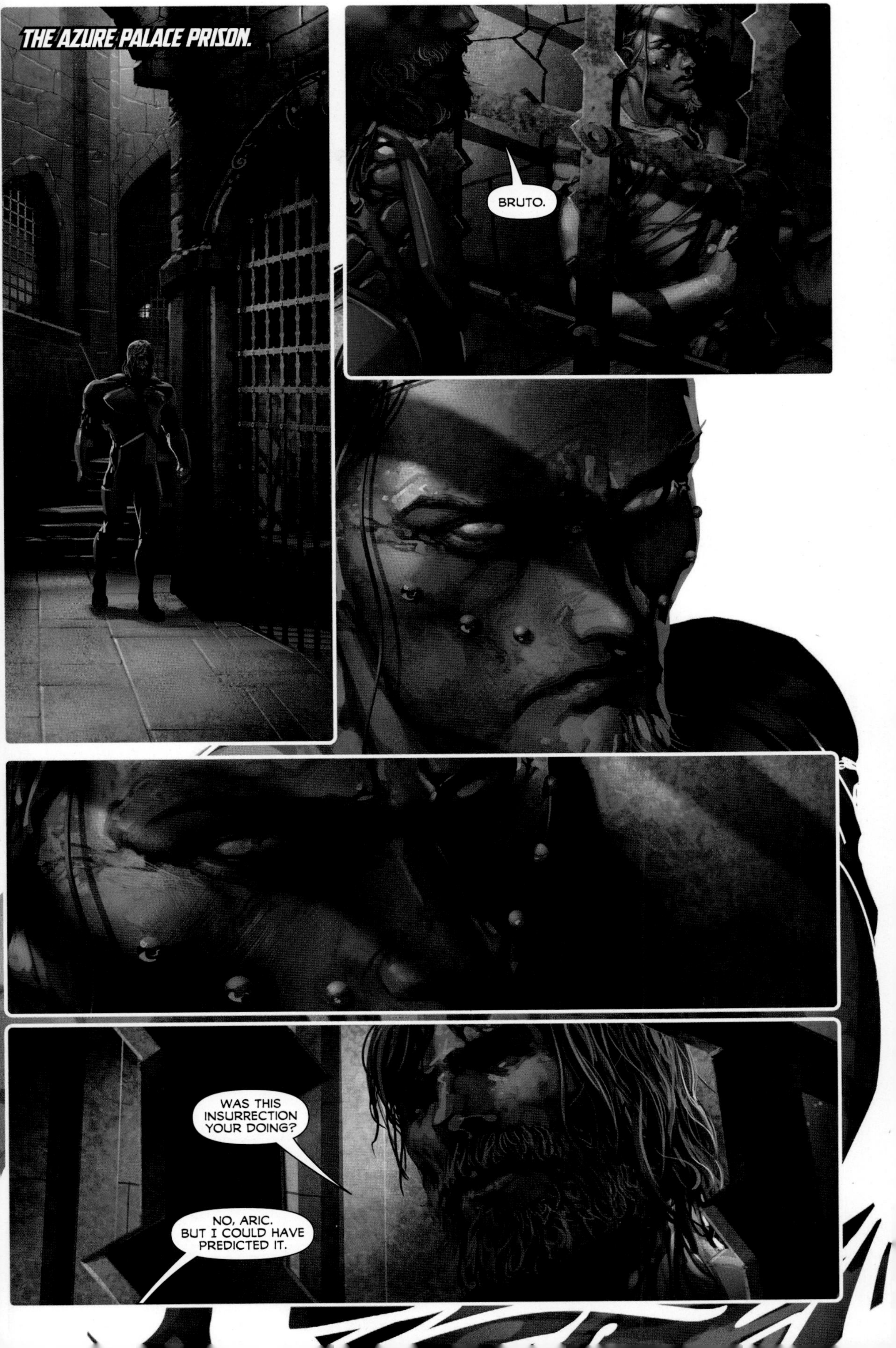
THE AZURE PALACE PRISON.
BRUTO.
WAS THIS INSURRECTION YOUR DOING?
NO, ARIC. BUT I COULD HAVE PREDICTED IT.

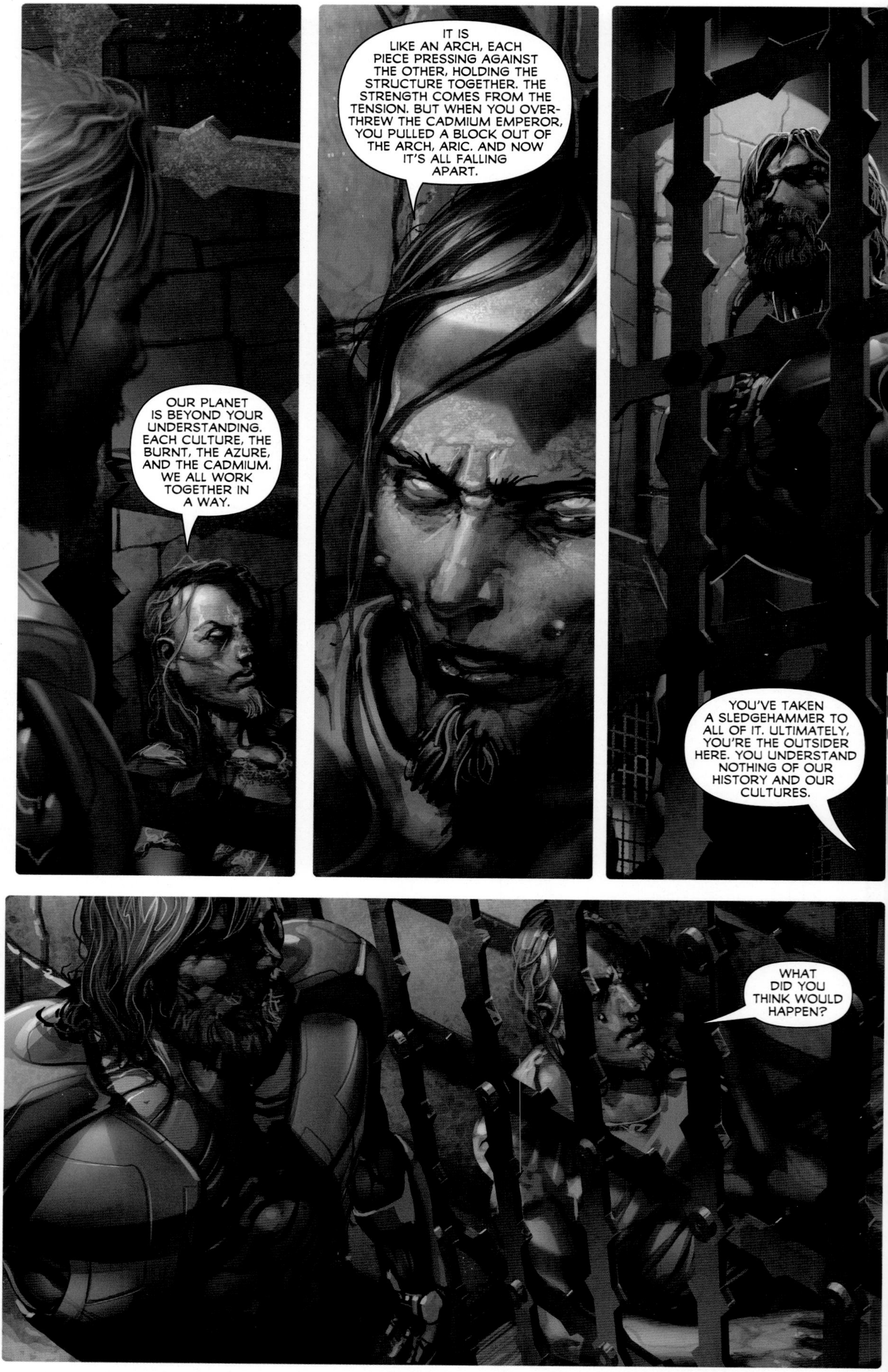
OUR PLANET IS BEYOND YOUR UNDERSTANDING. EACH CULTURE, THE BURNT, THE AZURE, AND THE CADMIUM. WE ALL WORK TOGETHER IN A WAY.
IT IS LIKE AN ARCH, EACH PIECE PRESSING AGAINST THE OTHER, HOLDING THE STRUCTURE TOGETHER. THE STRENGTH COMES FROM THE TENSION. BUT WHEN YOU OVERTHREW THE CADMIUM EMPEROR, YOU PULLED A BLOCK OUT OF THE ARCH, ARIC. AND NOW IT'S ALL FALLING APART.
YOU'VE TAKEN A SLEDGEHAMMER TO ALL OF IT. ULTIMATELY, YOU'RE THE OUTSIDER HERE. YOU UNDERSTAND NOTHING OF OUR HISTORY AND OUR CULTURES.
WHAT DID YOU THINK WOULD HAPPEN?

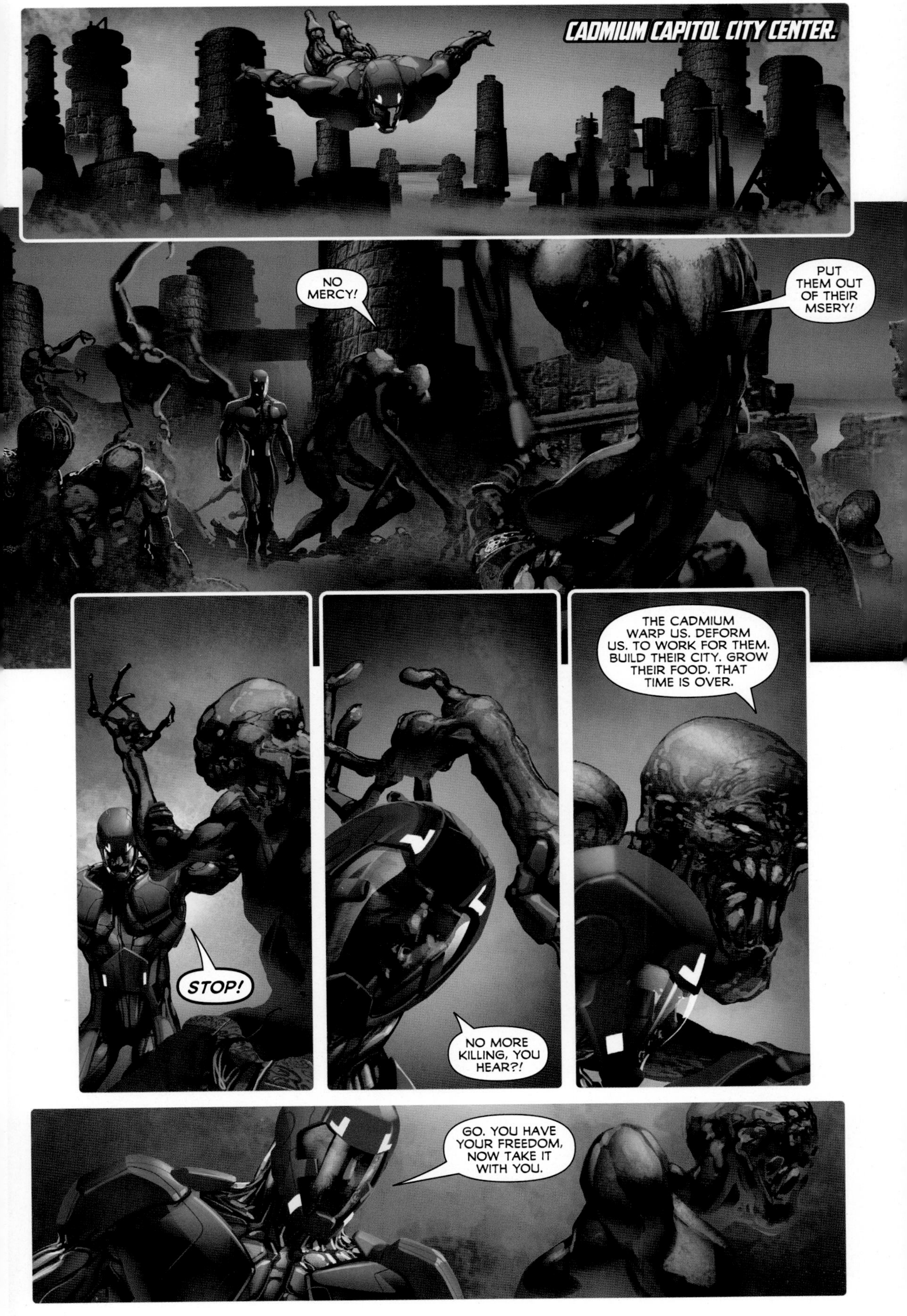
CADMIUM CAPITOL CITY CENTER.
NO MERCY!
PUT THEM OUT OF THEIR MSERY!
STOP!
NO MORE KILLING, YOU HEAR?!
THE CADMIUM WARP US. DEFORM US. TO WORK FOR THEM. BUILD THEIR CITY. GROW THEIR FOOD. THAT TIME IS OVER.
GO. YOU HAVE YOUR FREEDOM, NOW TAKE IT WITH YOU.

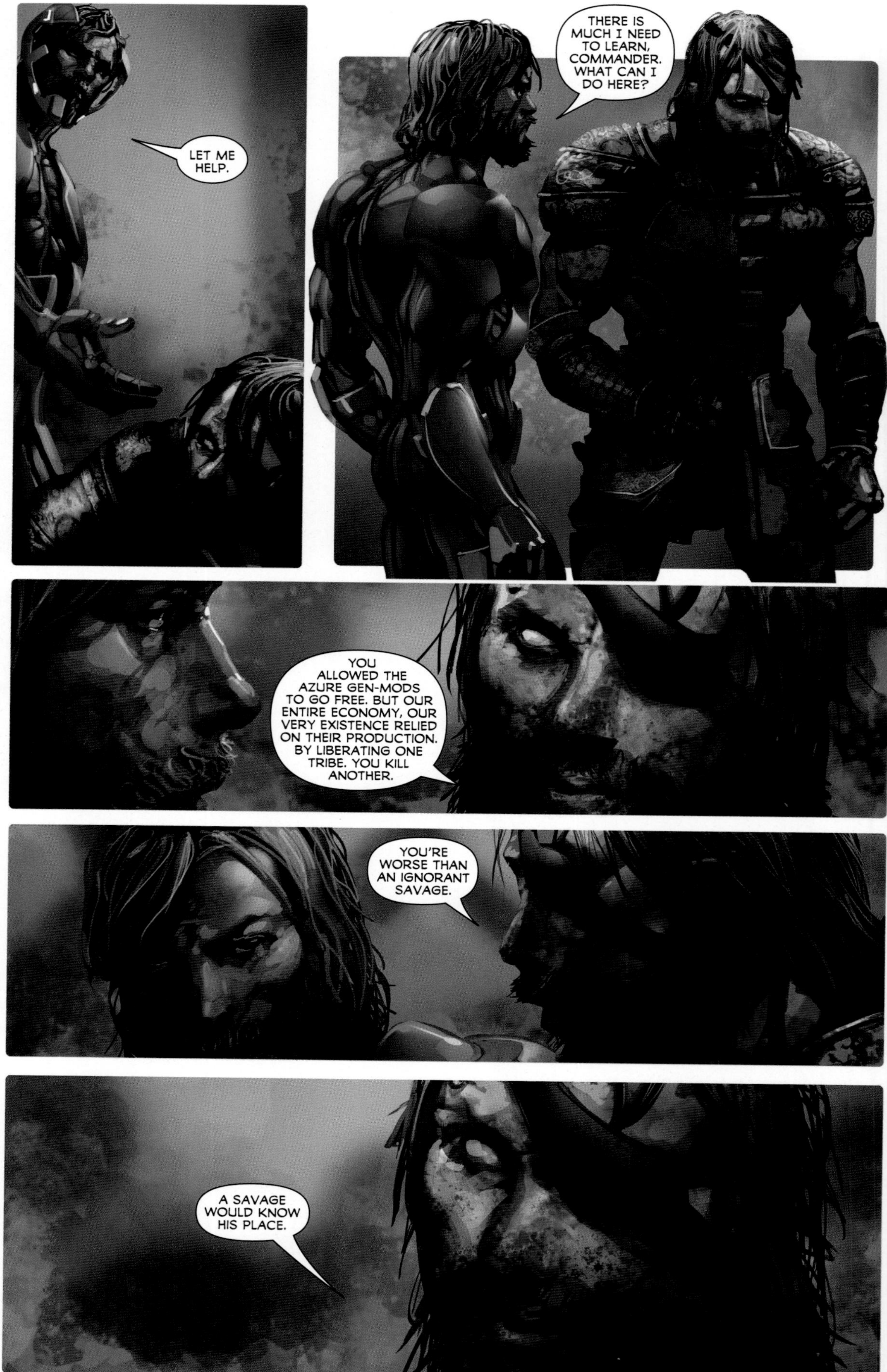
LET ME HELP.
THERE IS MUCH I NEED TO LEARN, COMMANDER. WHAT CAN I DO HERE?
YOU ALLOWED THE AZURE GEN-MODS TO GO FREE. BUT OUR ENTIRE ECONOMY, OUR VERY EXISTENCE RELIED ON THEIR PRODUCTION. BY LIBERATING ONE TRIBE. YOU KILL ANOTHER.
YOU'RE WORSE THAN AN IGNORANT SAVAGE.
A SAVAGE WOULD KNOW HIS PLACE.

SCHON?

SCHON, ARE YOU-- OH.

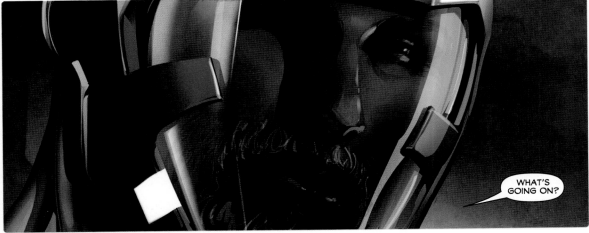

WHAT'S GOING ON?

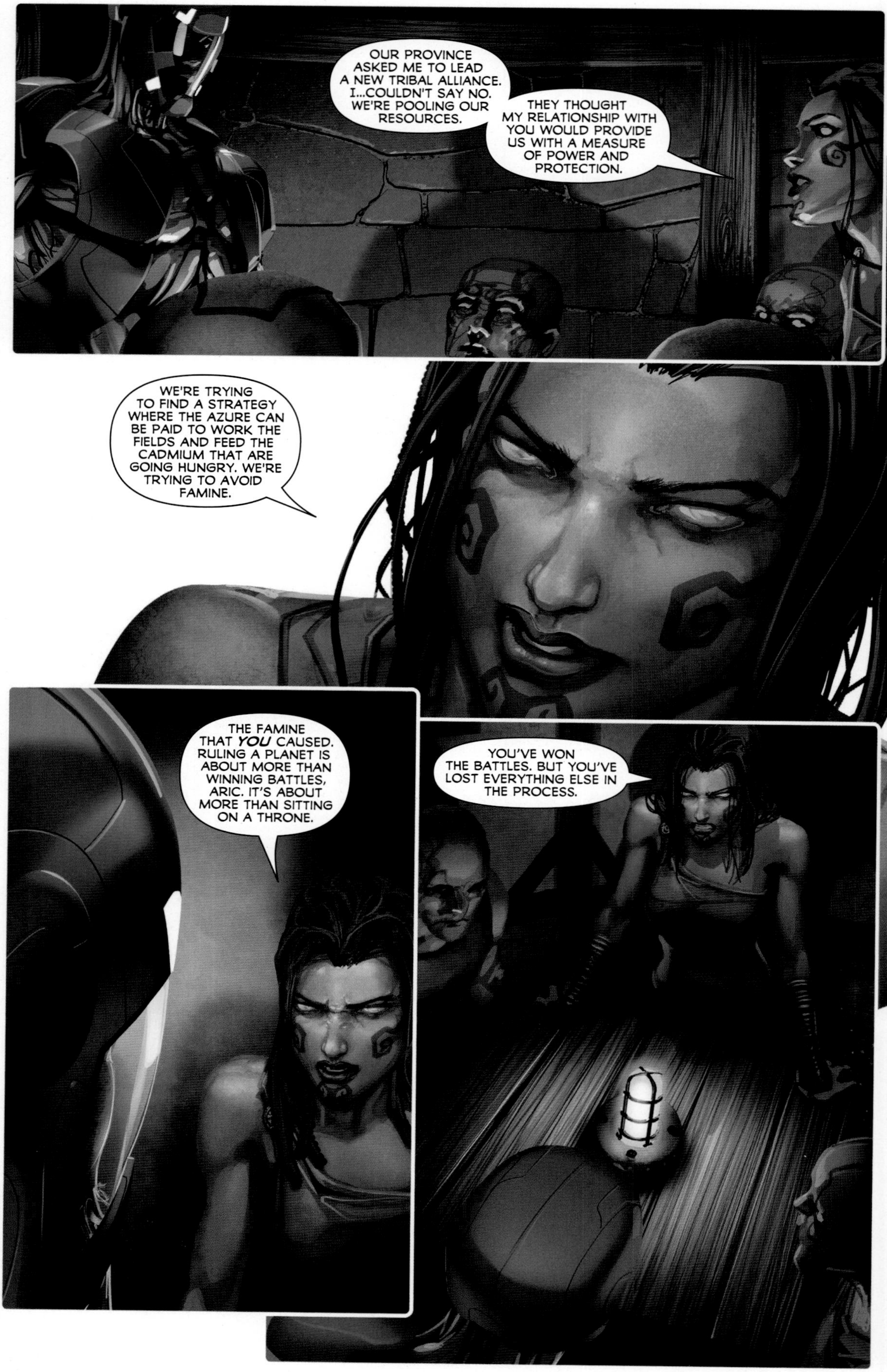
OUR PROVINCE ASKED ME TO LEAD A NEW TRIBAL ALLIANCE. I...COULDN'T SAY NO. WE'RE POOLING OUR RESOURCES.
THEY THOUGHT MY RELATIONSHIP WITH YOU WOULD PROVIDE US WITH A MEASURE OF POWER AND PROTECTION.
WE'RE TRYING TO FIND A STRATEGY WHERE THE AZURE CAN BE PAID TO WORK THE FIELDS AND FEED THE CADMIUM THAT ARE GOING HUNGRY. WE'RE TRYING TO AVOID FAMINE.
THE FAMINE THAT *YOU* CAUSED. RULING A PLANET IS ABOUT MORE THAN WINNING BATTLES, ARIC. IT'S ABOUT MORE THAN SITTING ON A THRONE.
YOU'VE WON THE BATTLES. BUT YOU'VE LOST EVERYTHING ELSE IN THE PROCESS.

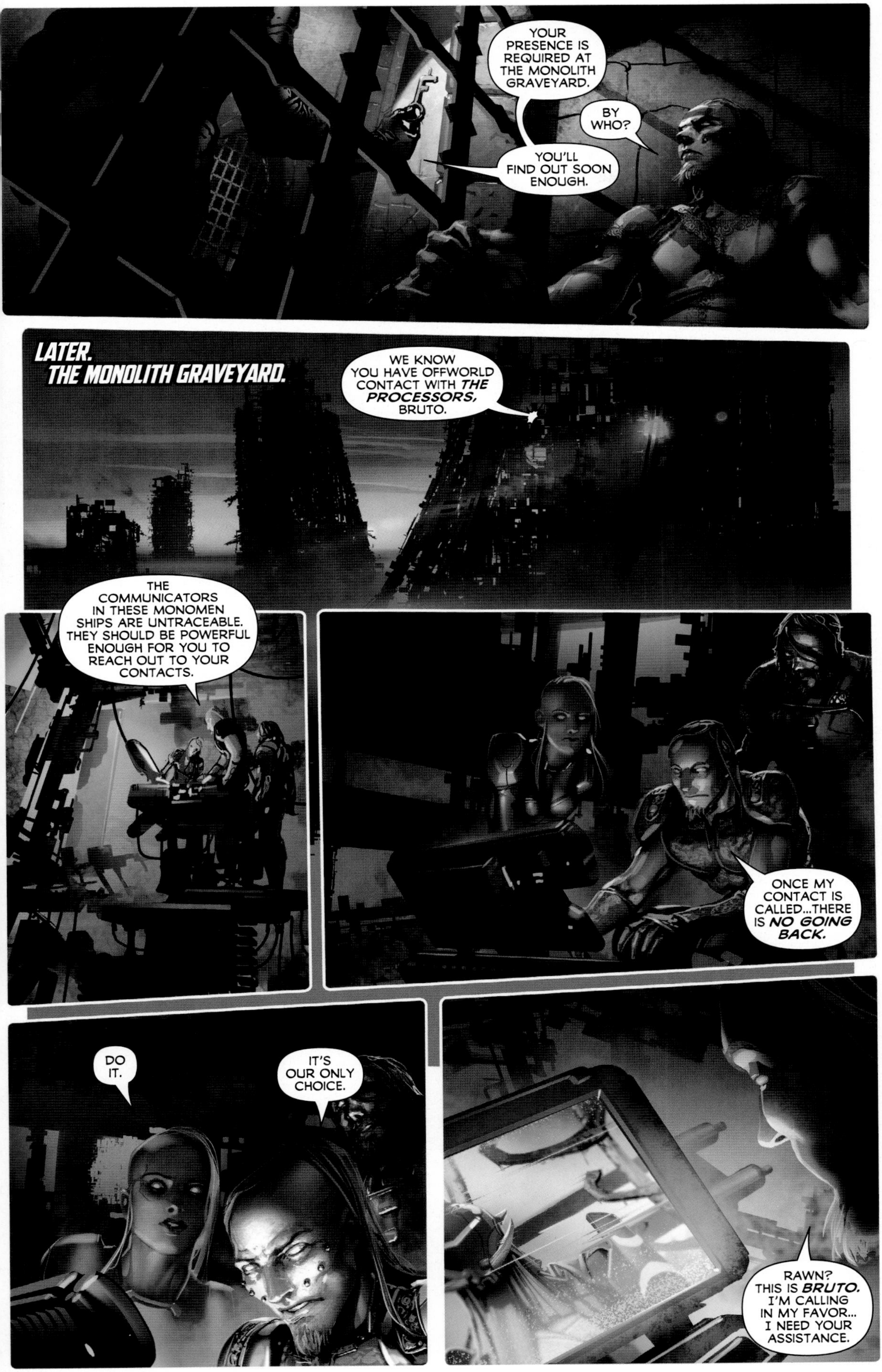
YOUR PRESENCE IS REQUIRED AT THE MONOLITH GRAVEYARD.
BY WHO?
YOU'LL FIND OUT SOON ENOUGH.
LATER. THE MONOLITH GRAVEYARD.
WE KNOW YOU HAVE OFFWORLD CONTACT WITH *THE PROCESSORS,* BRUTO.
THE COMMUNICATORS IN THESE MONOMEN SHIPS ARE UNTRACEABLE. THEY SHOULD BE POWERFUL ENOUGH FOR YOU TO REACH OUT TO YOUR CONTACTS.
ONCE MY CONTACT IS CALLED...THERE IS ***NO GOING BACK.***
DO IT.
IT'S OUR ONLY CHOICE.
RAWN? THIS IS ***BRUTO.*** I'M CALLING IN MY FAVOR... I NEED YOUR ASSISTANCE.

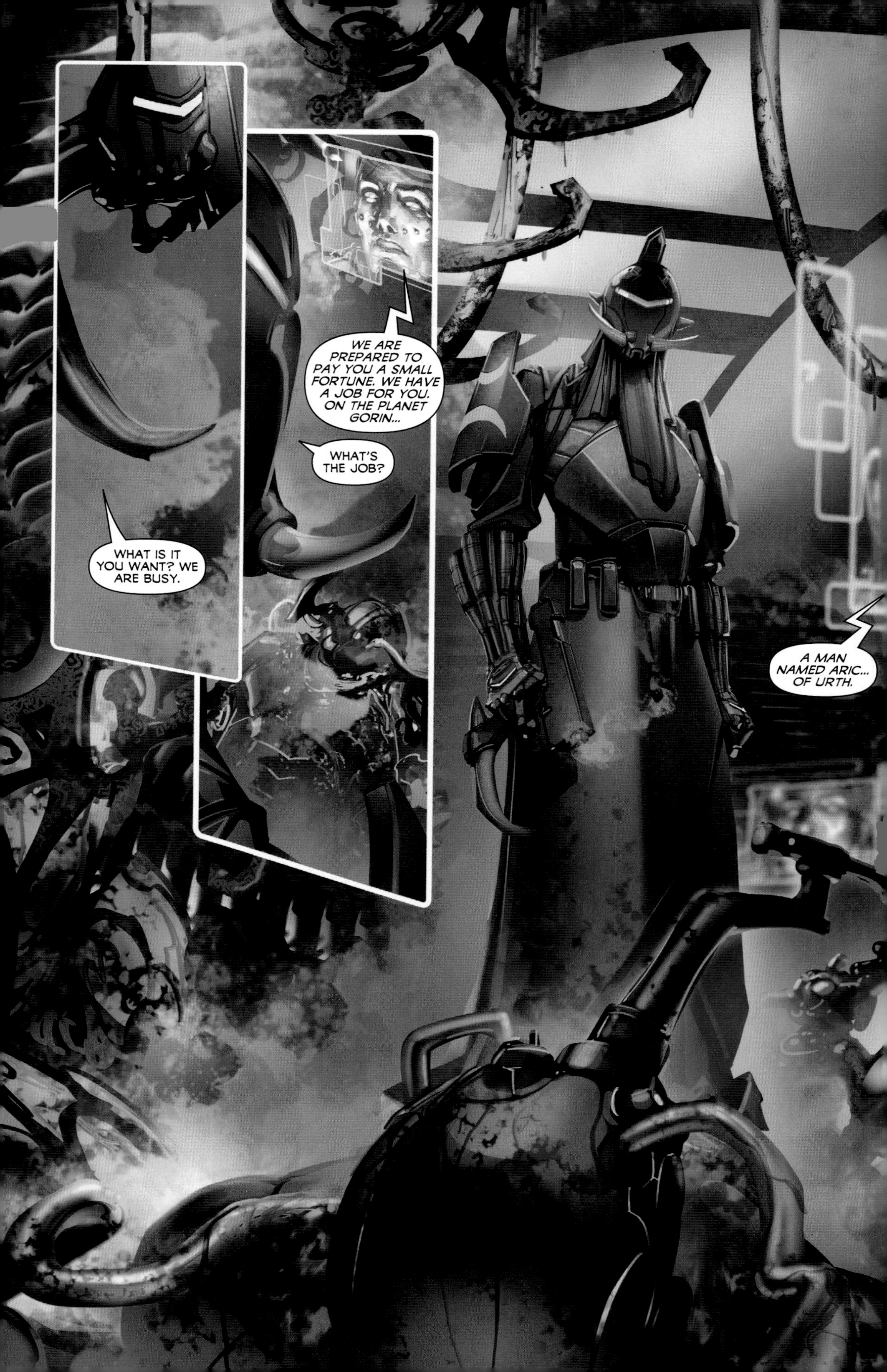
WHAT IS IT YOU WANT? WE ARE BUSY.
WE ARE PREPARED TO PAY YOU A SMALL FORTUNE. WE HAVE A JOB FOR YOU. ON THE PLANET GORIN...
WHAT'S THE JOB?
A MAN NAMED ARIC... OF URTH.

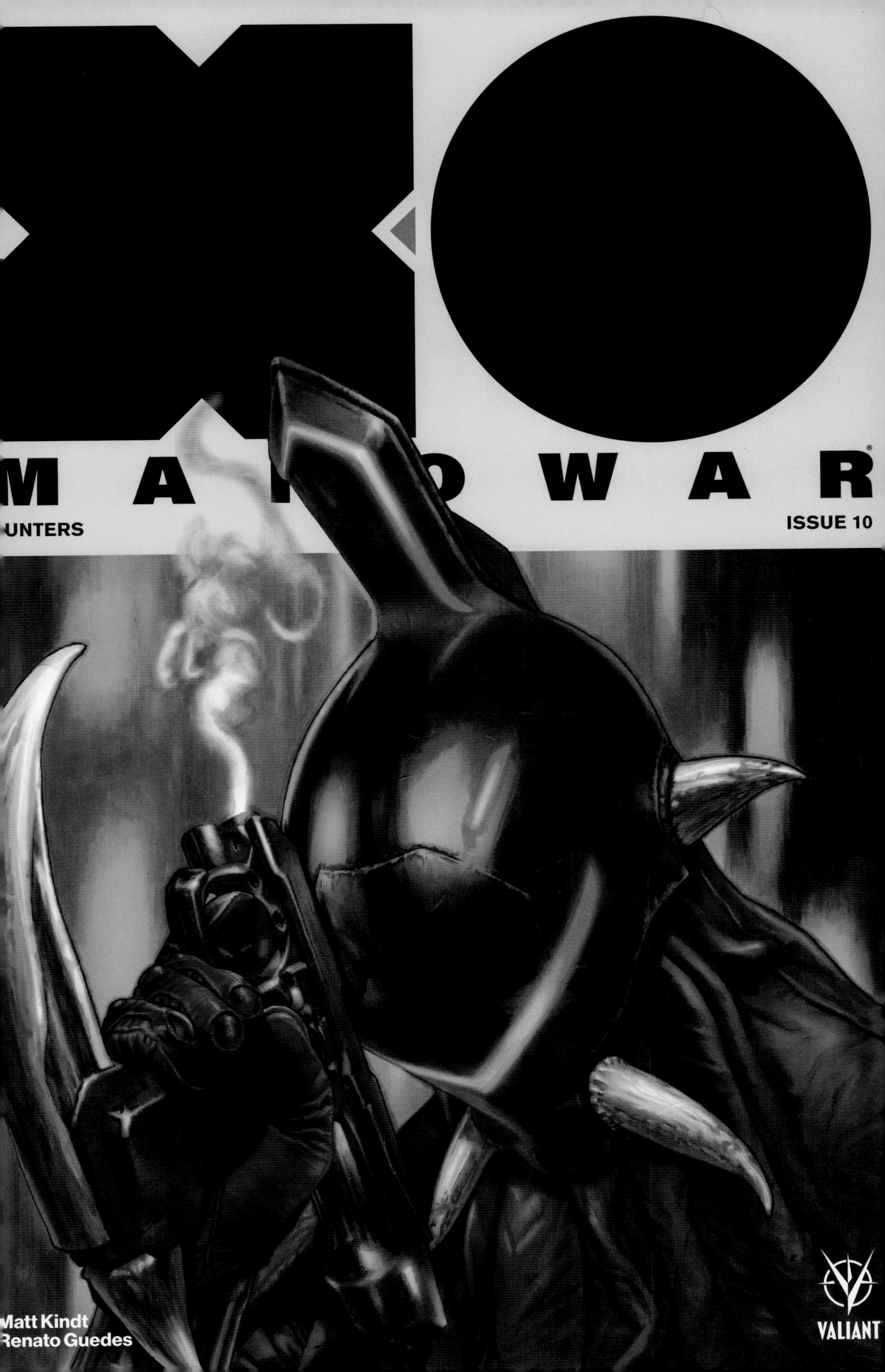
UNTERS
ISSUE 10
Matt Kindt
Renato Guedes
VALIANT

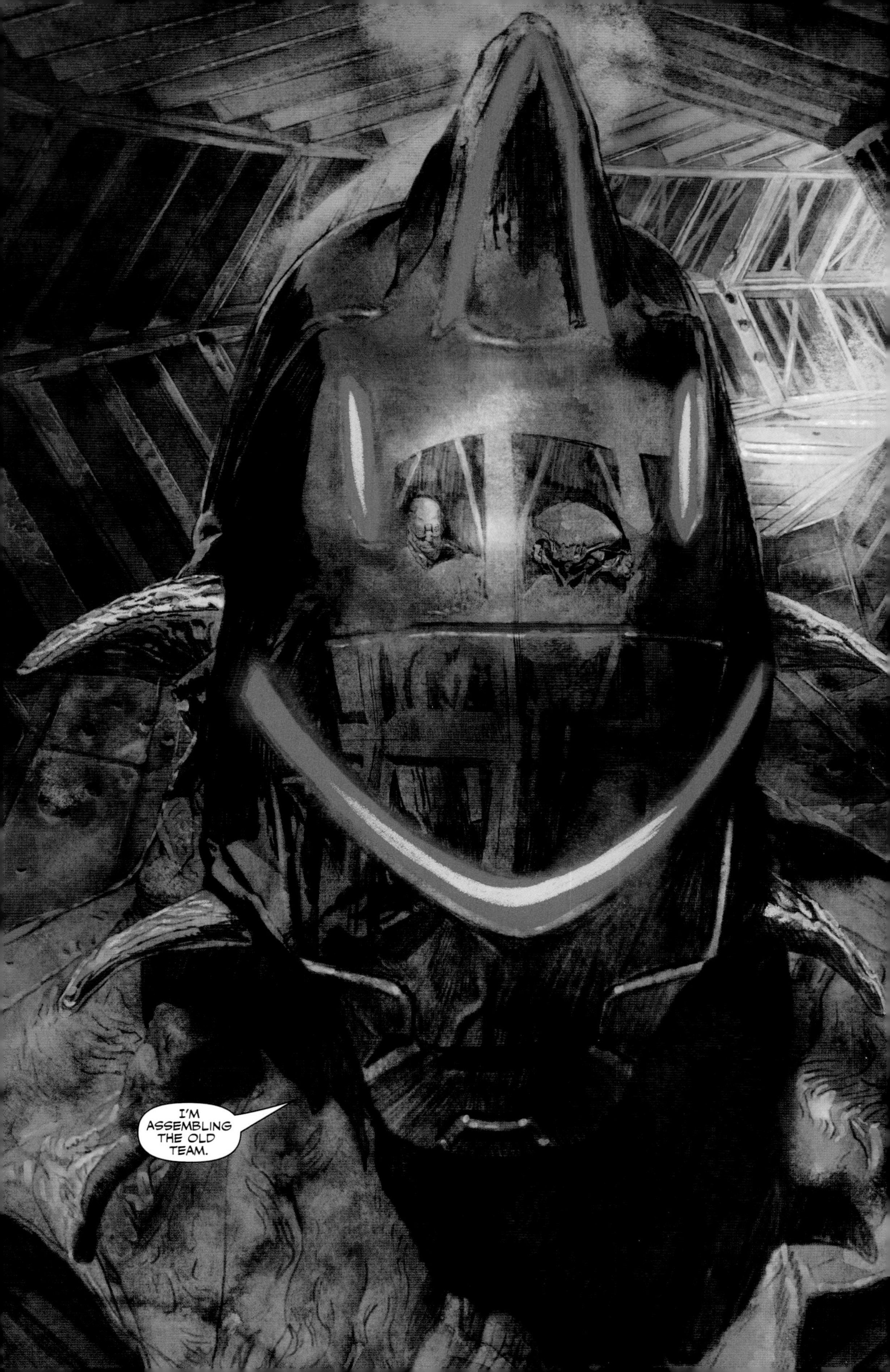
I'M ASSEMBLING THE OLD TEAM.

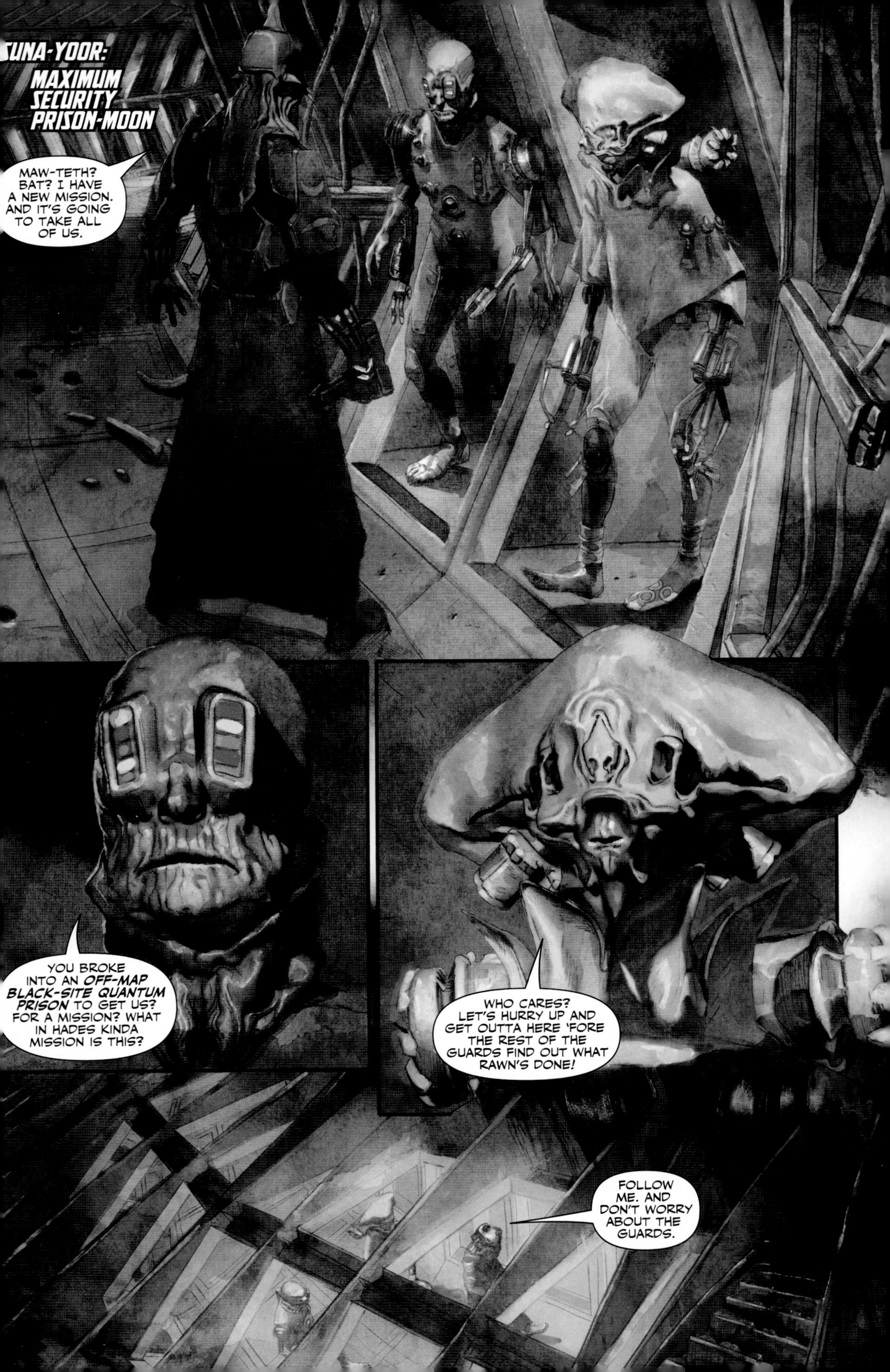

LUNA-YOOR:
MAXIMUM SECURITY PRISON-MOON
MAW-TETH? BAT? I HAVE A NEW MISSION. AND IT'S GOING TO TAKE ALL OF US.
YOU BROKE INTO AN *OFF-MAP BLACK-SITE QUANTUM PRISON* TO GET US? FOR A MISSION? WHAT IN HADES KINDA MISSION IS THIS?
WHO CARES? LET'S HURRY UP AND GET OUTTA HERE 'FORE THE REST OF THE GUARDS FIND OUT WHAT RAWN'S DONE!
FOLLOW ME. AND DON'T WORRY ABOUT THE GUARDS.

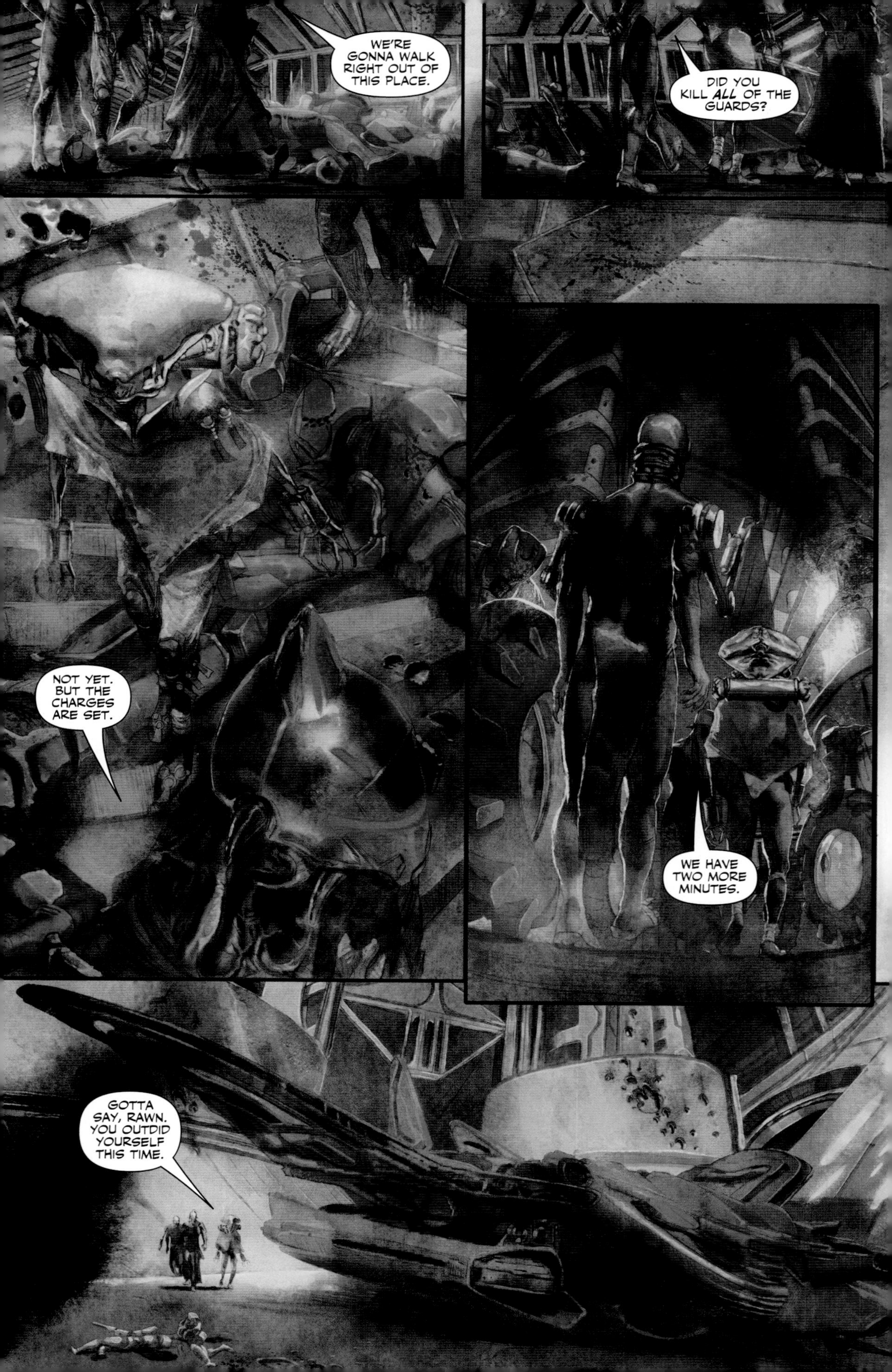
WE'RE GONNA WALK RIGHT OUT OF THIS PLACE.
DID YOU KILL ALL OF THE GUARDS?
NOT YET. BUT THE CHARGES ARE SET.
WE HAVE TWO MORE MINUTES.
GOTTA SAY, RAWN. YOU OUTDID YOURSELF THIS TIME.

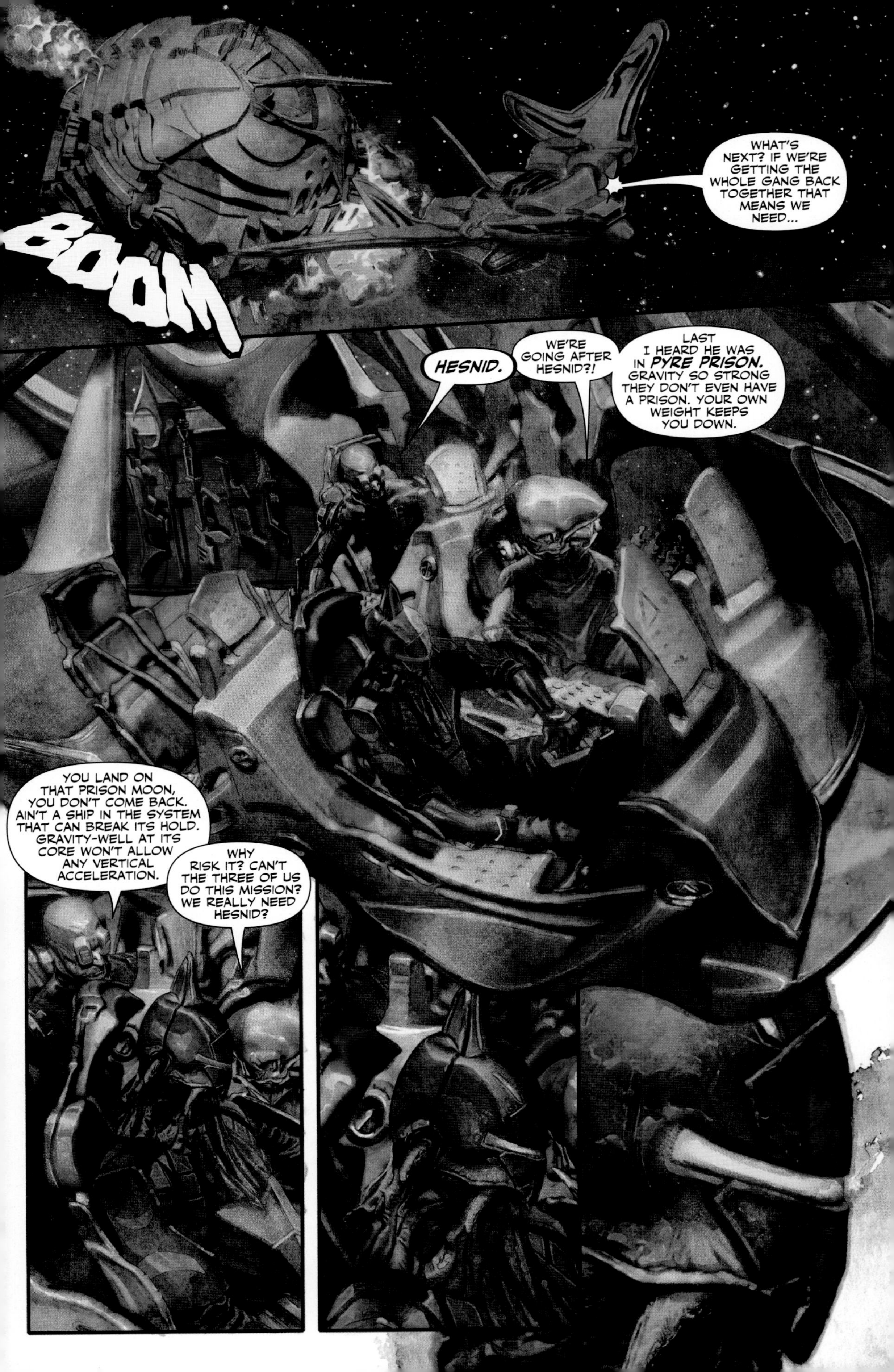
WHAT'S NEXT? IF WE'RE GETTING THE WHOLE GANG BACK TOGETHER THAT MEANS WE NEED...
BOOM
HESNID.
WE'RE GOING AFTER HESNID?!
LAST I HEARD HE WAS IN PYRE PRISON. GRAVITY SO STRONG THEY DON'T EVEN HAVE A PRISON. YOUR OWN WEIGHT KEEPS YOU DOWN.
YOU LAND ON THAT PRISON MOON, YOU DON'T COME BACK. AIN'T A SHIP IN THE SYSTEM THAT CAN BREAK ITS HOLD. GRAVITY-WELL AT ITS CORE WON'T ALLOW ANY VERTICAL ACCELERATION.
WHY RISK IT? CAN'T THE THREE OF US DO THIS MISSION? WE REALLY NEED HESNID?

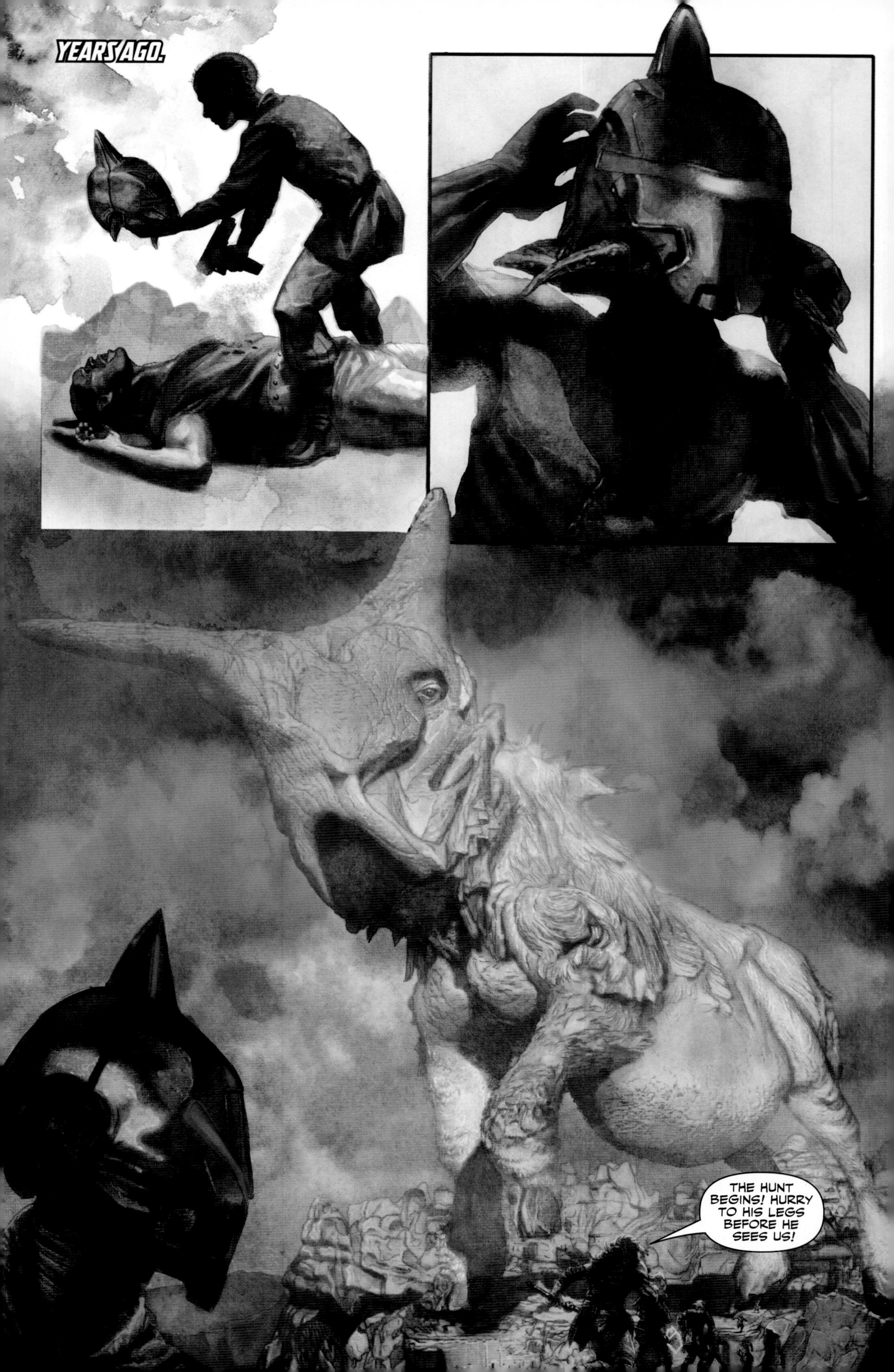
YEARS AGO.
THE HUNT BEGINS! HURRY TO HIS LEGS BEFORE HE SEES US!

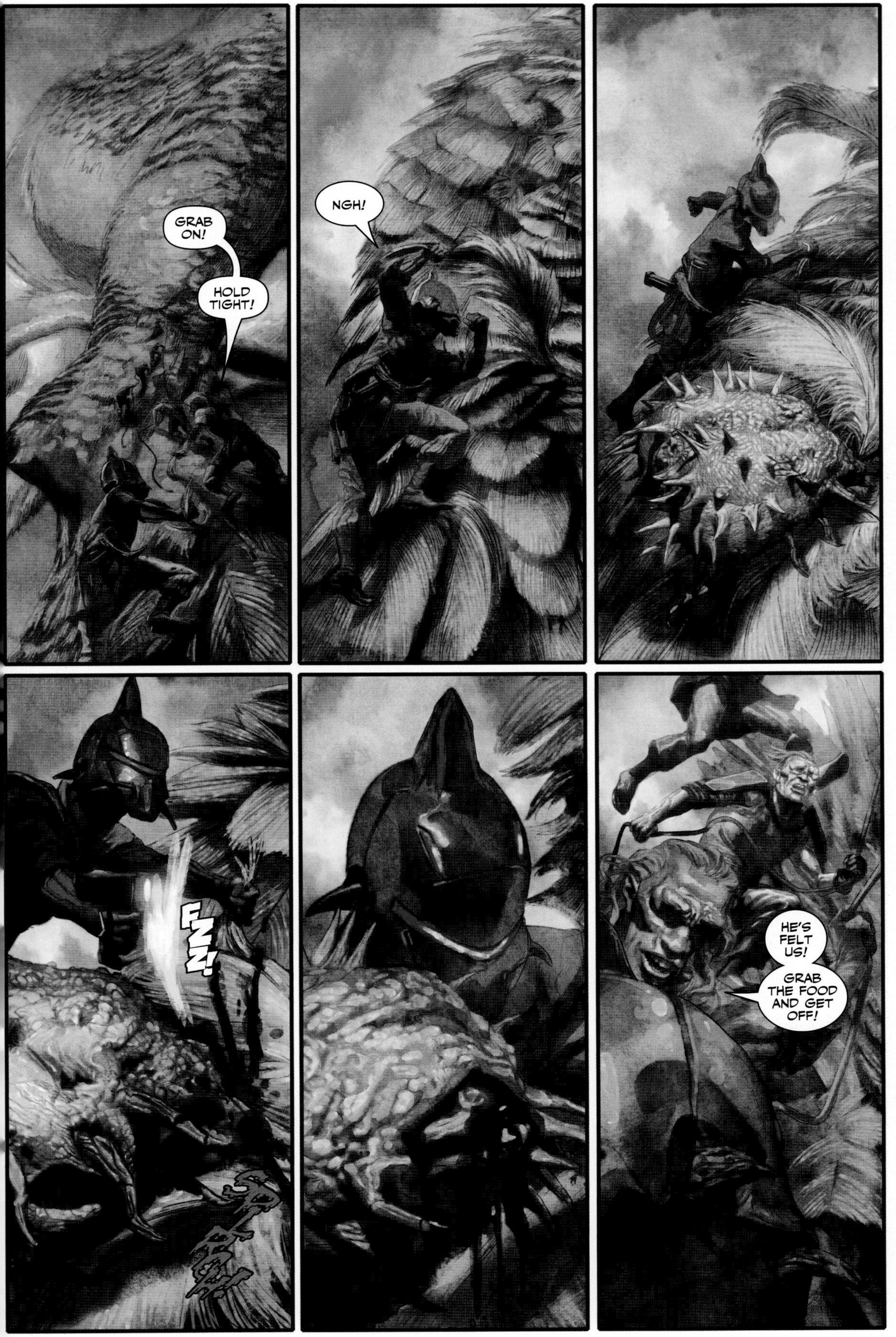
GRAB ON!
HOLD TIGHT!
NGH!
FZZ!
HE'S FELT US!
GRAB THE FOOD AND GET OFF!

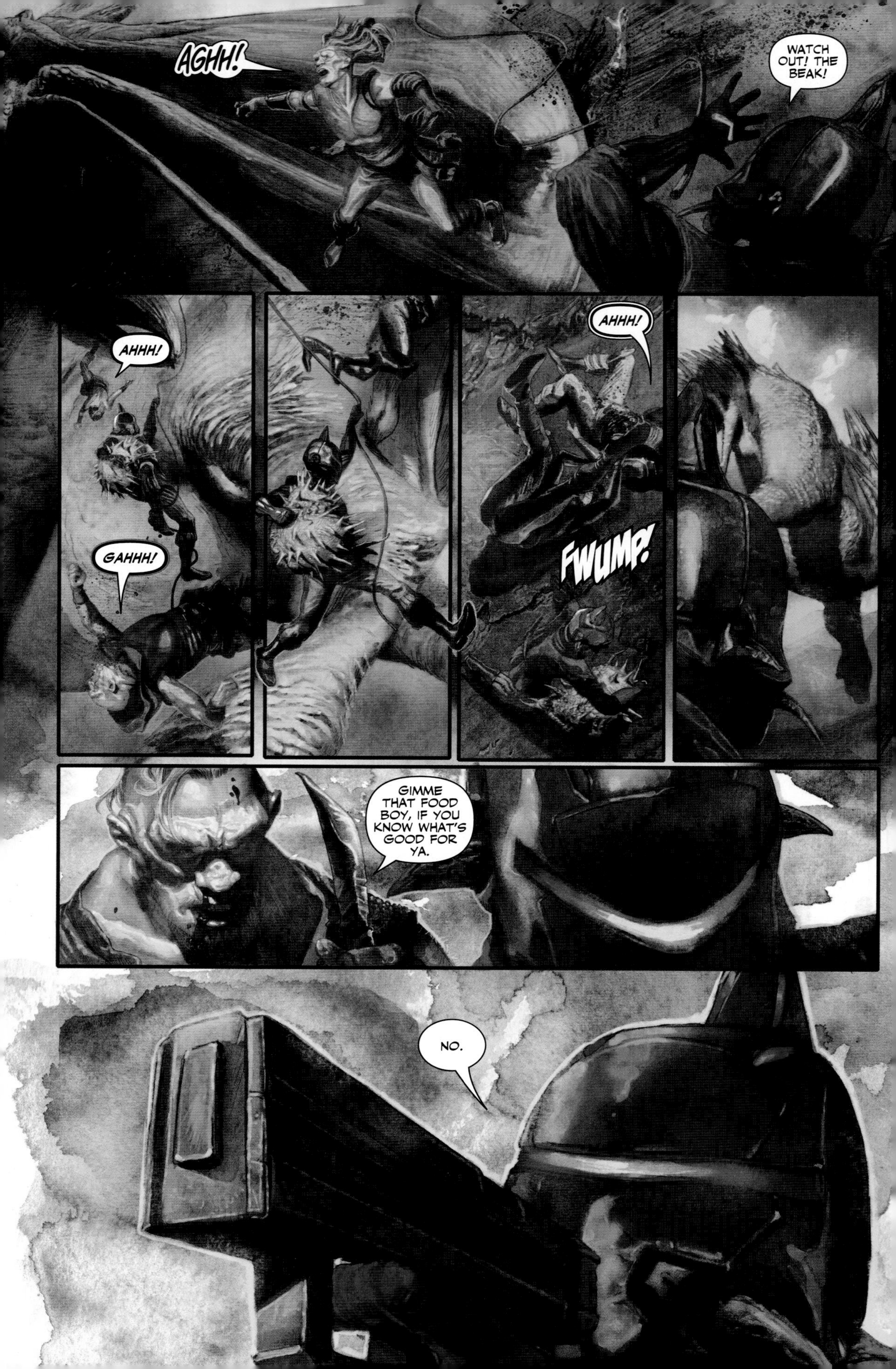
AGHH!
WATCH OUT! THE BEAK!
AHHH!
GAHHH!
AHHH!
FWUMP!
GIMME THAT FOOD BOY, IF YOU KNOW WHAT'S GOOD FOR YA.
NO.

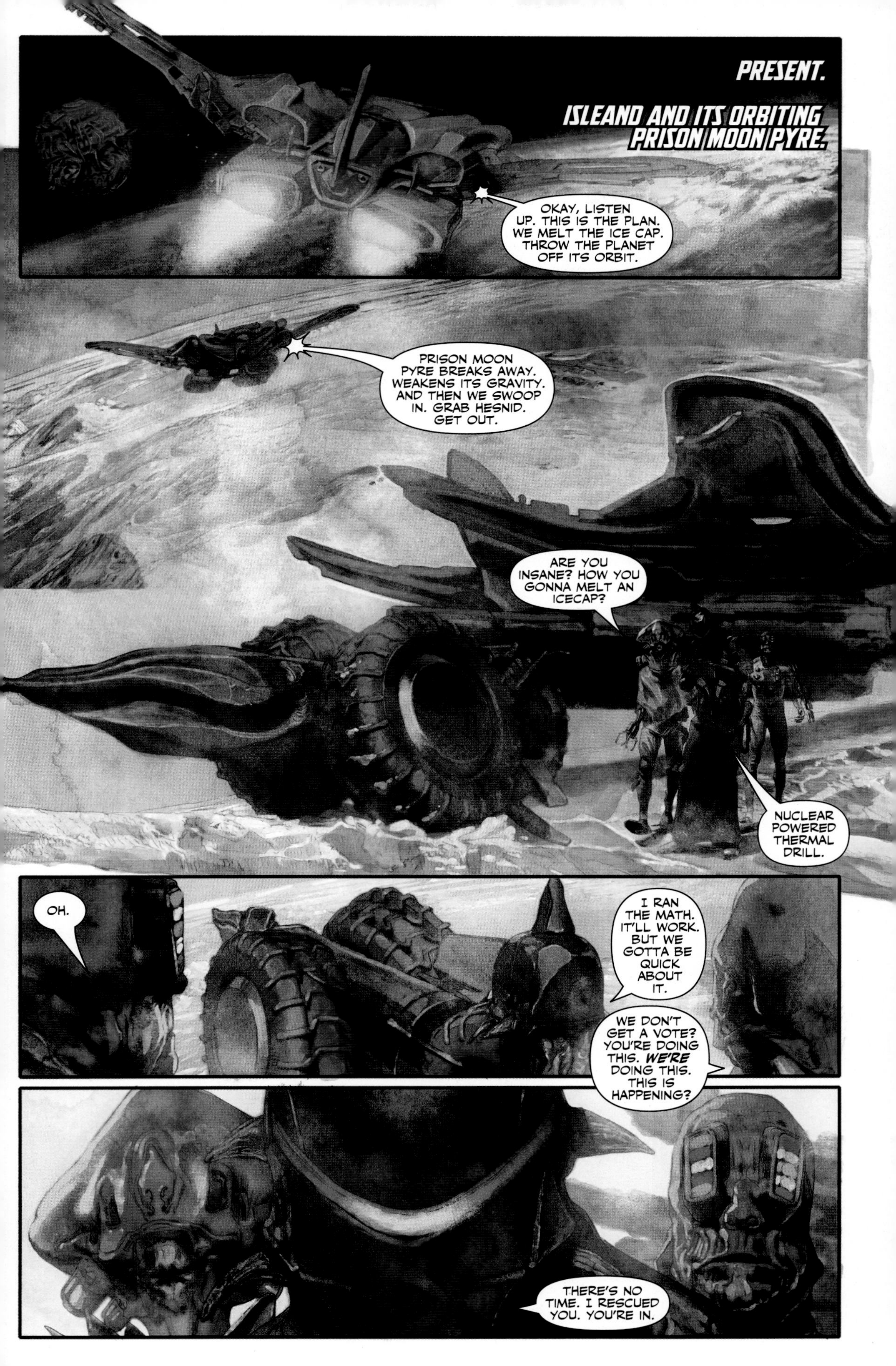
PRESENT.
ISLEAND AND ITS ORBITING PRISON MOON PYRE.
OKAY, LISTEN UP. THIS IS THE PLAN. WE MELT THE ICE CAP. THROW THE PLANET OFF ITS ORBIT.
PRISON MOON PYRE BREAKS AWAY. WEAKENS ITS GRAVITY. AND THEN WE SWOOP IN. GRAB HESNID. GET OUT.
ARE YOU INSANE? HOW YOU GONNA MELT AN ICECAP?
NUCLEAR POWERED THERMAL DRILL.
OH.
I RAN THE MATH. IT'LL WORK. BUT WE GOTTA BE QUICK ABOUT IT.
WE DON'T GET A VOTE? YOU'RE DOING THIS. *WE'RE* DOING THIS. THIS IS HAPPENING?
THERE'S NO TIME. I RESCUED YOU. YOU'RE IN.

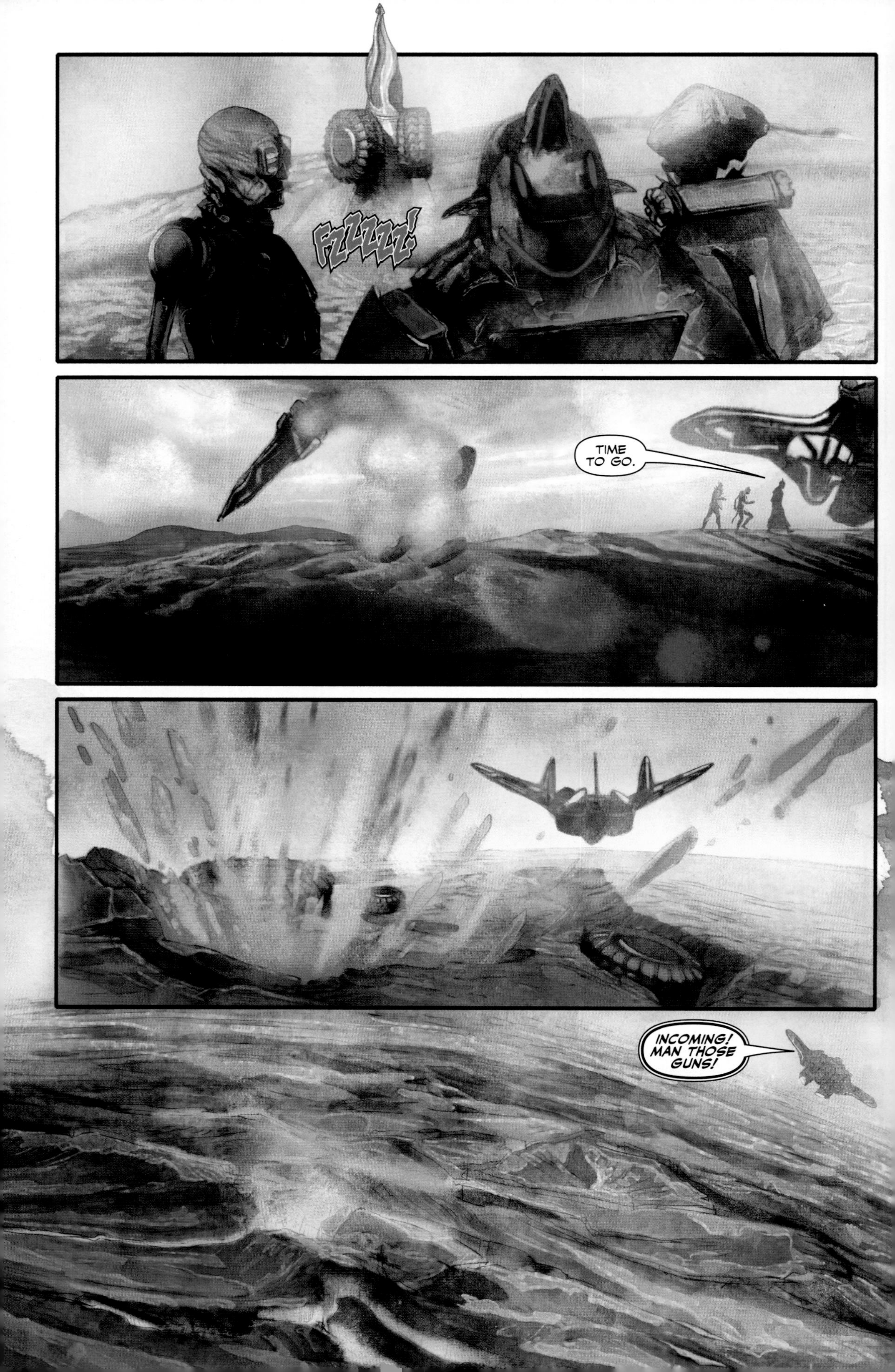
FZZZZZ!
TIME TO GO.
INCOMING! MAN THOSE GUNS!

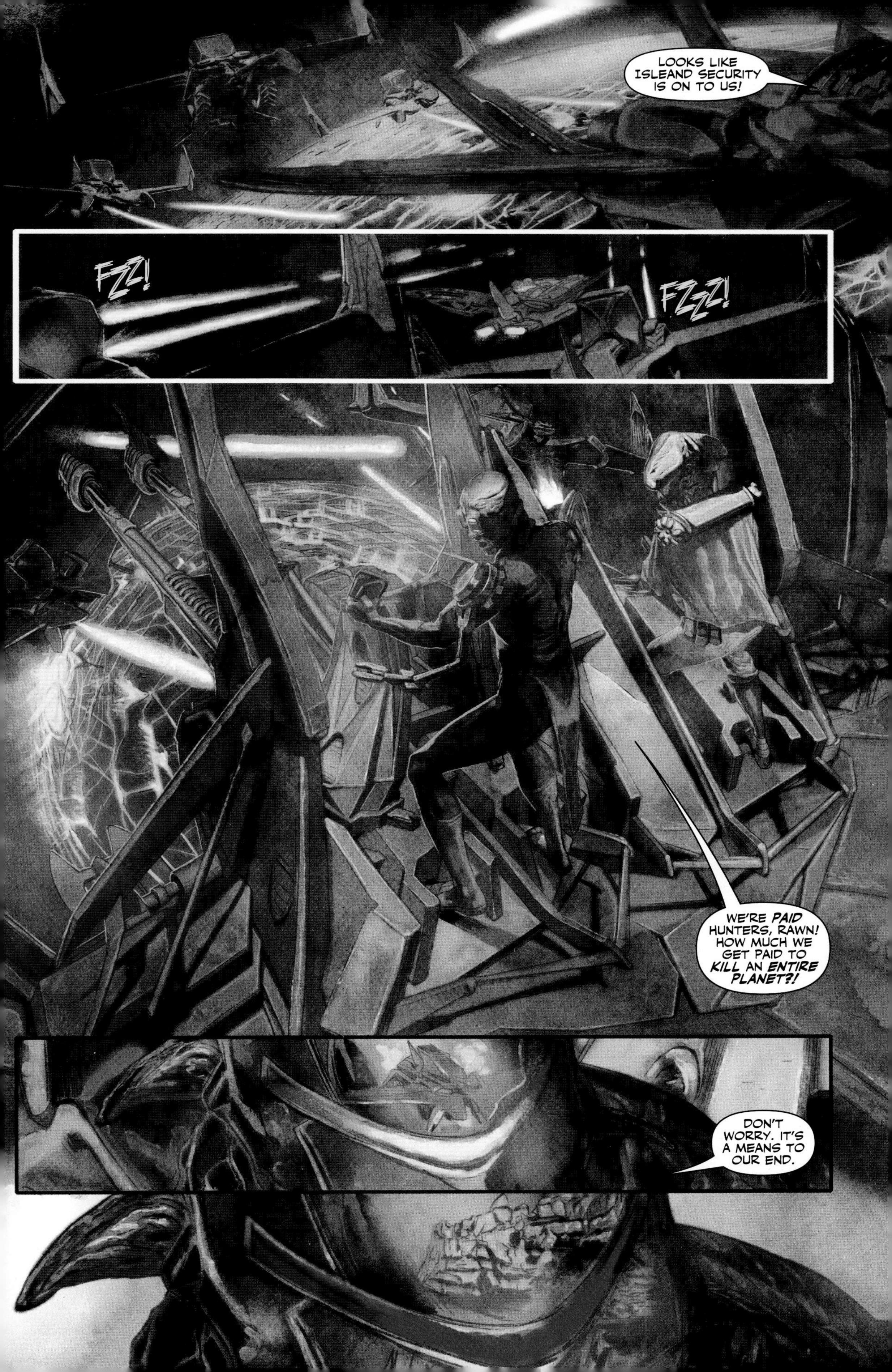

LOOKS LIKE ISLEAND SECURITY IS ON TO US!
FZZ!
FZZZ!
WE'RE *PAID* HUNTERS, RAWN! HOW MUCH WE GET PAID TO *KILL* AN *ENTIRE PLANET?!*
DON'T WORRY. IT'S A MEANS TO OUR END.

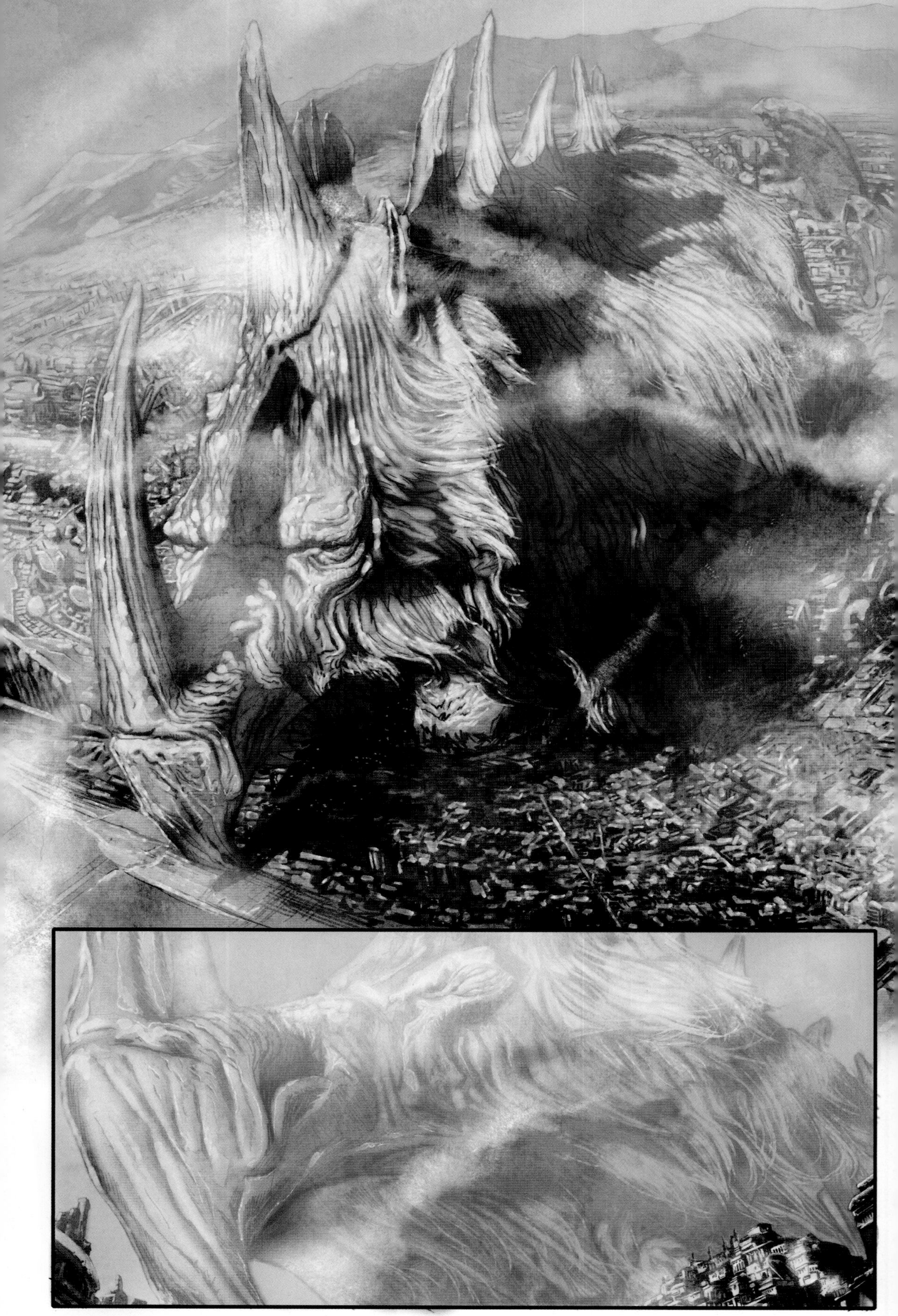

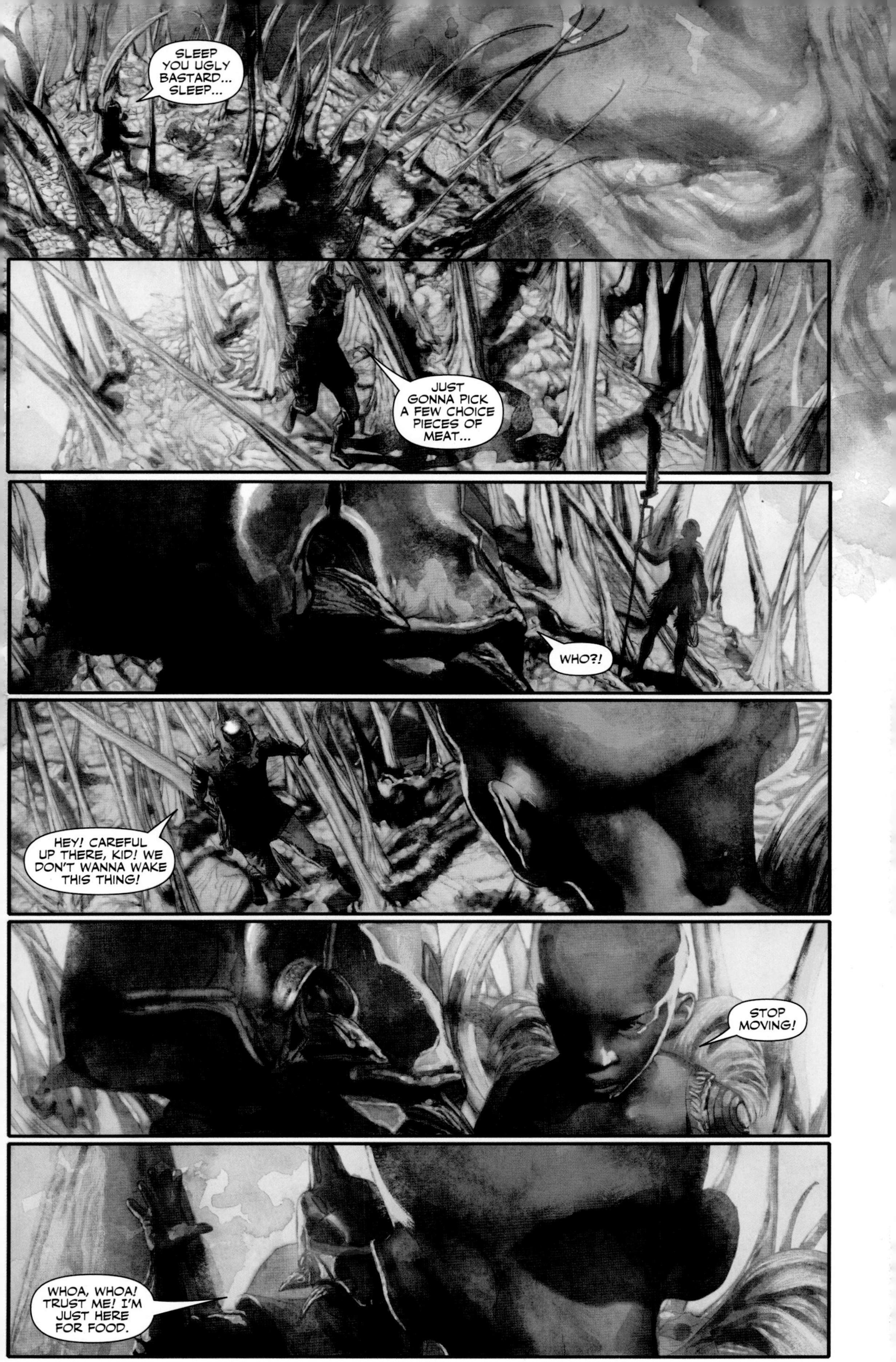
SLEEP YOU UGLY BASTARD... SLEEP...
JUST GONNA PICK A FEW CHOICE PIECES OF MEAT...
WHO?!
HEY! CAREFUL UP THERE, KID! WE DON'T WANNA WAKE THIS THING!
STOP MOVING!
WHOA, WHOA! TRUST ME! I'M JUST HERE FOR FOOD.

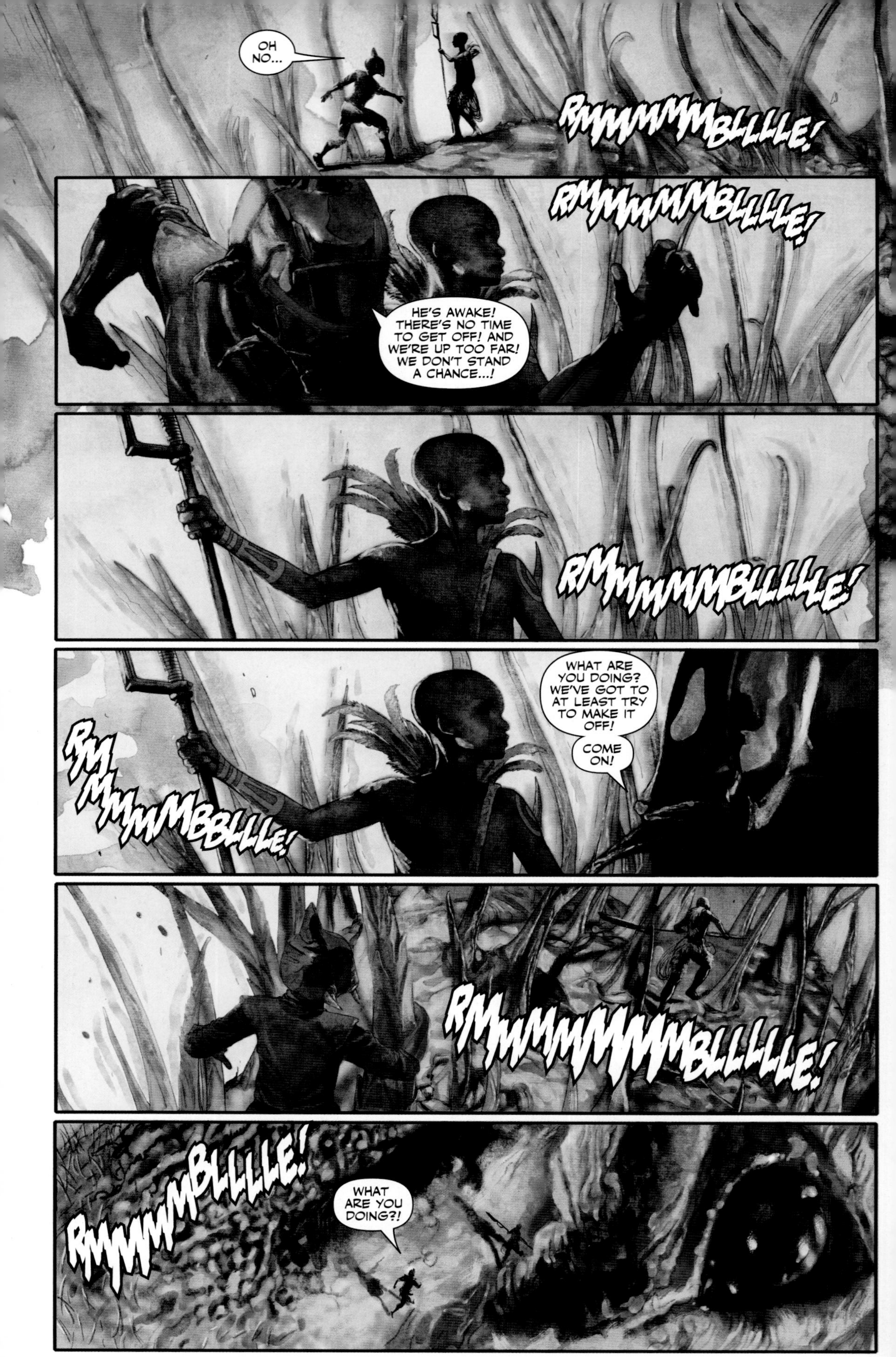
OH NO...
RMMMMMBLLLE!
RMMMMMBLLLE!
HE'S AWAKE! THERE'S NO TIME TO GET OFF! AND WE'RE UP TOO FAR! WE DON'T STAND A CHANCE...!
RMMMMMBLLLLE!
RMMMMMBBLLLE!
WHAT ARE YOU DOING? WE'VE GOT TO AT LEAST TRY TO MAKE IT OFF!
COME ON!
RMMMMMMMMBLLLLE!
RMMMMMBLLLLE!
WHAT ARE YOU DOING?!

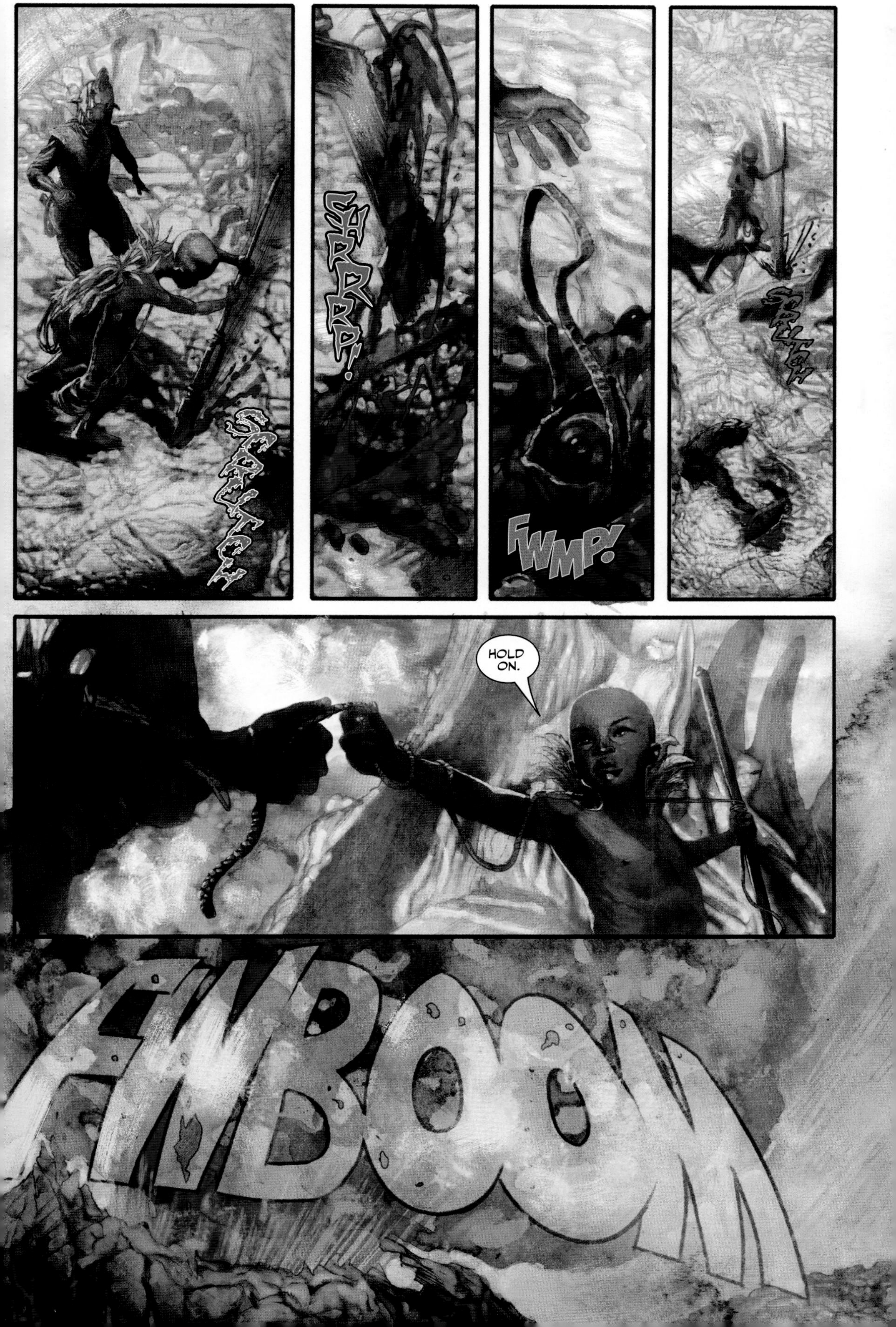
SHRRRD!
FWMP!
HOLD ON.

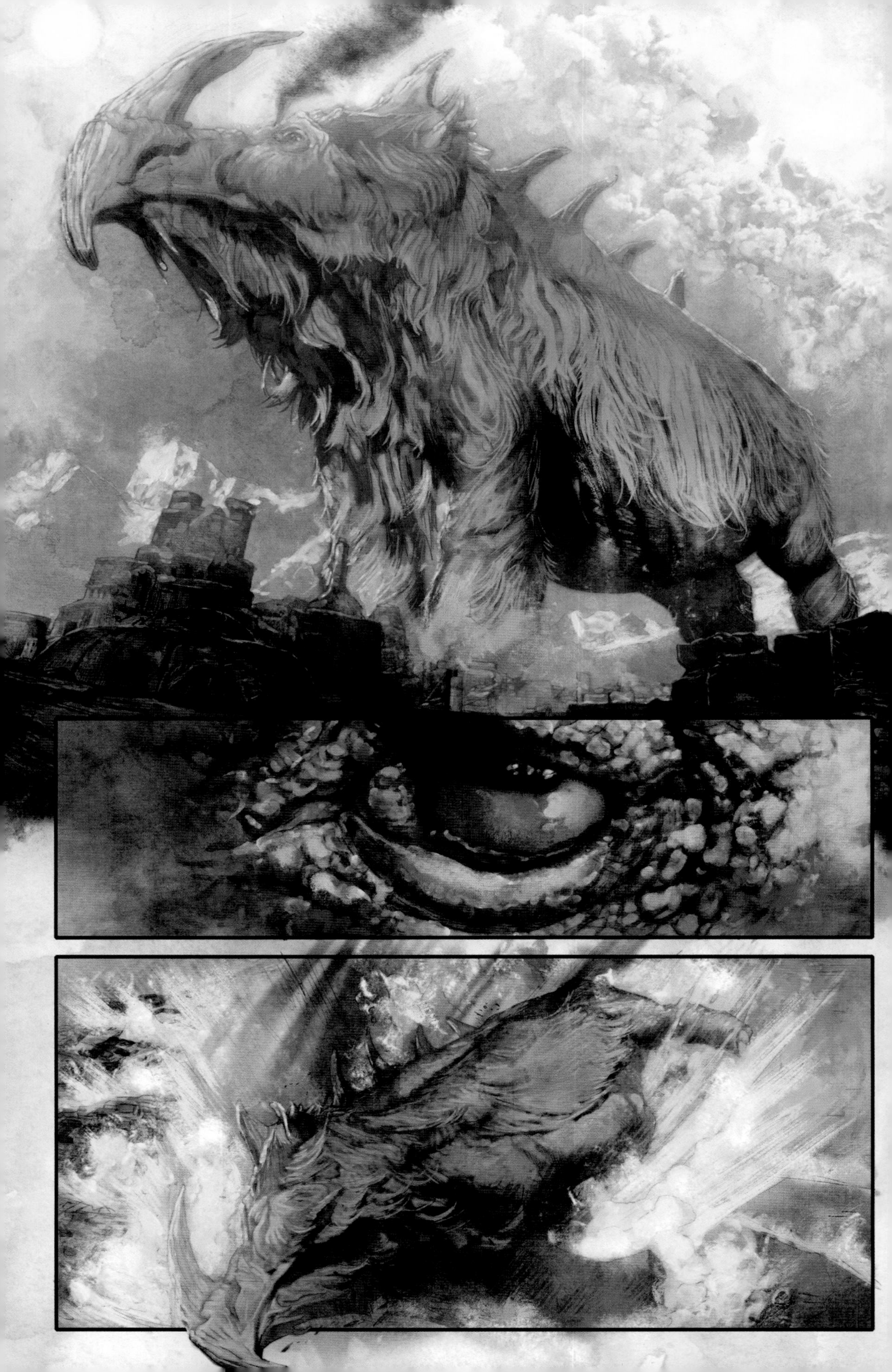

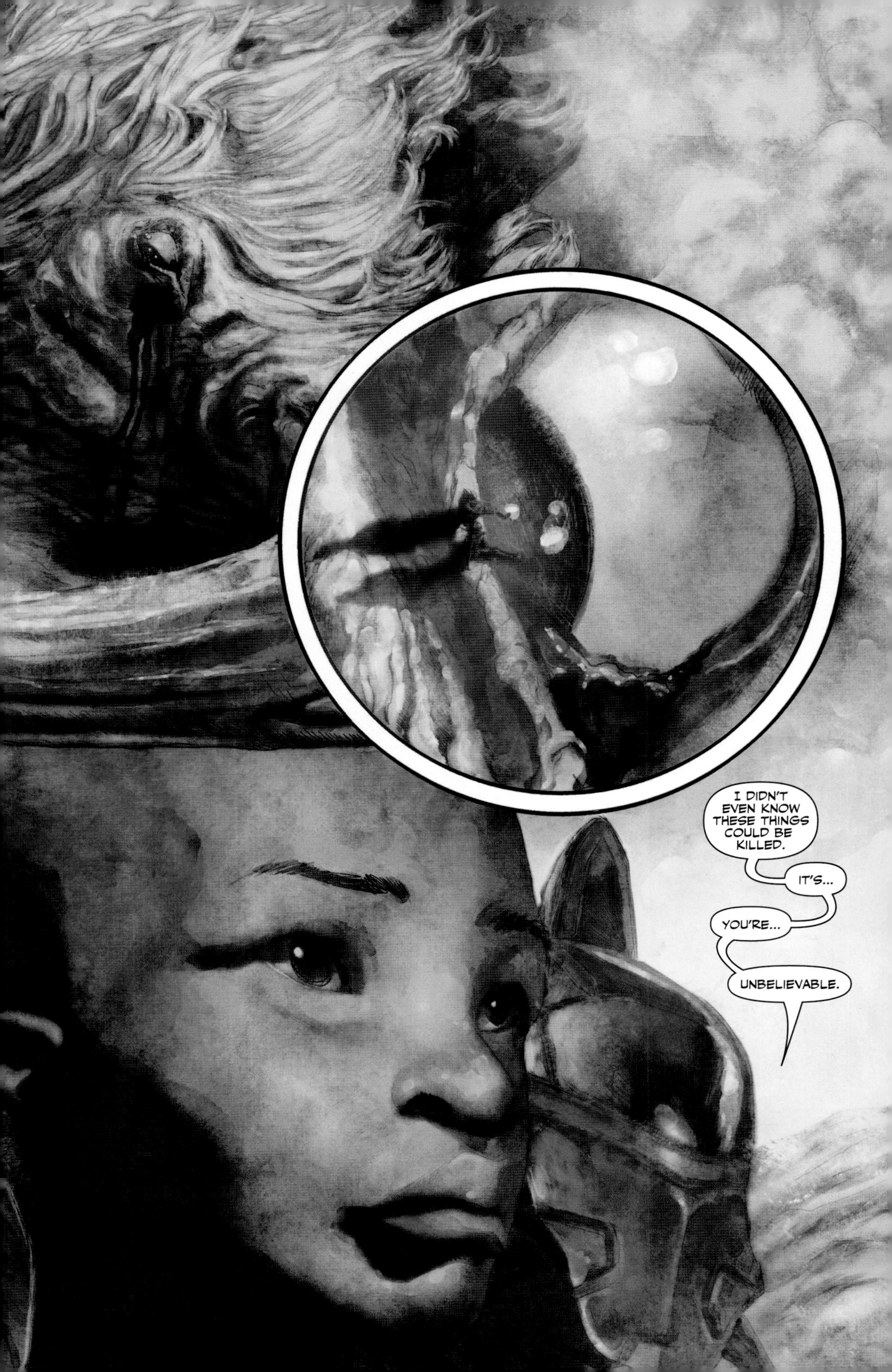
I DIDN'T EVEN KNOW THESE THINGS COULD BE KILLED.
IT'S...
YOU'RE...
UNBELIEVABLE.

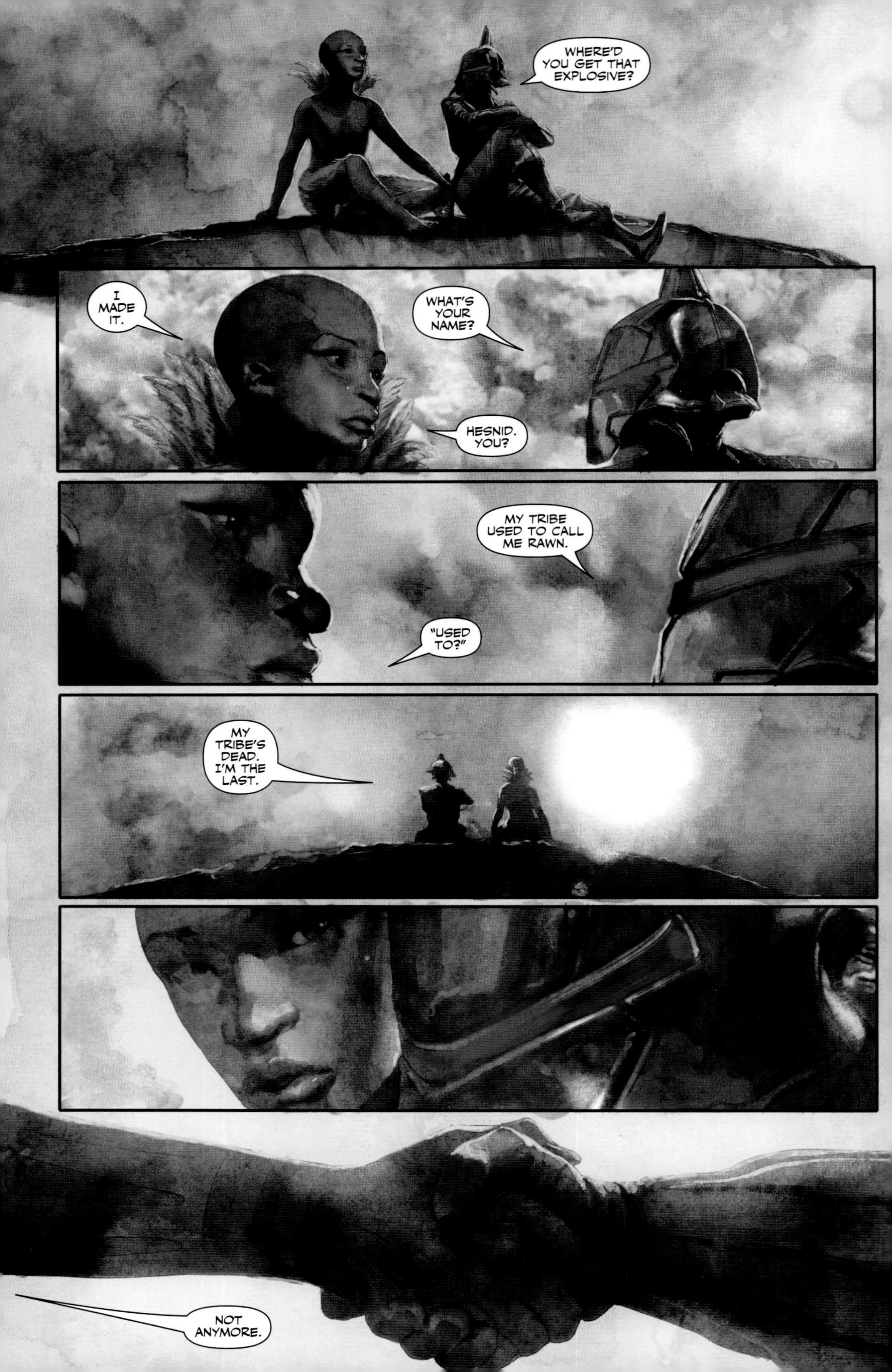
WHERE'D YOU GET THAT EXPLOSIVE?
I MADE IT.
WHAT'S YOUR NAME?
HESNID. YOU?
MY TRIBE USED TO CALL ME RAWN.
"USED TO?"
MY TRIBE'S DEAD. I'M THE LAST.
NOT ANYMORE.

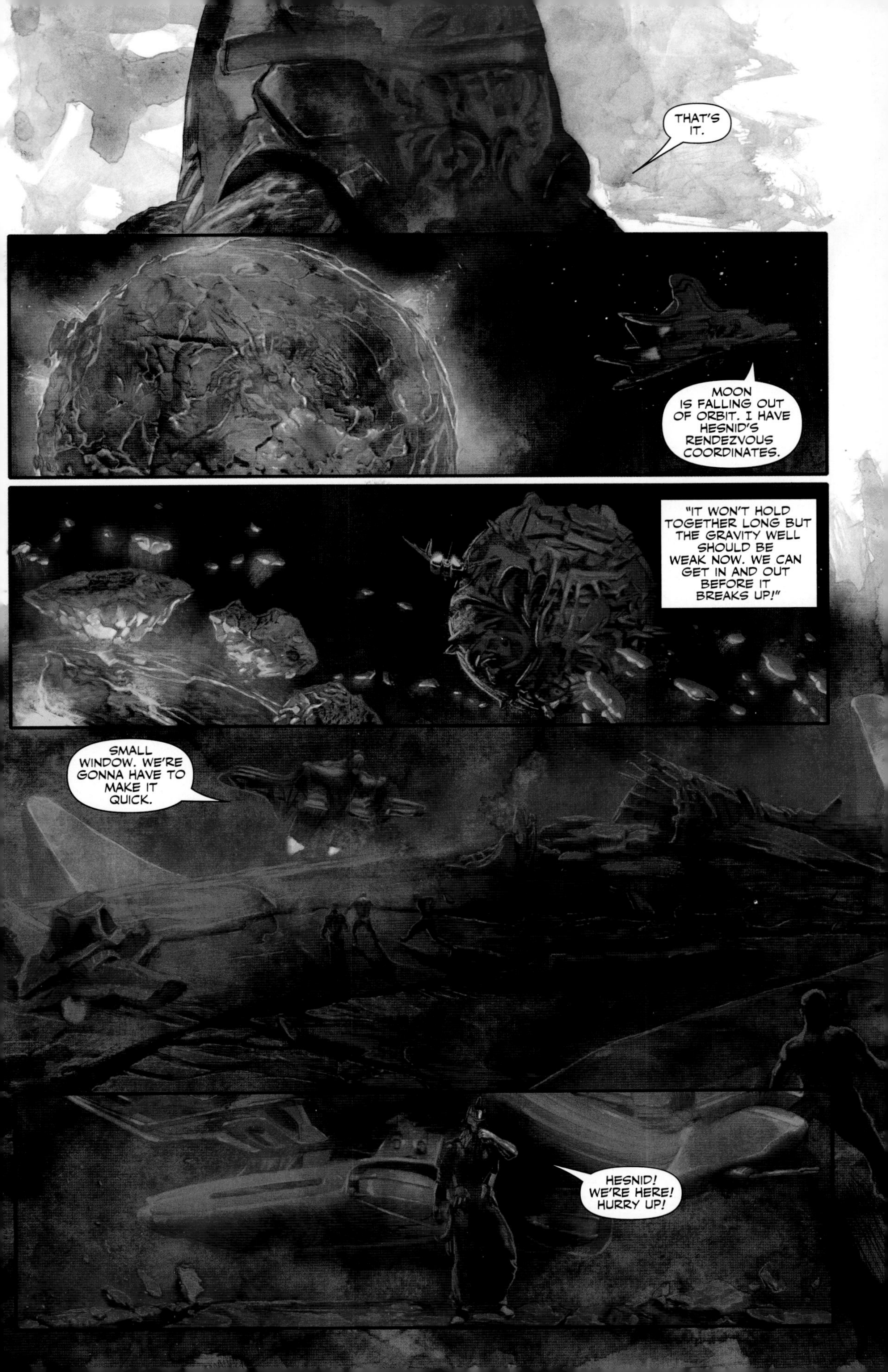
THAT'S IT.
MOON IS FALLING OUT OF ORBIT. I HAVE HESNID'S RENDEZVOUS COORDINATES.
"IT WON'T HOLD TOGETHER LONG BUT THE GRAVITY WELL SHOULD BE WEAK NOW. WE CAN GET IN AND OUT BEFORE IT BREAKS UP!"
SMALL WINDOW. WE'RE GONNA HAVE TO MAKE IT QUICK.
HESNID! WE'RE HERE! HURRY UP!

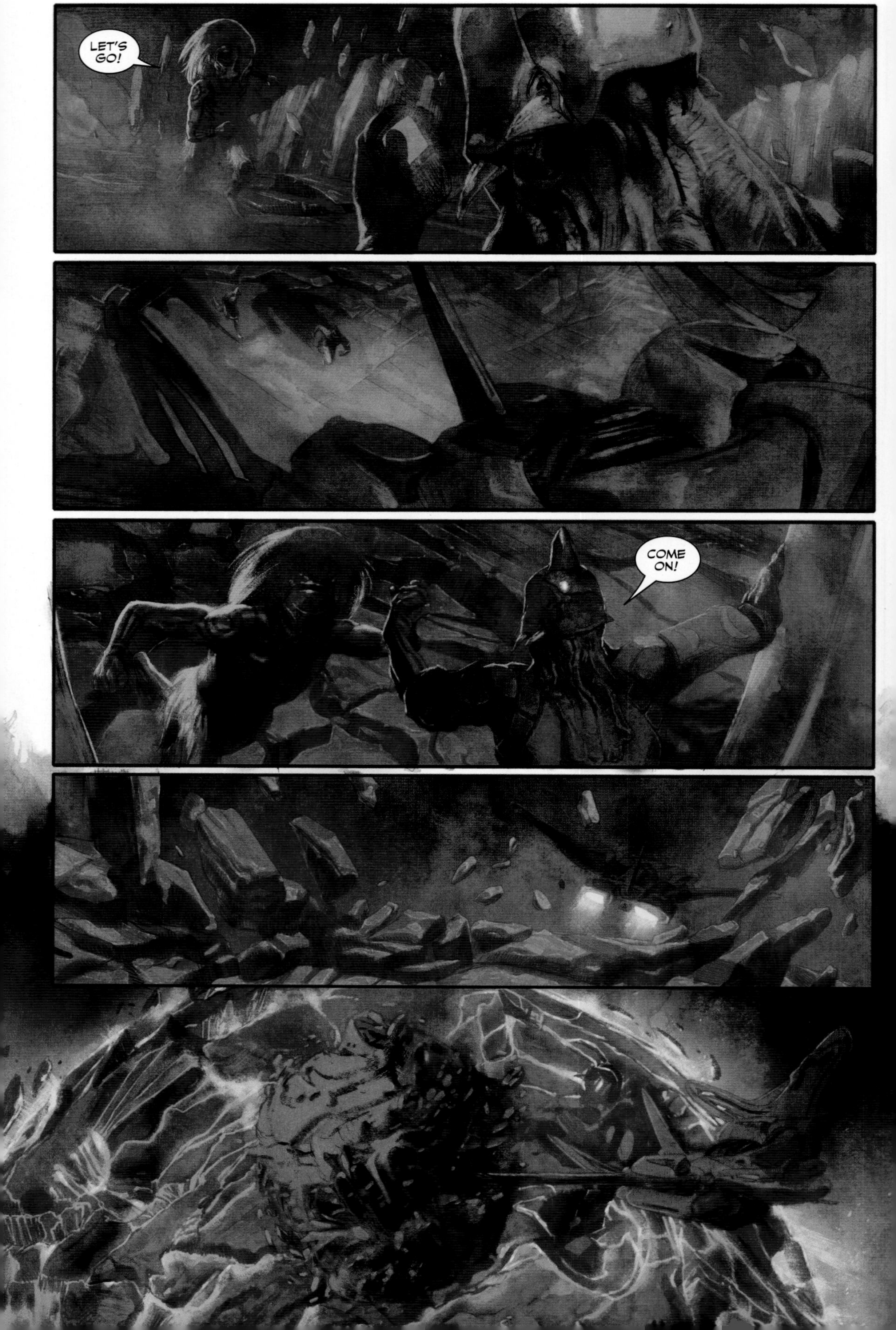
LET'S GO!
COME ON!

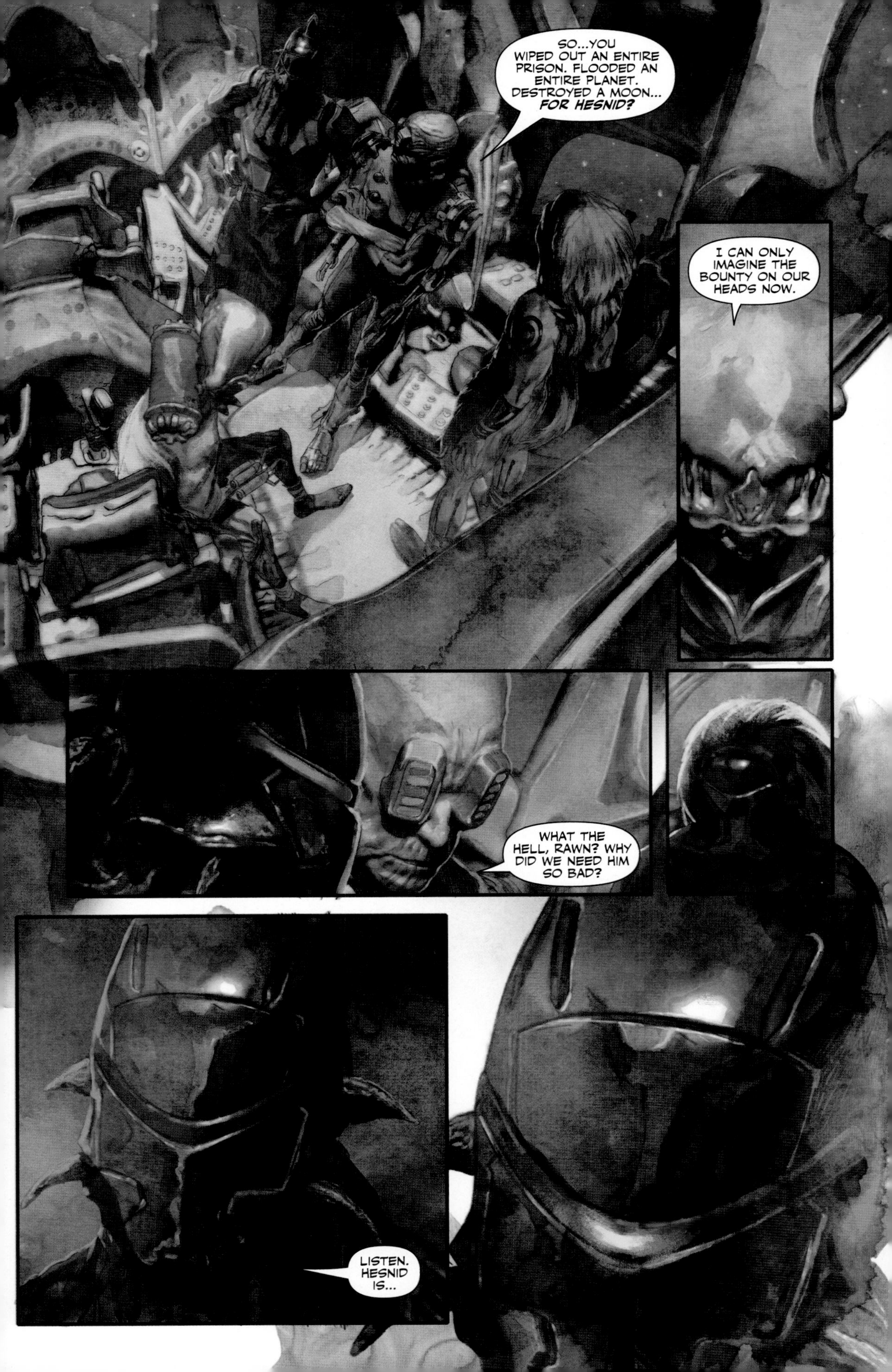
SO...YOU WIPED OUT AN ENTIRE PRISON. FLOODED AN ENTIRE PLANET. DESTROYED A MOON... *FOR HESNID?*
I CAN ONLY IMAGINE THE BOUNTY ON OUR HEADS NOW.
WHAT THE HELL, RAWN? WHY DID WE NEED HIM SO BAD?
LISTEN. HESNID IS...

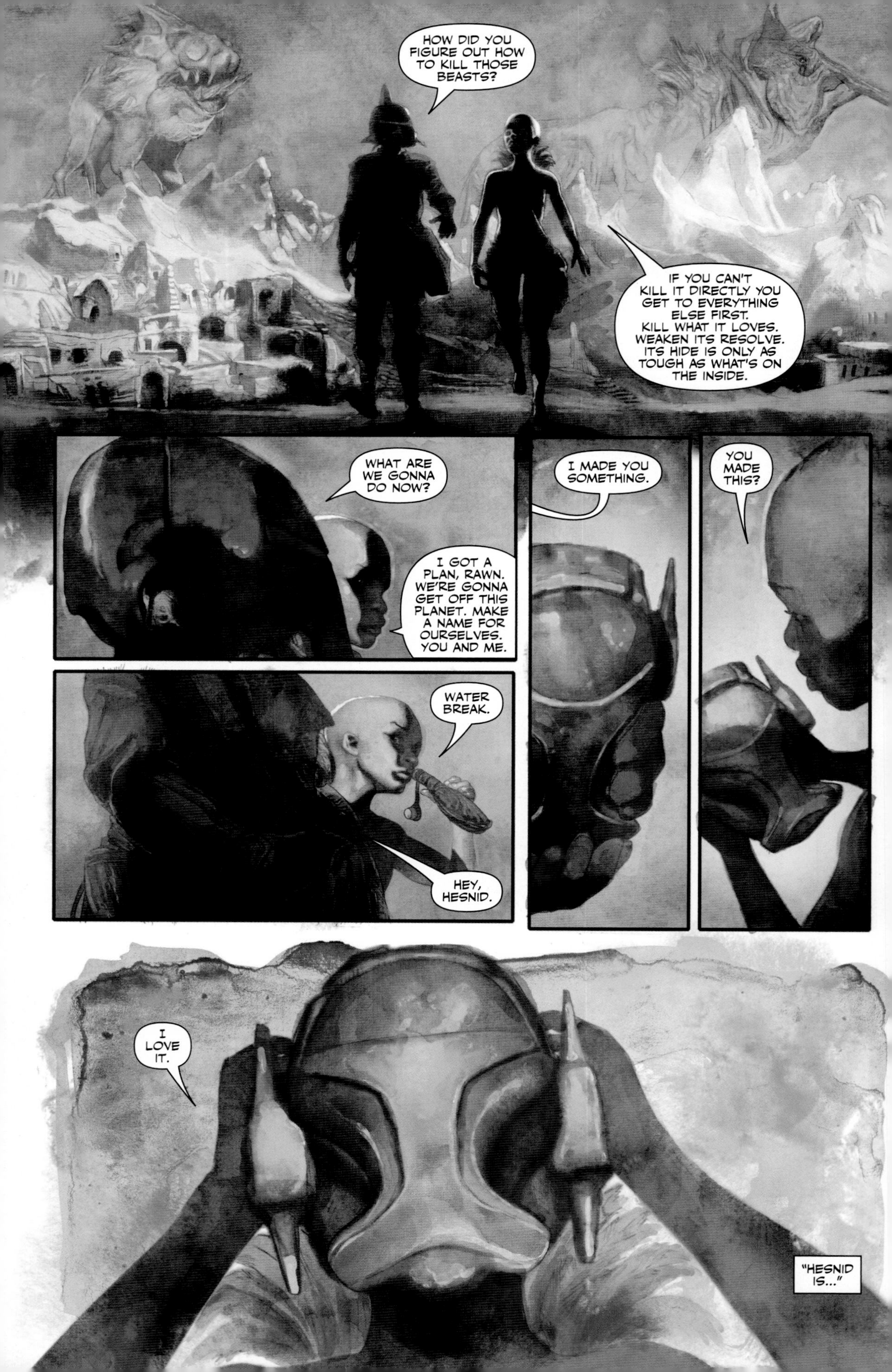
HOW DID YOU FIGURE OUT HOW TO KILL THOSE BEASTS?
IF YOU CAN'T KILL IT DIRECTLY YOU GET TO EVERYTHING ELSE FIRST. KILL WHAT IT LOVES. WEAKEN ITS RESOLVE. ITS HIDE IS ONLY AS TOUGH AS WHAT'S ON THE INSIDE.
WHAT ARE WE GONNA DO NOW?
I GOT A PLAN, RAWN. WE'RE GONNA GET OFF THIS PLANET. MAKE A NAME FOR OURSELVES. YOU AND ME.
WATER BREAK.
HEY, HESNID.
I MADE YOU SOMETHING.
YOU MADE THIS?
I LOVE IT.
"HESNID IS..."

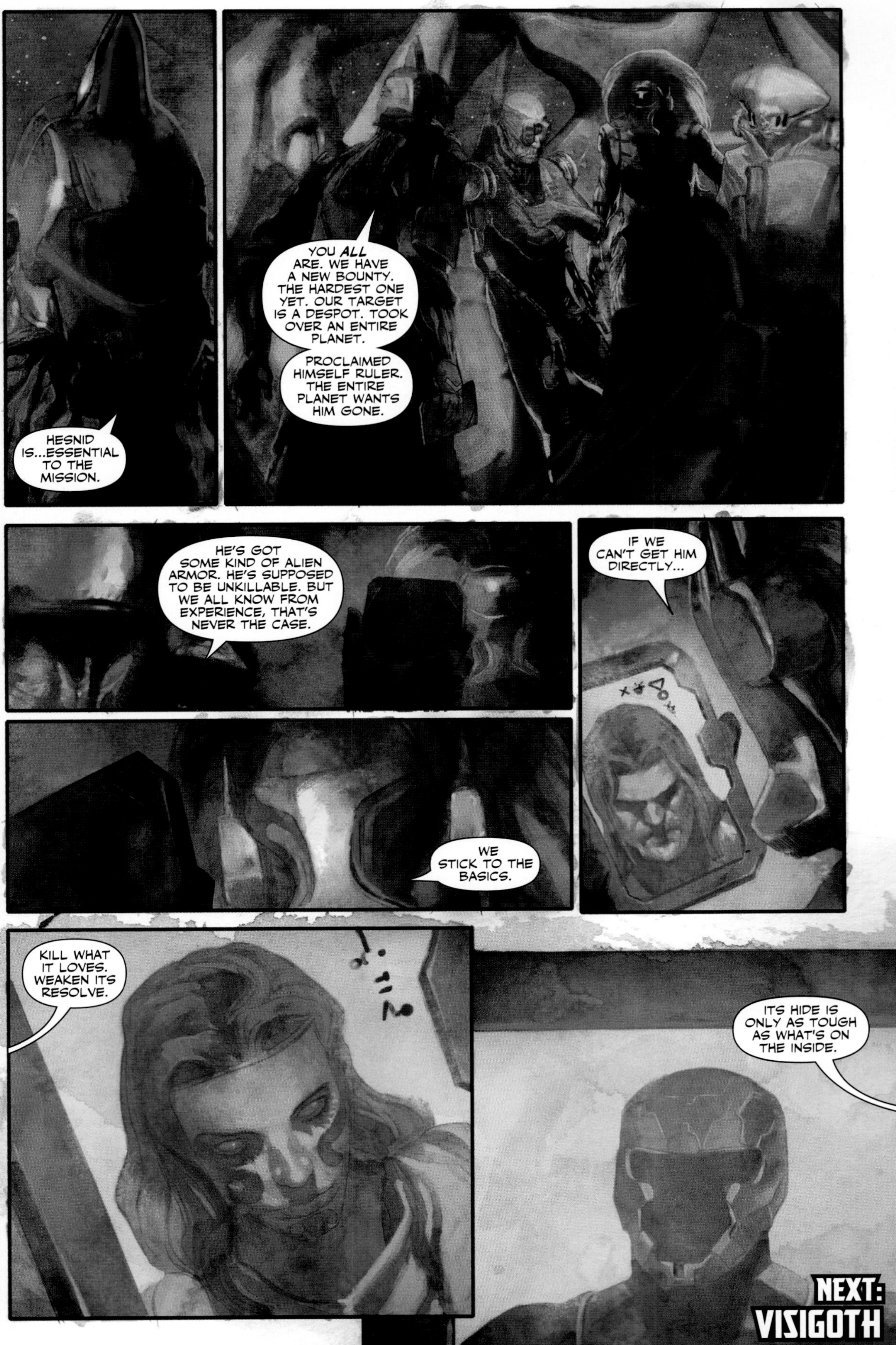

HESNID IS...ESSENTIAL TO THE MISSION.
YOU ALL ARE. WE HAVE A NEW BOUNTY. THE HARDEST ONE YET. OUR TARGET IS A DESPOT. TOOK OVER AN ENTIRE PLANET.
PROCLAIMED HIMSELF RULER. THE ENTIRE PLANET WANTS HIM GONE.
HE'S GOT SOME KIND OF ALIEN ARMOR. HE'S SUPPOSED TO BE UNKILLABLE. BUT WE ALL KNOW FROM EXPERIENCE, THAT'S NEVER THE CASE.
IF WE CAN'T GET HIM DIRECTLY...
WE STICK TO THE BASICS.
KILL WHAT IT LOVES. WEAKEN ITS RESOLVE.
ITS HIDE IS ONLY AS TOUGH AS WHAT'S ON THE INSIDE.
NEXT: VISIGOTH

X-O MANOWAR #7 | DESIGNS BY MATT KINDT AND LEWIS LAROSA
ARTWORK BY CLAYTON CRAIN

DESIGNING THE MONO-MEN

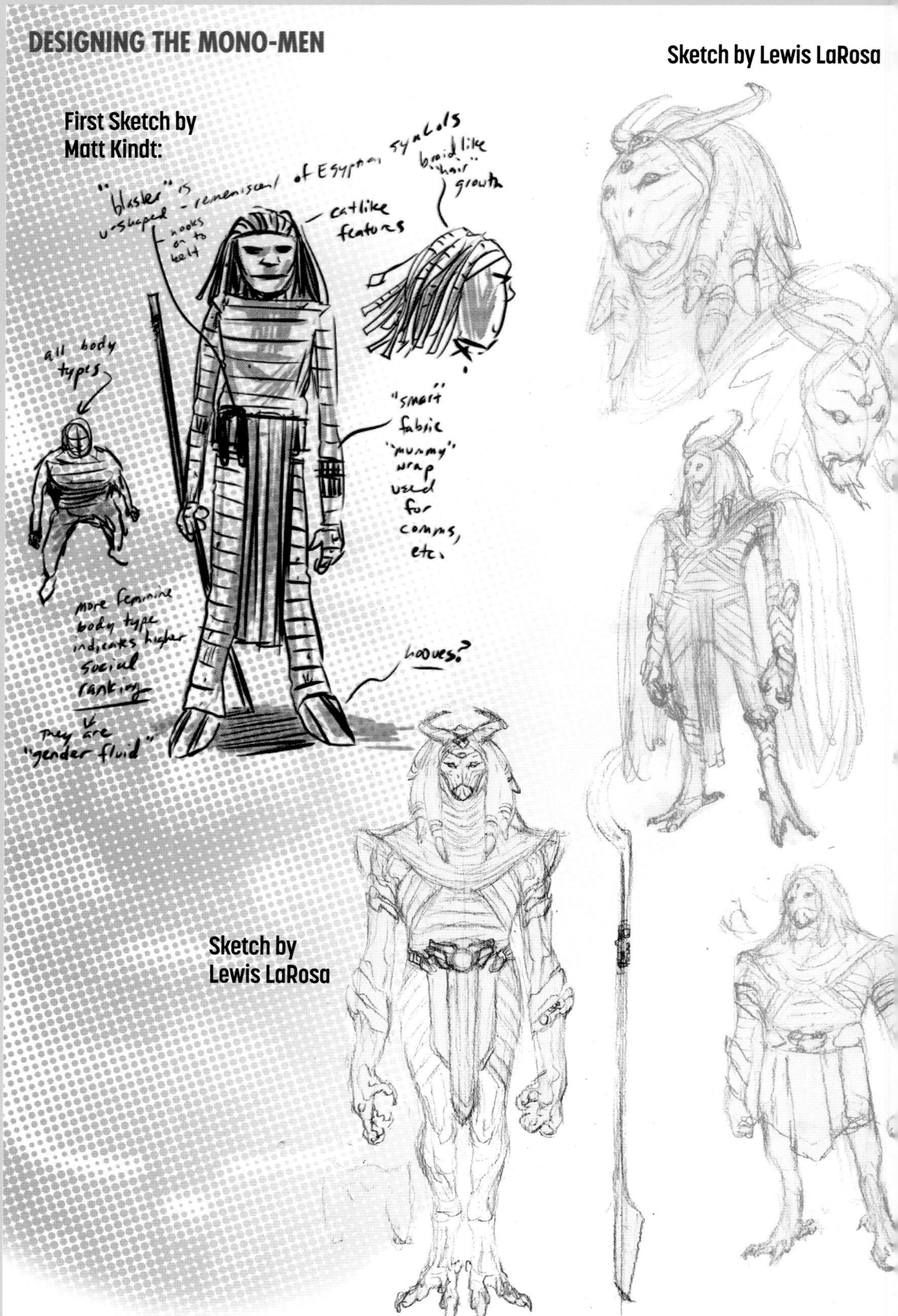
"blaster" is u-shaped - reminiscent of Egyptian symbols
hooks on to belt
catlike features
braid like "hair" growth
all body types
"smart" fabric "mummy" wrap used for comms, etc.
more feminine body type indicates higher social ranking
they are "gender fluid"
hooves?

First Sketch by Matt Kindt:

Sketch by Lewis LaRosa

Sketch by Lewis LaRosa

Originally published in *X-O MANOWAR (2017) #7 PRE-ORDER EDITION*

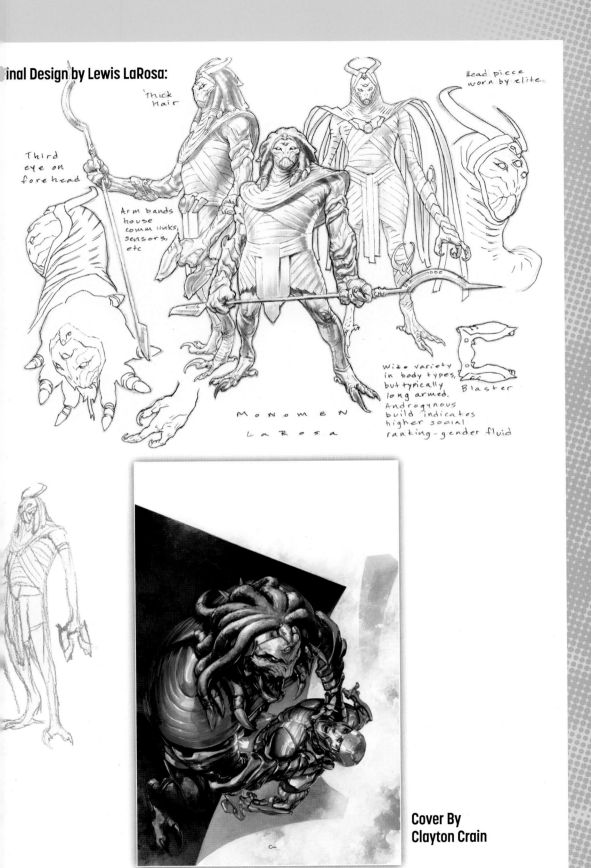

Final Design by Lewis LaRosa:

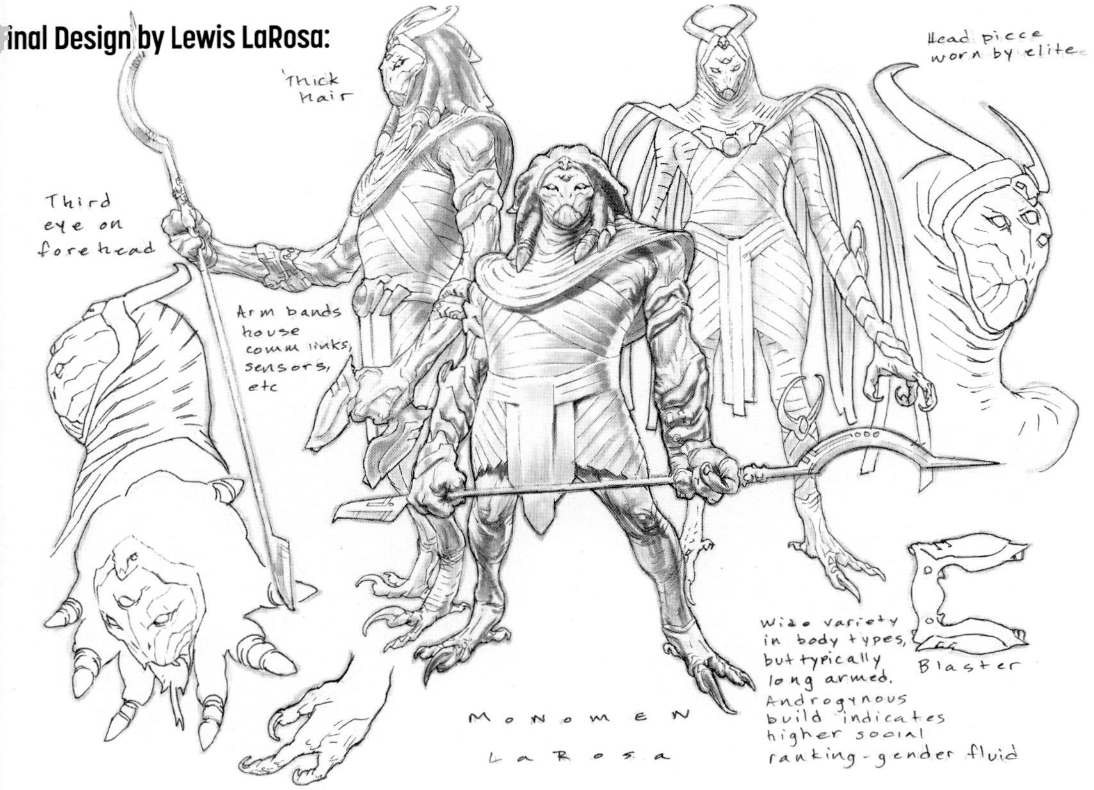
Thick Hair
Third eye on forehead
Arm bands house comm links, sensors, etc
Head piece worn by elite
Wide variety in body types, but typically long armed. Androgynous build indicates higher social ranking - gender fluid
Blaster
MONOMEN
LaRosa

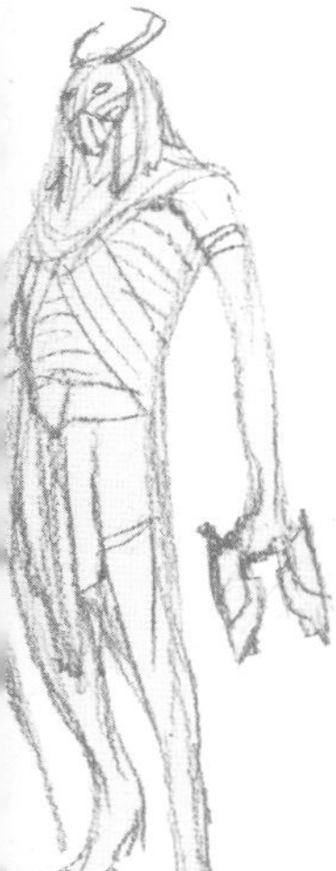

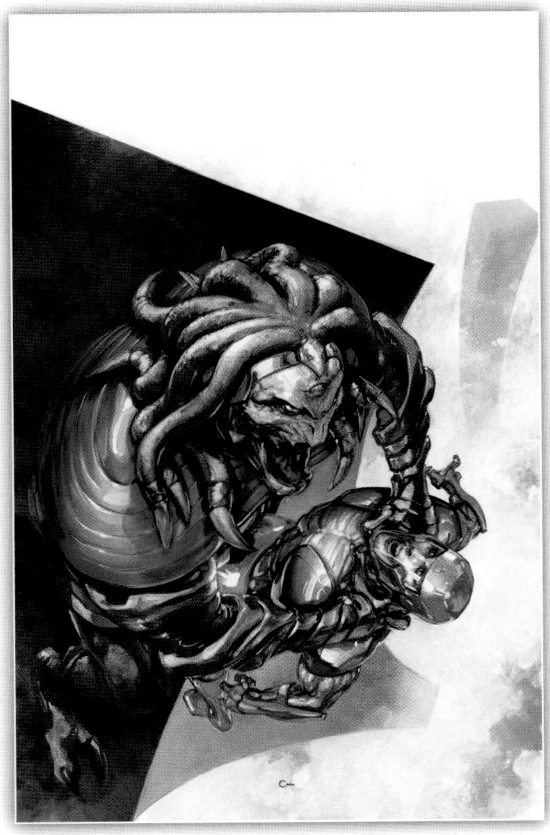

Cover By Clayton Crain

MATT KINDT ON THE CHARACTER AND WORLD OF X-O MANOWAR

The idea I came up with for the series was to take Aric off Earth, throw him on an alien planet, and see what happens. To sort of strip him back down to his basic barbarian phase, and then take the armor away, and figure out what he is as a human being first, before introducing the armor back into the equation. That's what I like, I'm a big fan of barbarians, so just getting him back into barbarian-mode was the thing I was most excited about. But also to build a world, go to an alien planet, sort of fleshing it all out, and making it real. Doing something that wasn't just him flying through space and landing on a planet, doing his mission, and coming back home, but to actually spend some time developing Planet Gorin.

I was excited to develop an alien planet that felt real, that felt lived on and had a history to it. So there are three different distinct races of beings that live on the planet, they all have their own histories and their own way of interacting. So to have that existing when we meet Aric, we don't really know what's happened on Earth or why he's here, we sort of just throw him onto this planet and have him deal with this alien culture. I think seeing that character on an alien planet and out of his comfort zone -- rather than having him be a man on Earth in modern times -- and seeing him react to the strangeness of it all, helps us see him in a different way. The stuff that is alien to him is also alien to us, and I think you lose sight of that fact when his character is on earth in the twenty-first century. The twenty-first century is foreign to him because he hasn't seen a cell phone or used a computer. Stuff like that. So getting to put him on an alien planet, where we can feel what he feels, and everything is as alien to us as it is to him, helps the reader get into his character a little bit more. ■

ARTWORK BY CLAYTON CRAIN

Originally published in *X-O MANOWAR (2017) #7 PRE-ORDER EDITION*

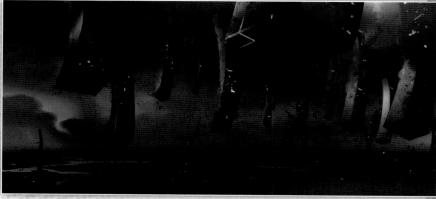

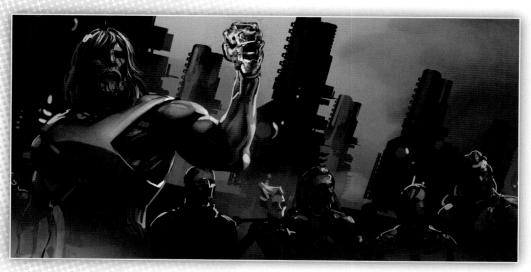

MATT KINDT ON ARIC'S PROGRESSION AND WHAT'S TO COME

Writing comics is a weird process because, theoretically, the story never ends. Like, what's the last issue? We don't know what it is. So it's odd as a writer to approach a book like X-O Manowar and have unlimited space to tell it. That part of it is challenging, but also fun. That's when we came up with the idea to throw him onto an alien planet and have all these cultures, and all this room to build new things. So I think what I was excited about doing then was showing him progress, both mentally and emotionally. The beauty of comics and that big canvas is that you can show a character start in one place and then grow, and I think that's kind of what we're doing. After Aric arrives on the planet, he's just a farmer and the story gets looped back into this war that he doesn't want to fight in, but he's recruited as a foot soldier in the first arc. Every arc is structured in a way where we see him progress because he's a born fighter, so he's not going to be a foot soldier forever. So he does that, proves himself, and gets upgraded to captain, and then general, and then we're going to get to emperor. We'll get to see how a person progresses from guy on a farm to an emperor, and what he has to do to get there. How does it change him? Is he fit to be emperor by the time he gets to that position?

But I think in any sort of long-form storytelling can you do a story like that. Where you just have a character evolve over time, and show him go from a foot soldier to an emperor. In comics it's hard to do because you've got a character like X-O -- he's the flagship character who everyone loves the most, and to do that, to get to show the evolution of that character for a company like Valiant, is unique.

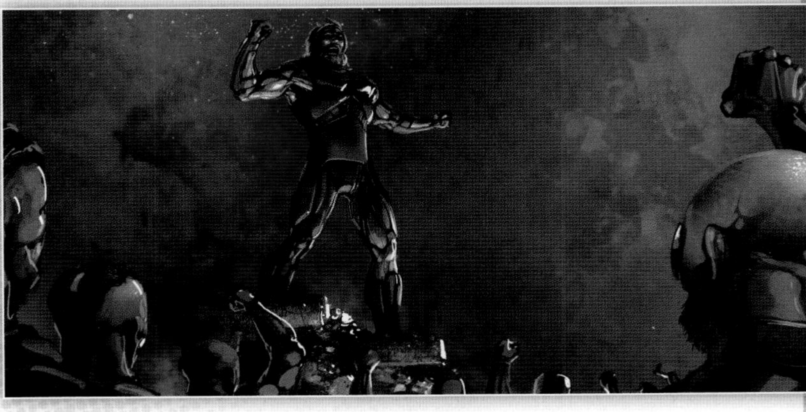

Part of what's happening for Aric to get to emperor is that he's going to have to do some things that aren't popular with some of the planet's residents. I think it's up to the reader in a lot of ways to decide, "Did he do the right thing? Did he not?" But I think these bounty hunters are after Aric because they think he did not do the right thing. The bounty hunters are bad news. I've loved bounty hunters since I was seven years old, watching Empire Strikes Back and I've been dying to get them into a book ever since. ■

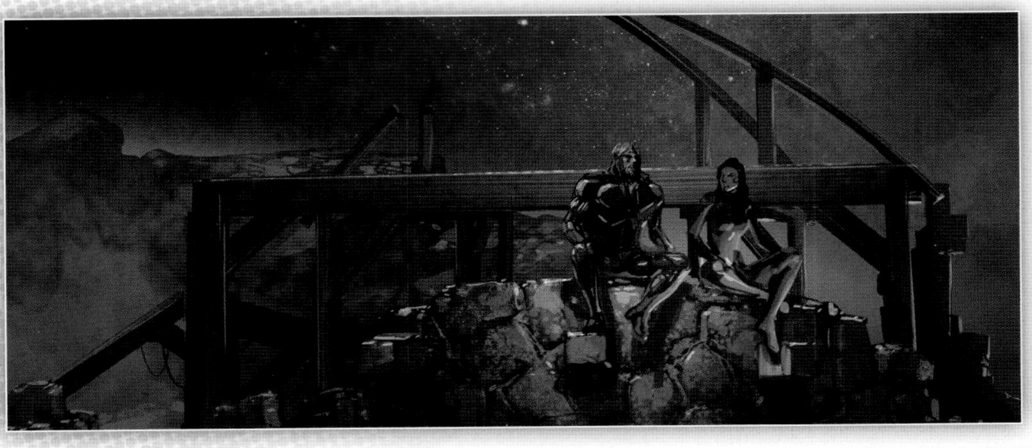

ARTWORK BY CLAYTON CRAIN

Originally published in *X-O MANOWAR (2017) #8 PRE-ORDER EDITION*

DESIGNING THE MONOLITH DEFENSES

Design by Clayton Crain

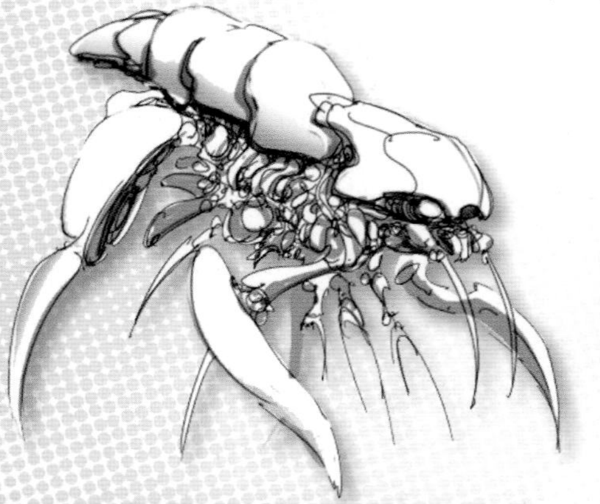

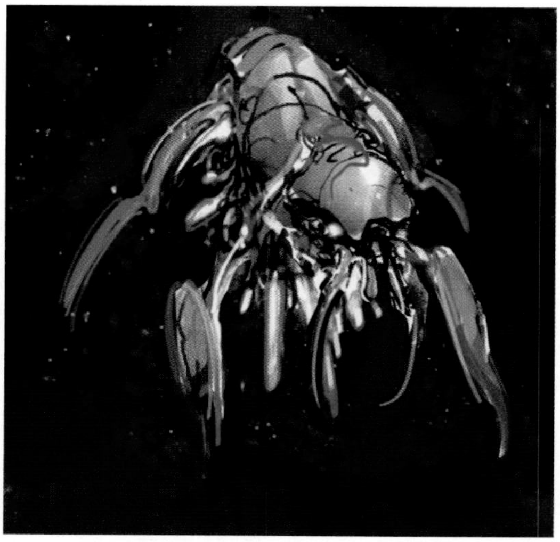

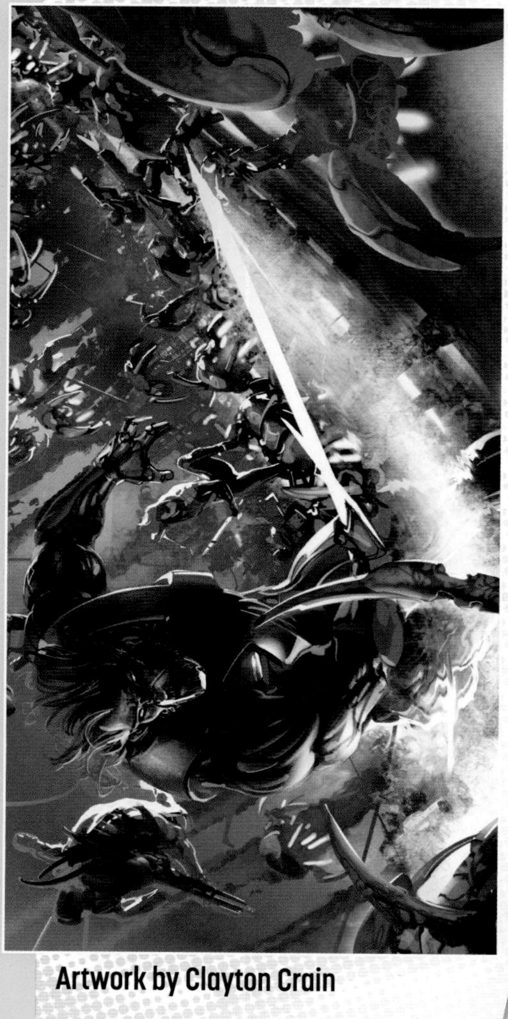

Artwork by Clayton Crain

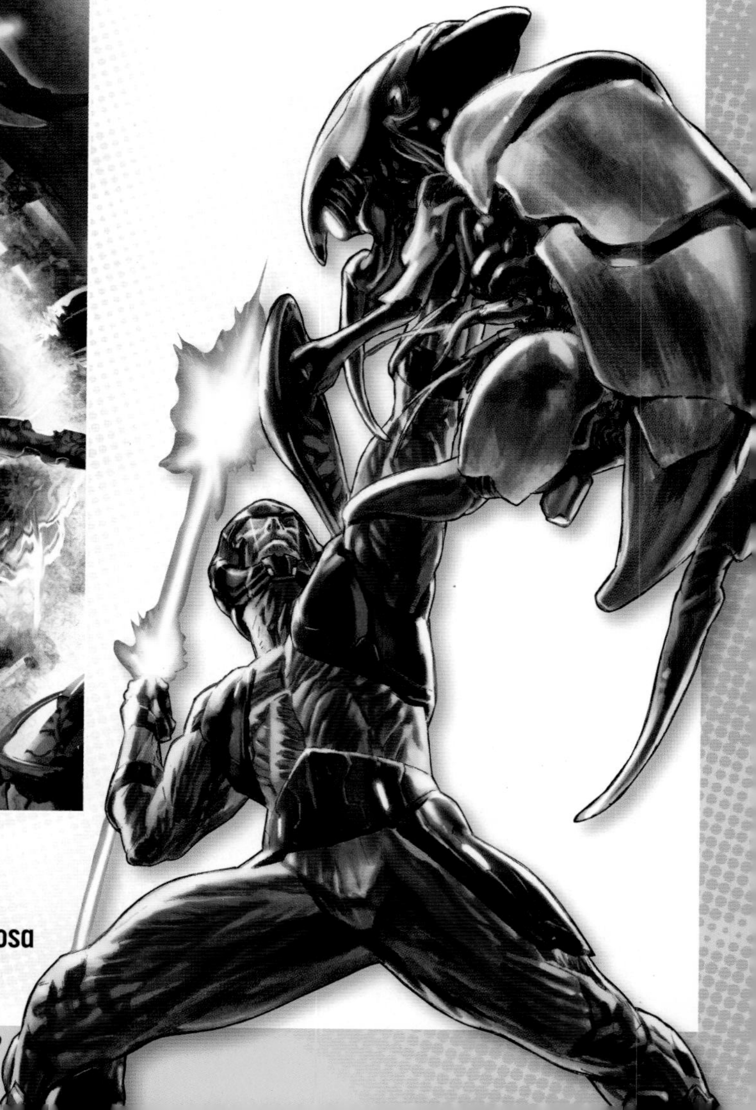

Artwork by Lewis LaRosa
with Diego Rodriguez

Originally published in *X-O MANOWAR (2017) #9*
PRE-ORDER EDITION

THE MYTHOLOGY OF PYRE PRISON

WITH COMMENTARY BY **MATT KINDT**

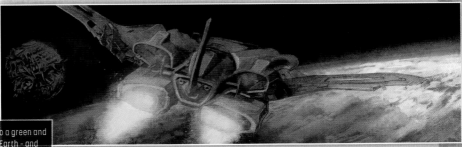

We see the ship flying to a green and blue planet - similar to Earth - and orbiting it we see a red moon - the prison moon of this planet, Pyre.

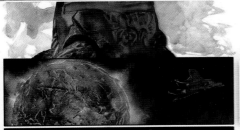

There are no structures on the moon prison - the moon in this case IS the prison. Its gravity is so powerful that it's hard to move, let alone breathe or land on it. Once you're rocketed to this moon - you don't come back.

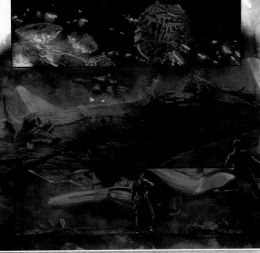

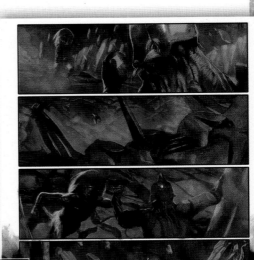

The ship almost lands on the moon- it's hovering just above the surface - the moon is cracking up - big crevices and cracks everywhere - it's desolate - just dust and a few surviving prisoners wandering around...they look pretty bulky/strong - the gravity building their muscles.

On this moon we see wrecked space ships and rockets everywhere - the gravity sucked them in and they just crash-landed - there was no getting off this moon once you were on it. They fed prisoners by shooting food/supply rockets on one-way-trips so they're littered everywhere as well. I kinda want to do an entire book about this prison moon!!!!! Oh well, it's blown up now.

ARTWORK BY RENATO GUEDES

Originally published in *X-O MANOWAR (2017) #10 PRE-ORDER EDITION*

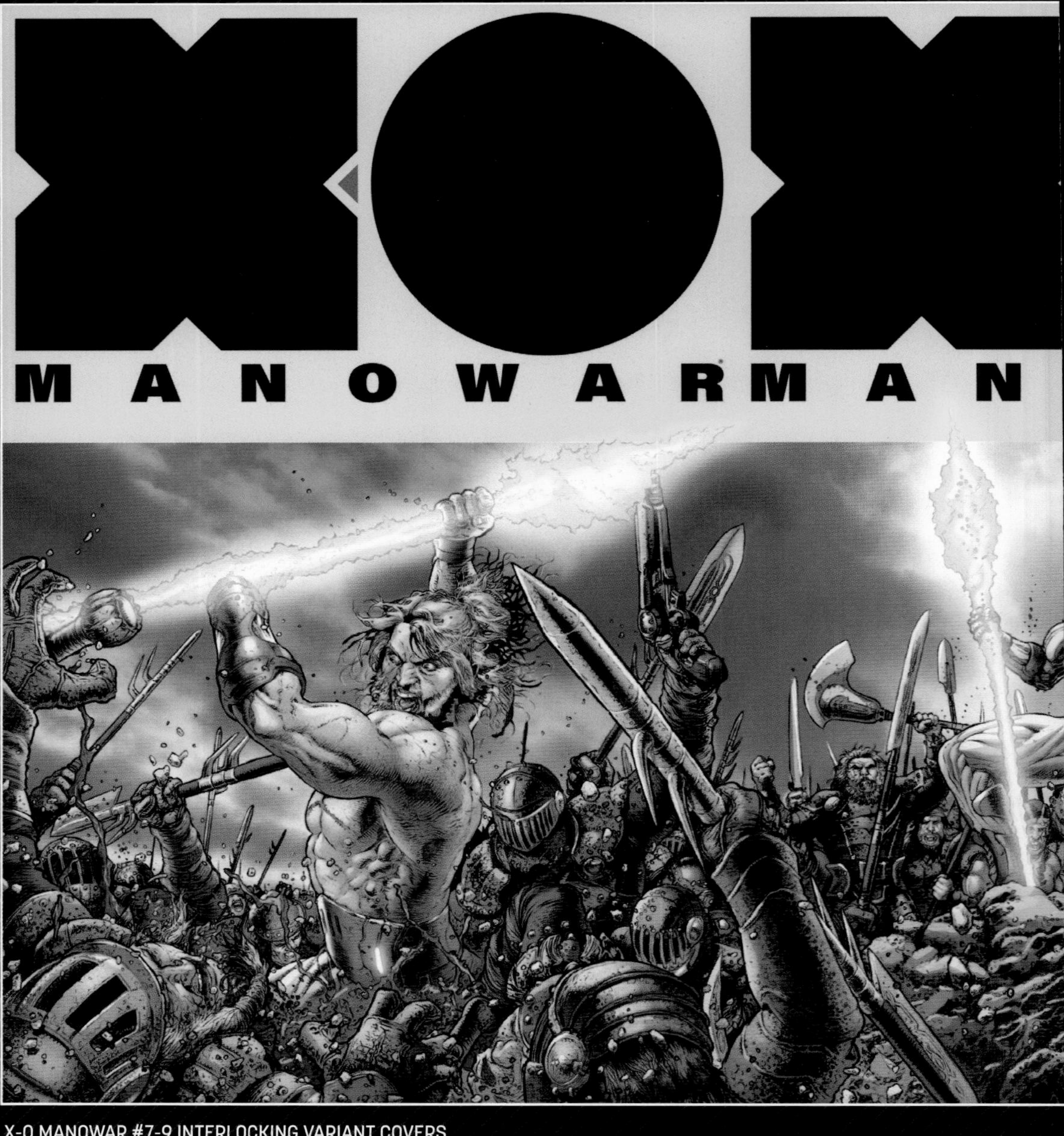
M A N O W A R M A N

X-O MANOWAR #7-9 INTERLOCKING VARIANT COVERS
Art by JUAN JOSÉ RYP with BRIAN REBER

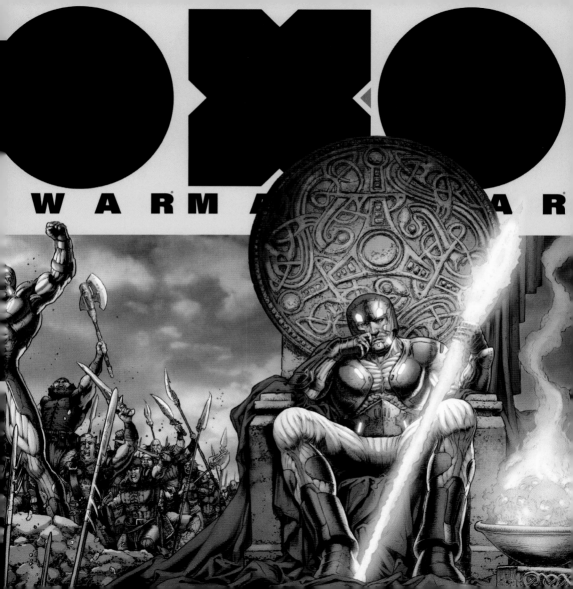

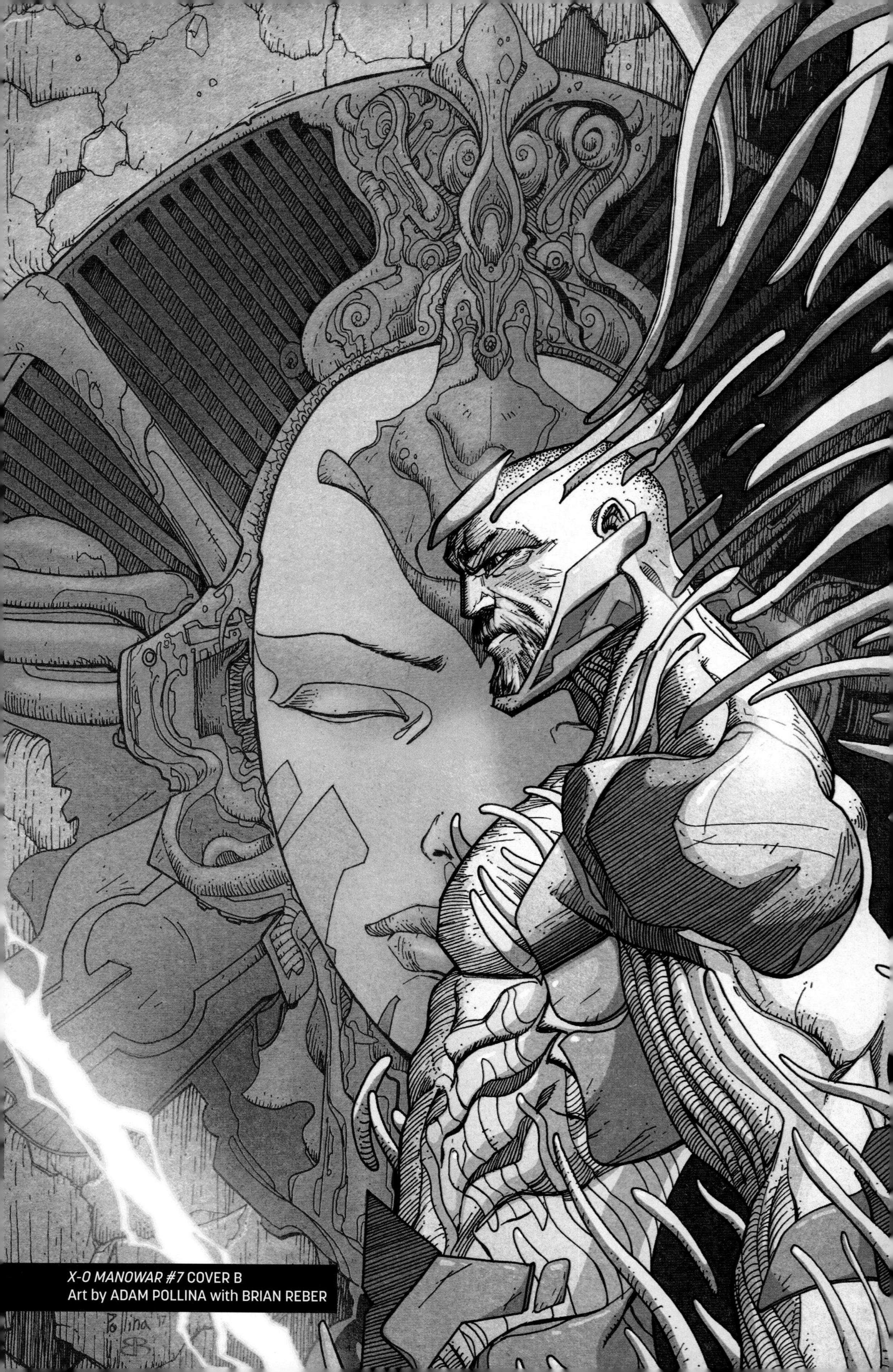

X-O MANOWAR #7 COVER B
Art by ADAM POLLINA with BRIAN REBER

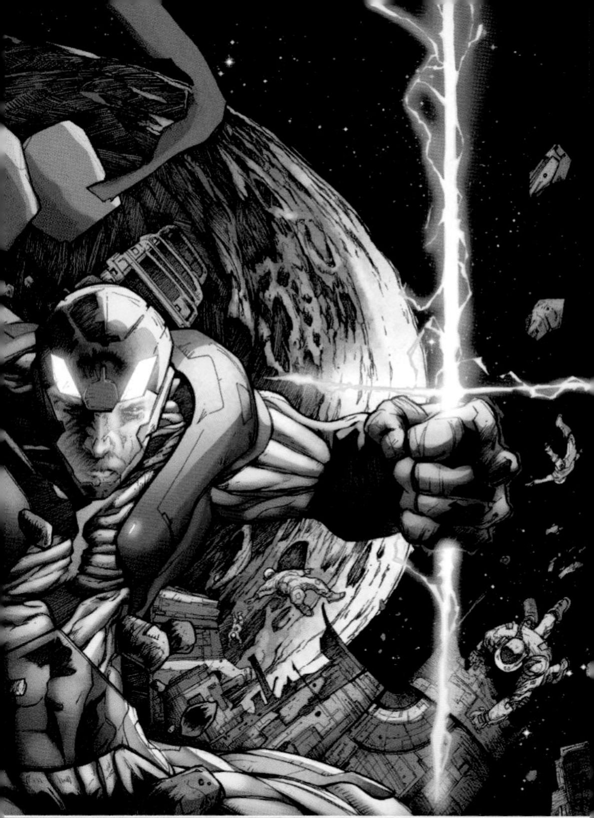

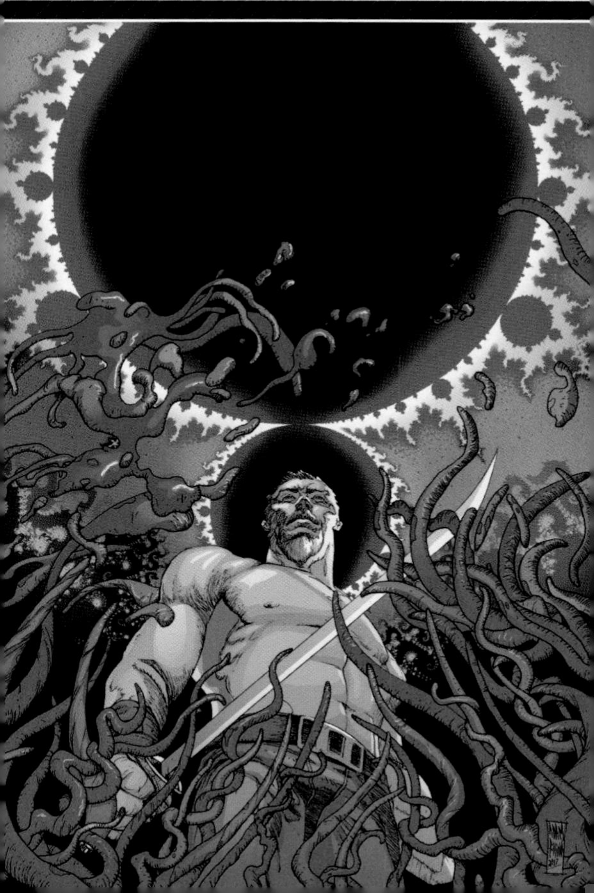

X-O MANOWAR #7 ICON VARIANT COVER
Art by BEN TEMPLESMITH

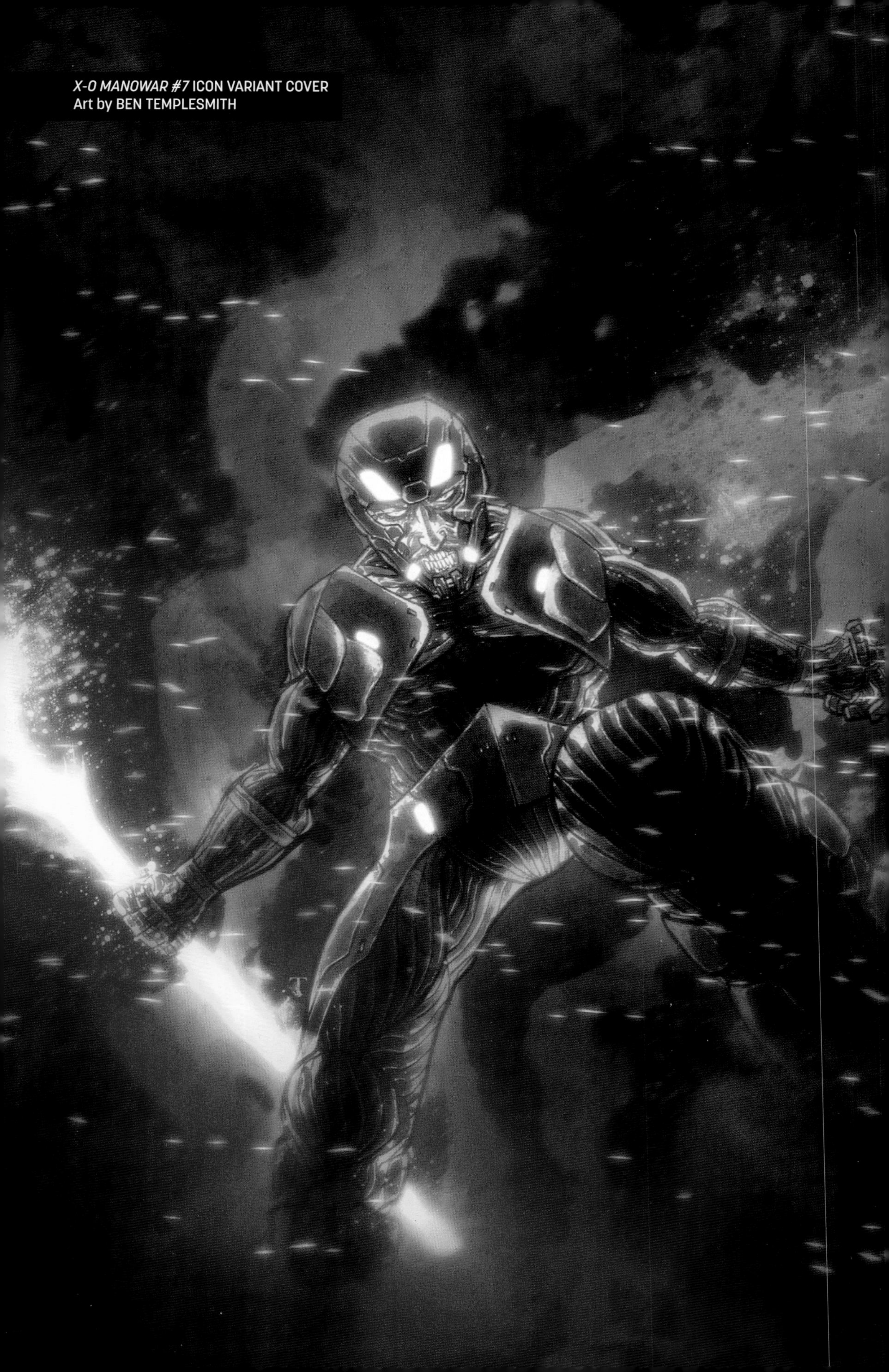

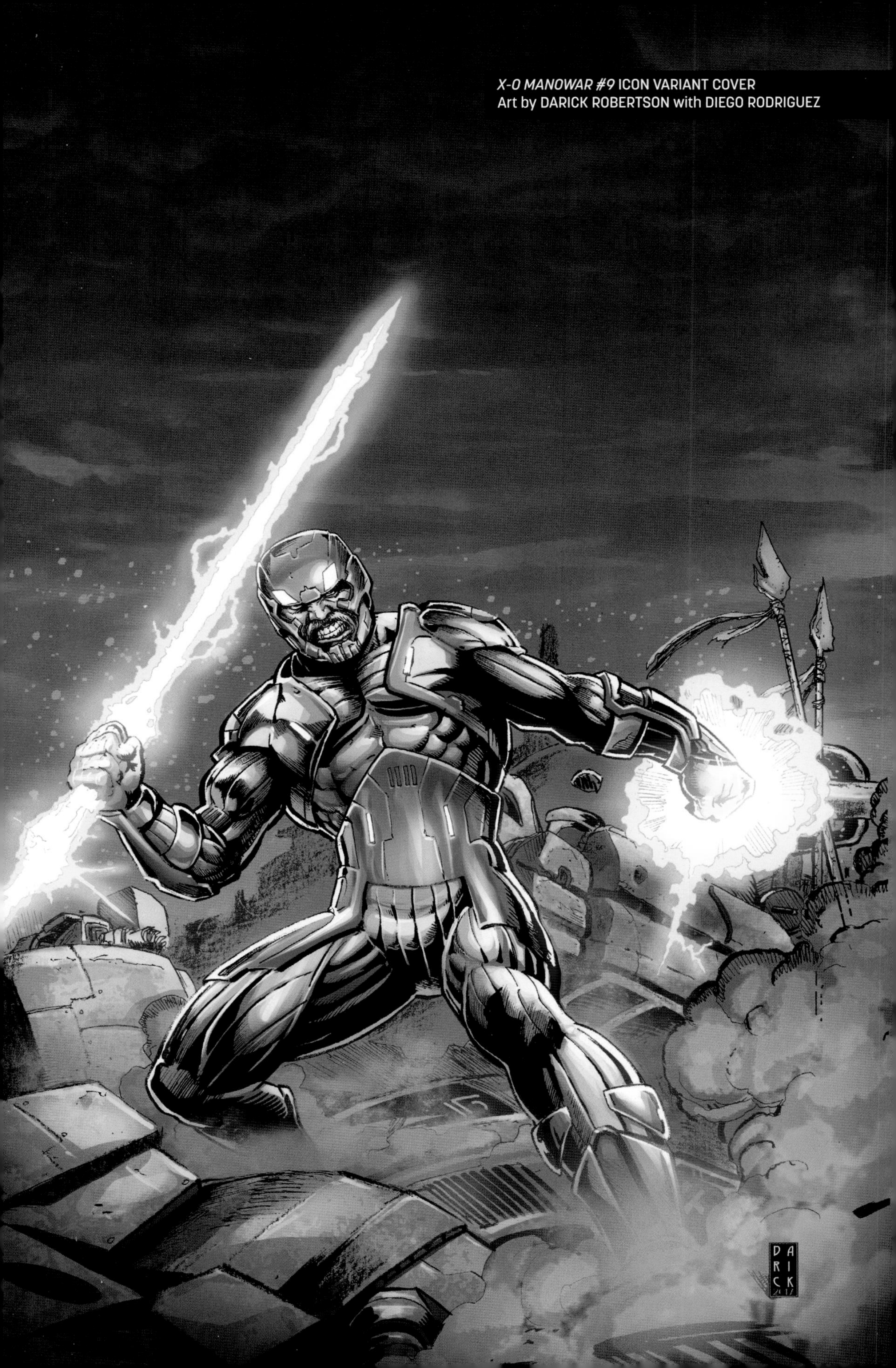

X-O MANOWAR #9 ICON VARIANT COVER
Art by DARICK ROBERTSON with DIEGO RODRIGUEZ

X-O MANOWAR #10 COVER B
Art by KENNETH ROCAFORT

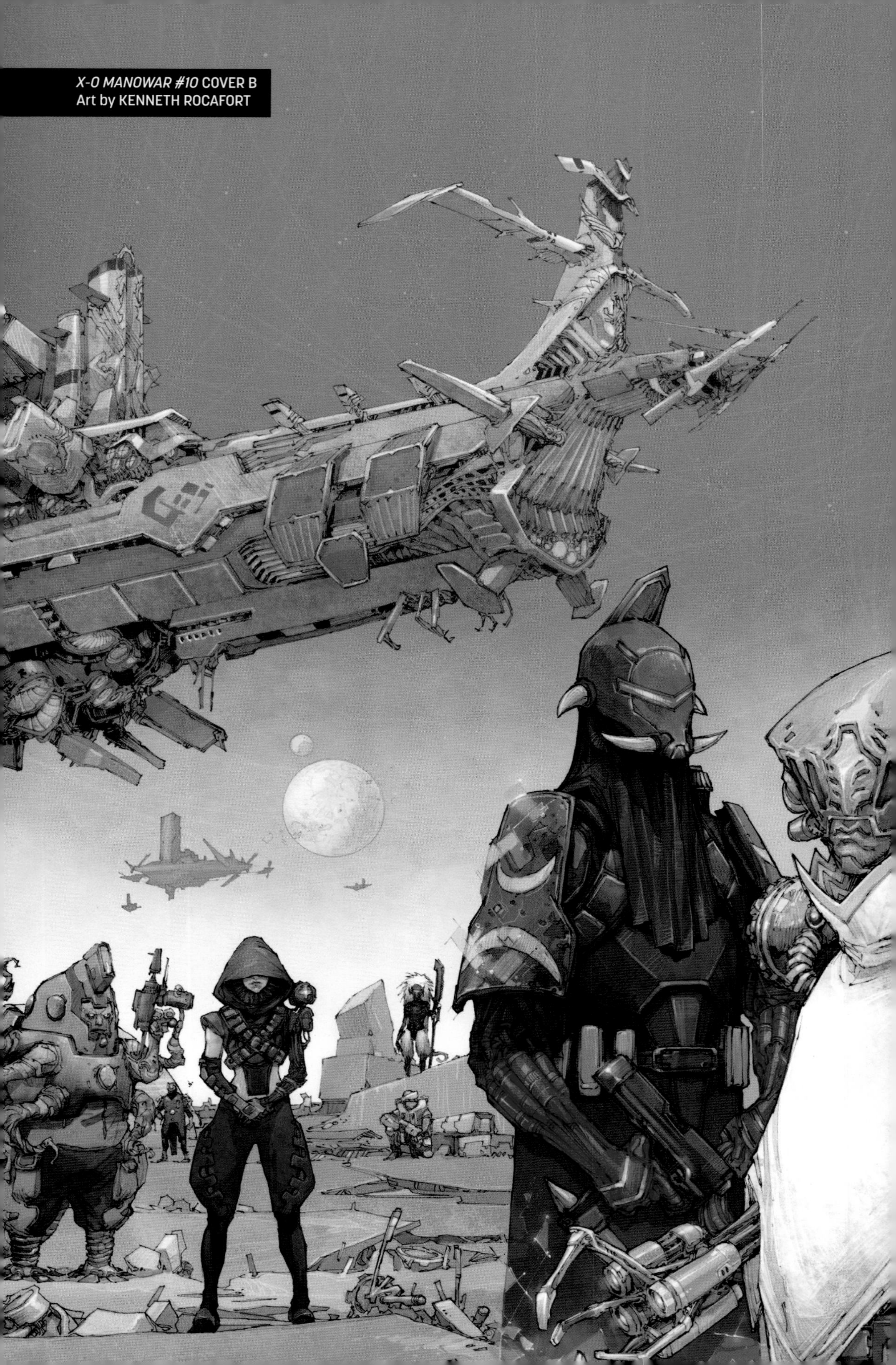

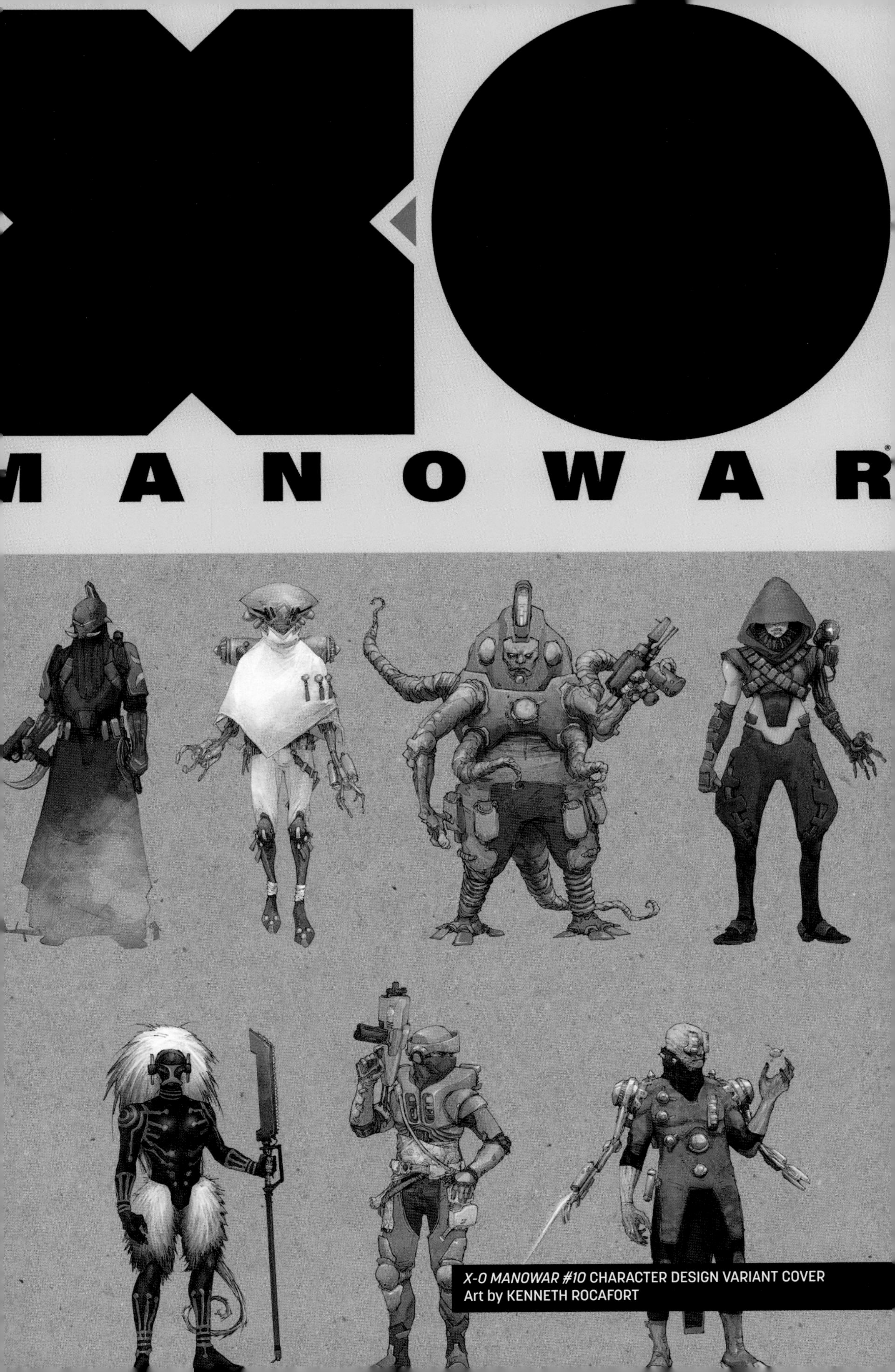
X-O
MANOWAR

X-O MANOWAR #10 CHARACTER DESIGN VARIANT COVER
Art by KENNETH ROCAFORT

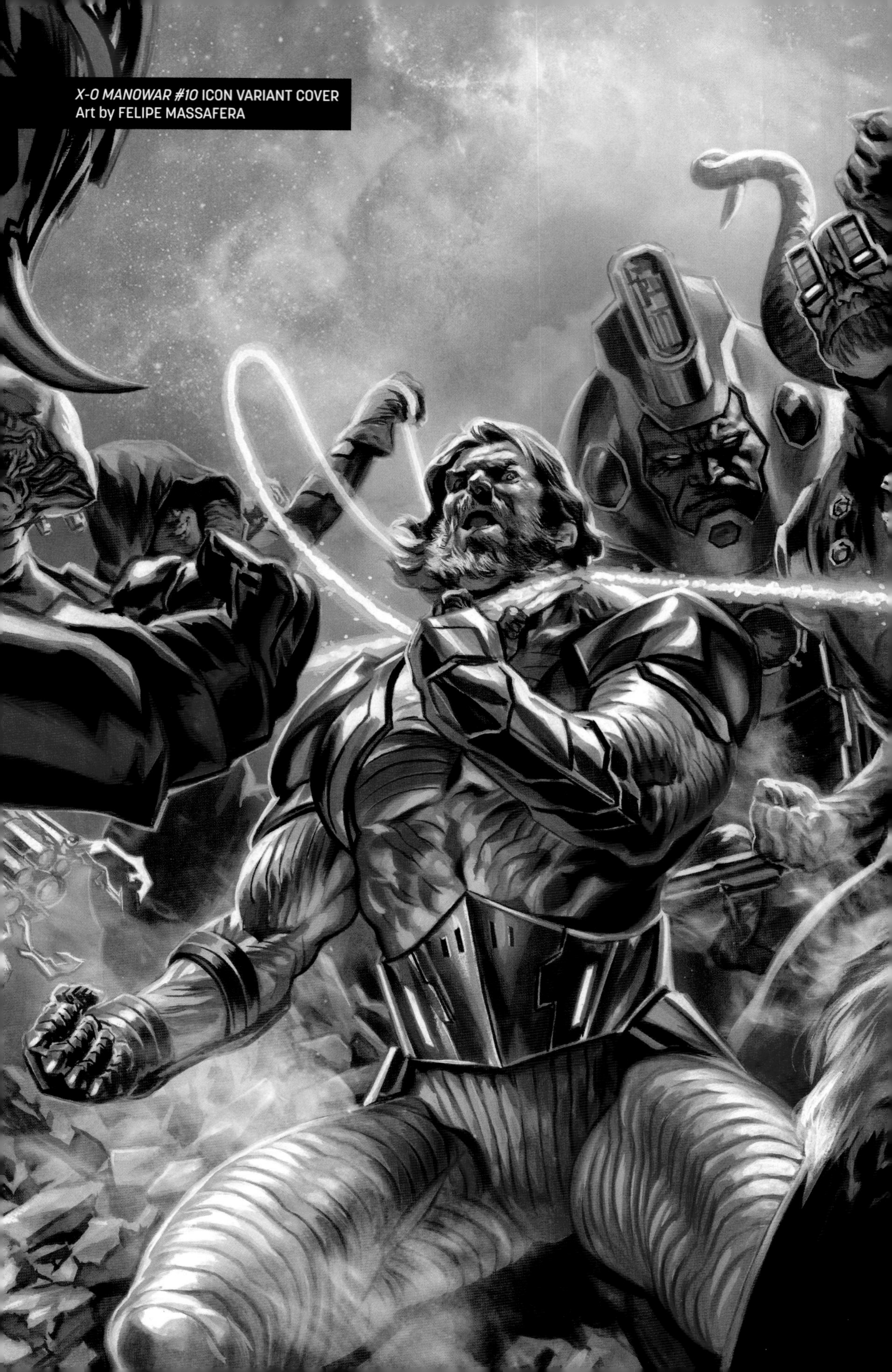

X-O MANOWAR #10 ICON VARIANT COVER
Art by FELIPE MASSAFERA

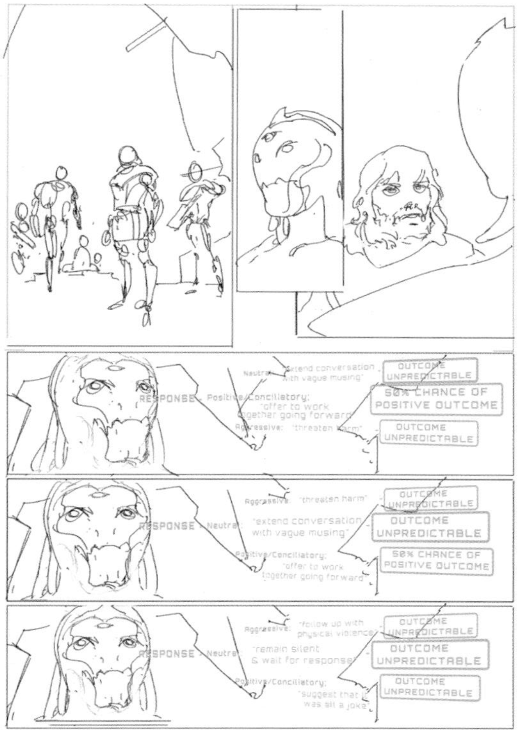
RESPONSE - Positive/Conciliatory:
"offer to work together going forward"
Neutral: "extend conversation with vague musing"
Aggressive: "threaten harm"
OUTCOME UNPREDICTABLE
50% CHANCE OF POSITIVE OUTCOME
OUTCOME UNPREDICTABLE
RESPONSE - Neutral: "extend conversation with vague musing"
Aggressive: "threaten harm"
Positive/Conciliatory: "offer to work together going forward"
OUTCOME UNPREDICTABLE
OUTCOME UNPREDICTABLE
50% CHANCE OF POSITIVE OUTCOME
RESPONSE - Neutral: "remain silent & wait for response"
Aggressive: "follow up with physical violence"
Positive/Conciliatory: "suggest that it was all a joke"
OUTCOME UNPREDICTABLE
OUTCOME UNPREDICTABLE
OUTCOME UNPREDICTABLE

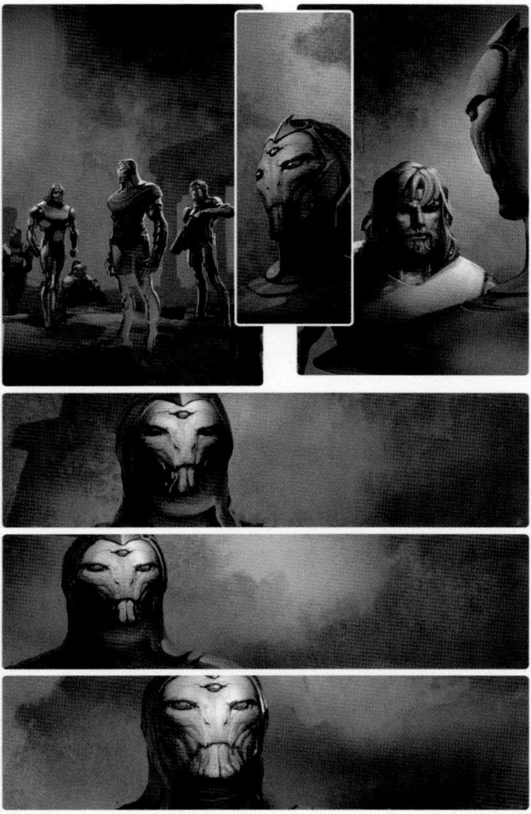

X-O MANOWAR #7, p. 17
Process and final art by CLAYTON CRAIN

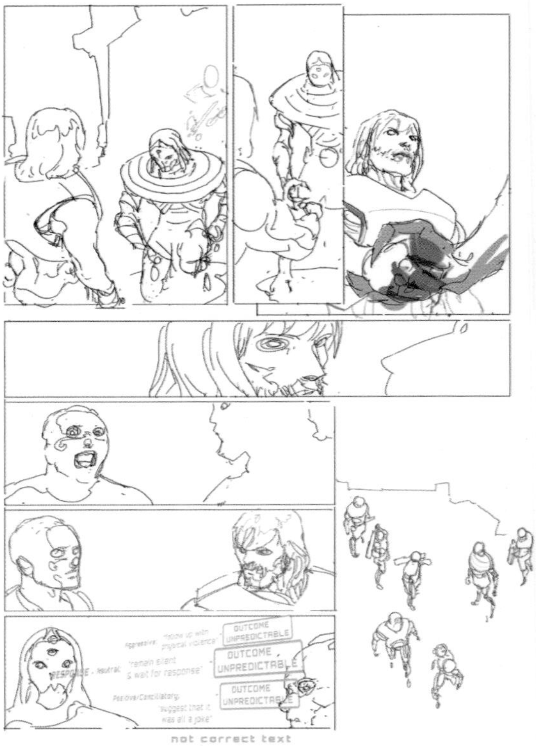

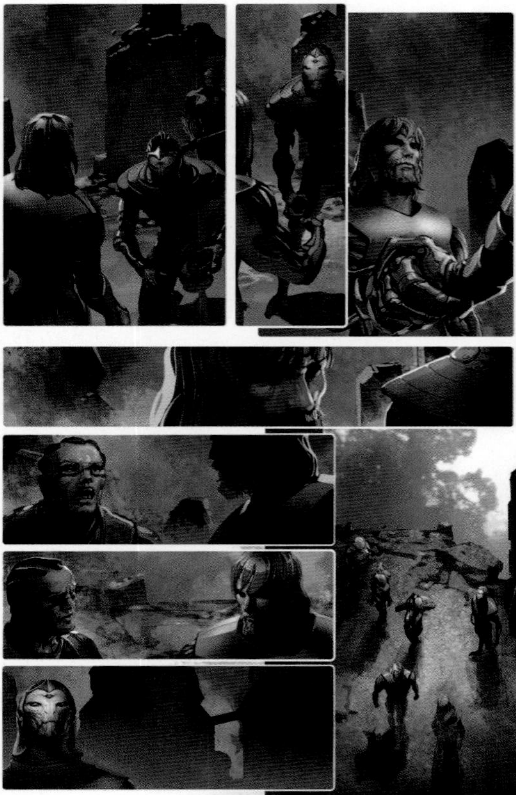

X-O MANOWAR #7, p. 18
Process and final art by CLAYTON CRAIN

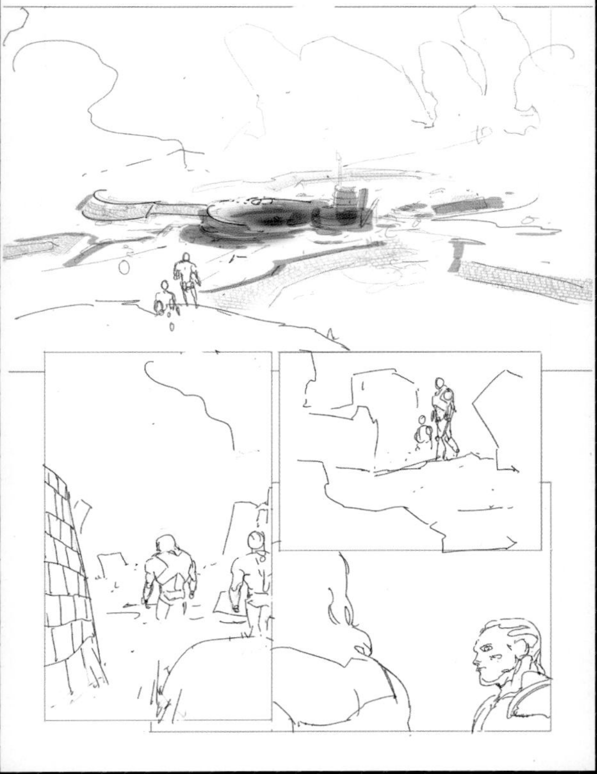

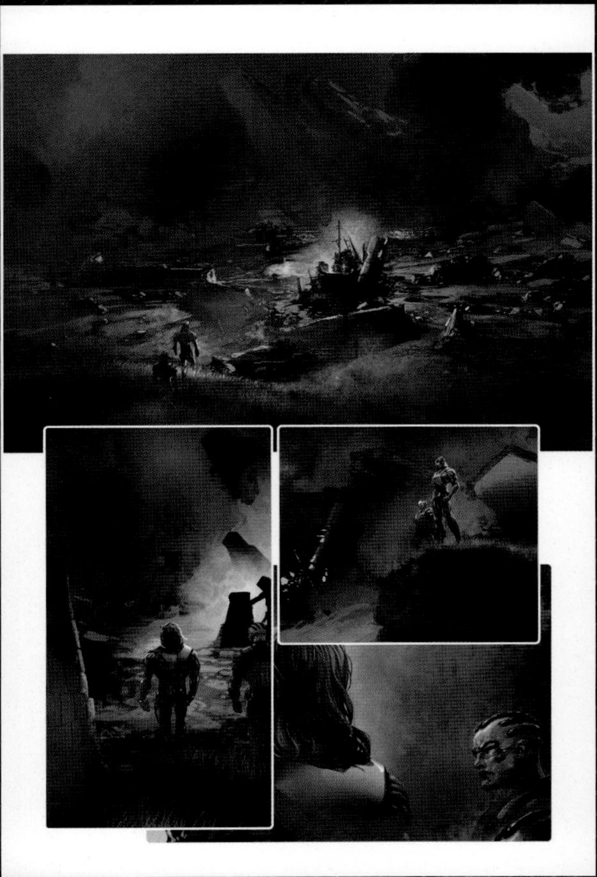

X-O MANOWAR #7, p. 19
Process and final art by CLAYTON CRAIN

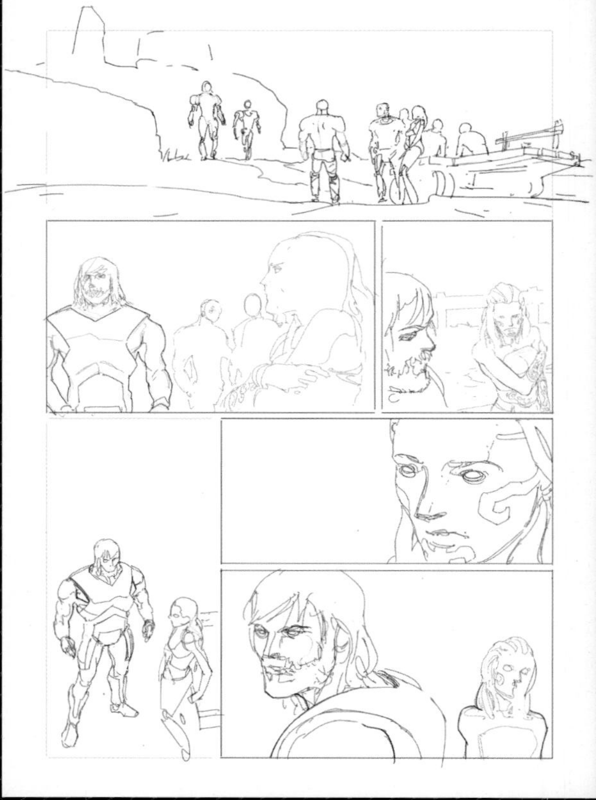

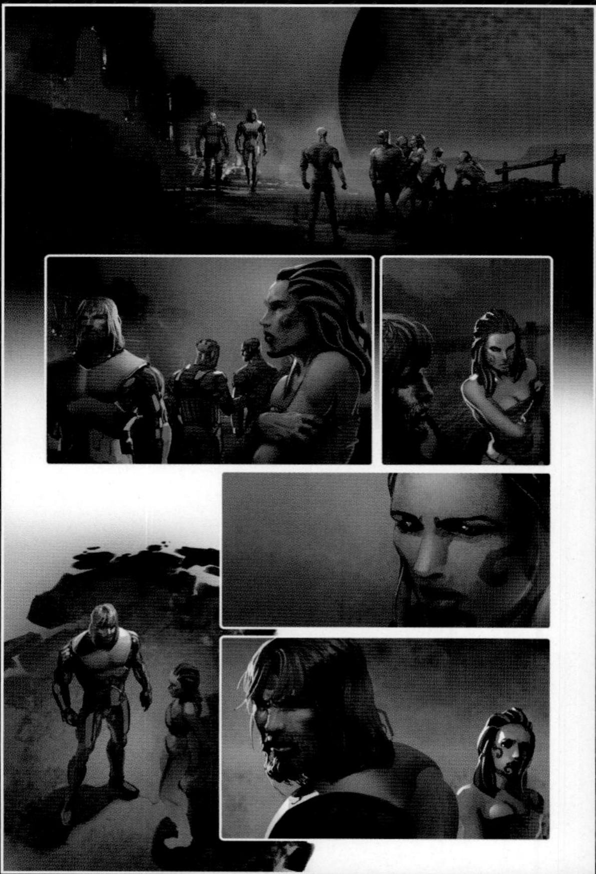

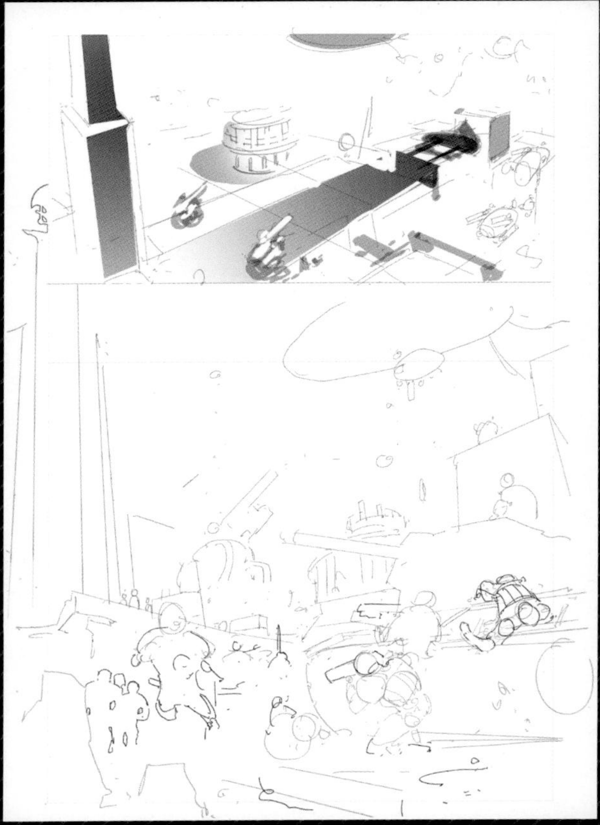

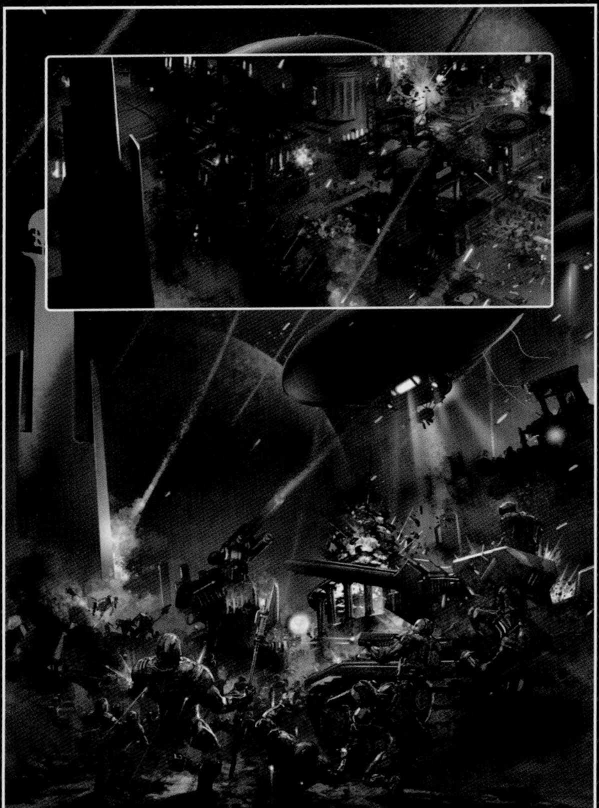

X-O MANOWAR #7, p. 20
Process and final art by CLAYTON CRAIN

X-O MANOWAR #7, p. 121
Process and final art by CLAYTON CRAIN

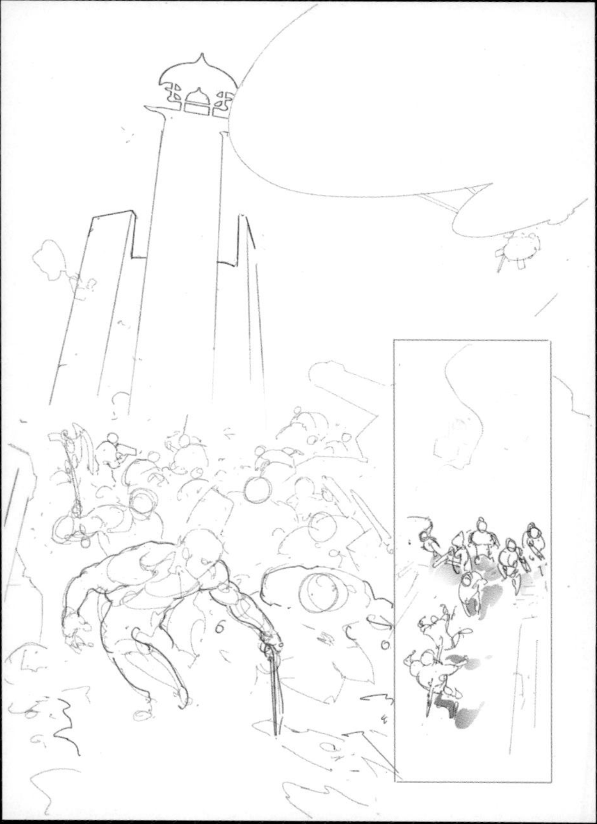

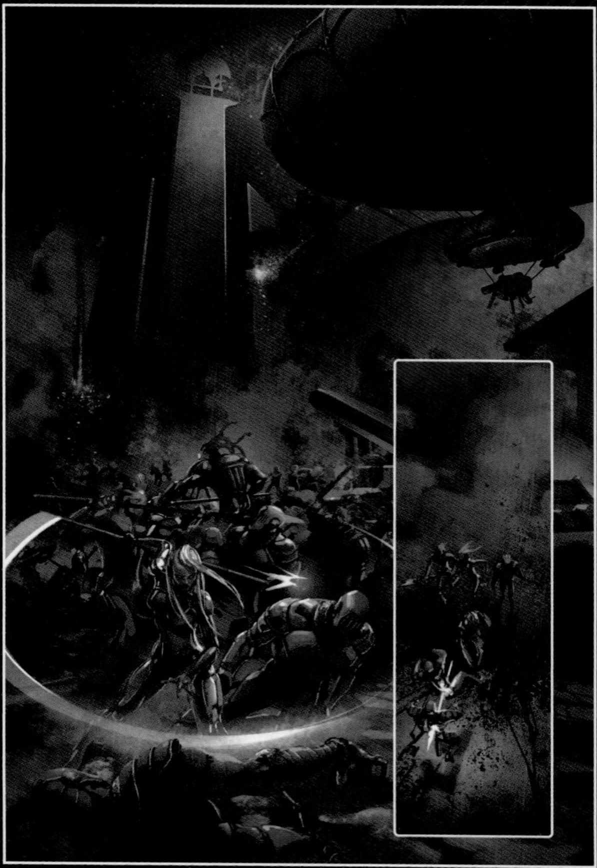

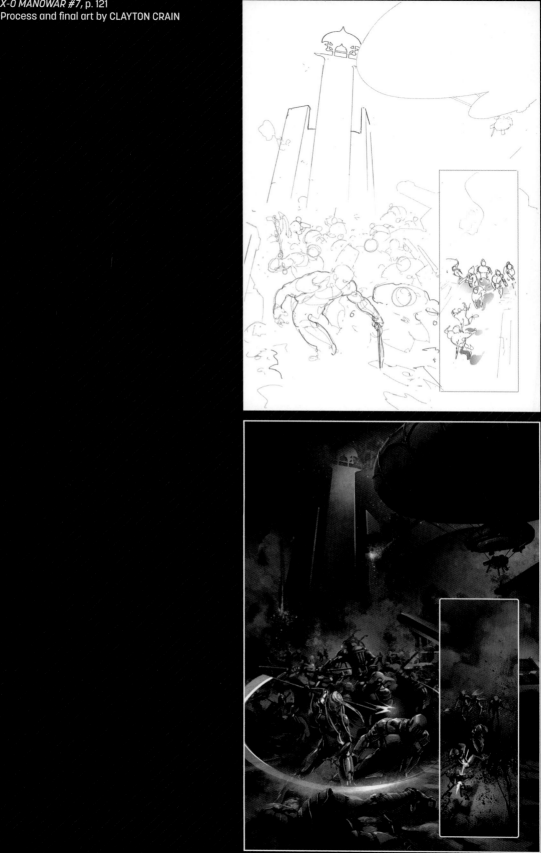

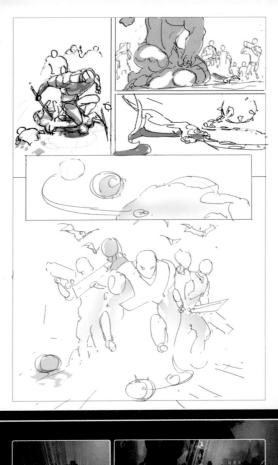

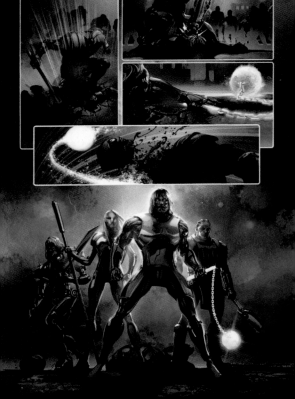

EXPLORE THE VALIANT UNIVERSE

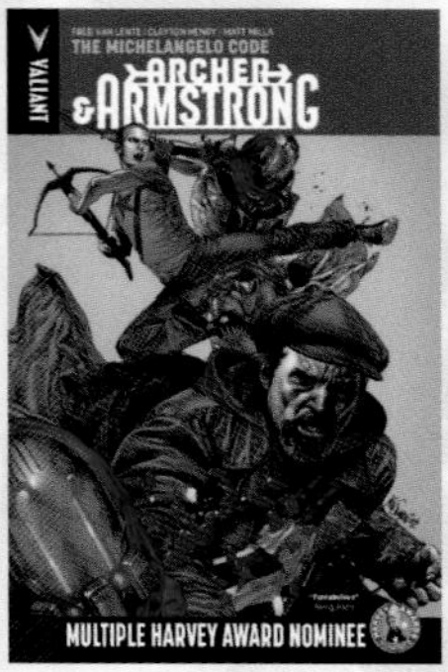
VALIANT
THE MICHELANGELO CODE
ARCHER & ARMSTRONG
MULTIPLE HARVEY AWARD NOMINEE

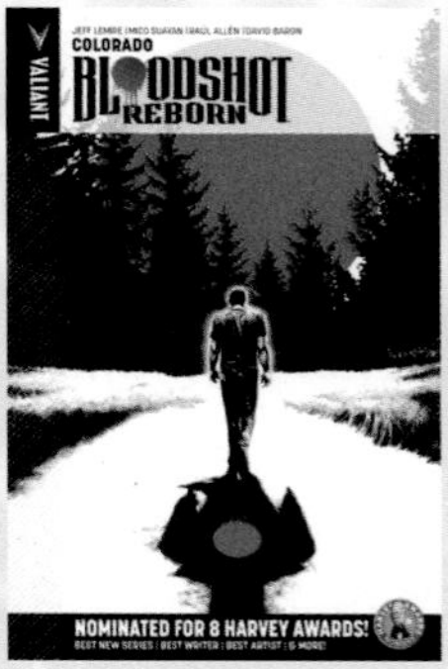
VALIANT
COLORADO
BLOODSHOT REBORN
NOMINATED FOR 8 HARVEY AWARDS!

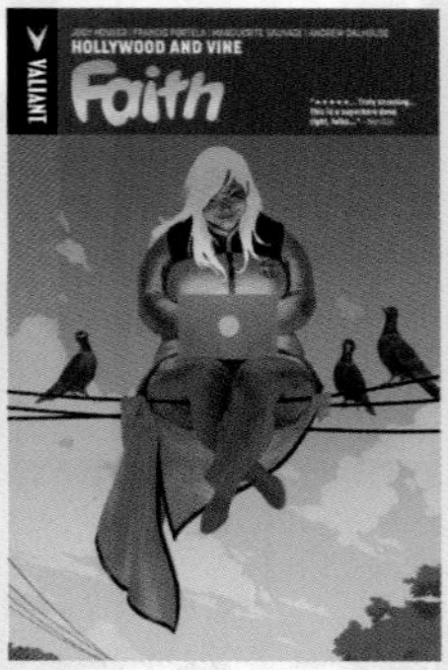
VALIANT
HOLLYWOOD AND VINE
Faith

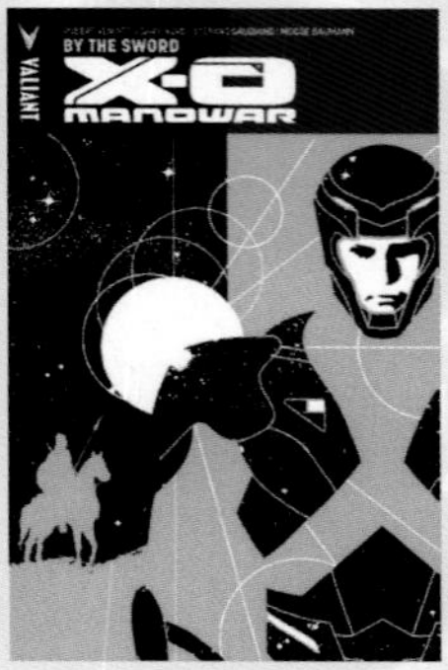
VALIANT
BY THE SWORD
X-O MANOWAR

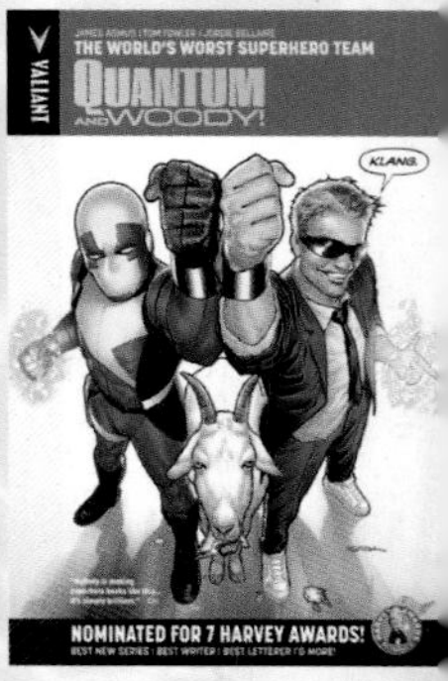
VALIANT
THE WORLD'S WORST SUPERHERO TEAM
QUANTUM AND WOODY!
KLANG
NOMINATED FOR 7 HARVEY AWARDS!

4001 A.D.

4001 A.D.
ISBN: 9781682151433

4001 A.D.: Beyond New Japan
ISBN: 9781682151464

Rai Vol 4: 4001 A.D.
ISBN: 9781682151471

A&A: THE ADVENTURES OF ARCHER AND ARMSTRONG

Volume 1: In the Bag
ISBN: 9781682151495

Volume 2: Romance and Road Trips
ISBN: 9781682151716

Volume 3: Andromeda Estranged
ISBN: 9781682152034

ARCHER & ARMSTRONG

Volume 1: The Michelangelo Code
ISBN: 9780979640988

Volume 2: Wrath of the Eternal Warrior
ISBN: 9781939346049

Volume 3: Far Faraway
ISBN: 9781939346148

Volume 4: Sect Civil War
ISBN: 9781939346254

Volume 5: Mission: Improbable
ISBN: 9781939346353

Volume 6: American Wasteland
ISBN: 9781939346421

Volume 7: The One Percent and Other Tales
ISBN: 9781939346537

ARMOR HUNTERS

Armor Hunters
ISBN: 9781939346452

Armor Hunters: Bloodshot
ISBN: 9781939346469

Armor Hunters: Harbinger
ISBN: 9781939346506

Unity Vol. 3: Armor Hunters
ISBN: 9781939346445

X-O Manowar Vol. 7: Armor Hunters
ISBN: 9781939346476

BLOODSHOT

Volume 1: Setting the World on Fire
ISBN: 9780979640964

Volume 2: The Rise and the Fall
ISBN: 9781939346032

Volume 3: Harbinger Wars
ISBN: 9781939346124

Volume 4: H.A.R.D. Corps
ISBN: 9781939346193

Volume 5: Get Some!
ISBN: 9781939346315

Volume 6: The Glitch and Other Tales
ISBN: 9781939346711

BLOODSHOT REBORN

Volume 1: Colorado
ISBN: 9781939346674

Volume 2: The Hunt
ISBN: 9781939346827

Volume 3: The Analog Man
ISBN: 9781682151334

Volume 4: Bloodshot Island
ISBN: 9781682151952

BLOODSHOT U.S.A.

ISBN: 9781682151952

BOOK OF DEATH

Book of Death
ISBN: 9781939346971

Book of Death: The Fall of the Valiant Universe
ISBN: 9781939346988

BRITANNIA

Volume 1
ISBN: 9781682151853

Volume 2: We Who Are About to Die
ISBN: 9781682152133

DEAD DROP

ISBN: 9781939346858

THE DEATH-DEFYING DOCTOR MIRAGE

Volume 1
ISBN: 9781939346490

Volume 2: Second Lives
ISBN: 9781682151297

THE DELINQUENTS

ISBN: 9781939346513

DIVINITY

Divinity I
ISBN: 9781939346766

Divinity II
ISBN: 9781682151518

Divinity III
ISBN: 9781682151914

Divinity III: Glorious Heroes of the Stalinverse
ISBN: 9781682152072

ETERNAL WARRIOR

Volume 1: Sword of the Wild
ISBN: 9781939346209

Volume 2: Eternal Emperor
ISBN: 9781939346292

Volume 3: Days of Steel
ISBN: 9781939346742

WRATH OF THE ETERNAL WARRIOR

Volume 1: Risen
ISBN: 9781682151235

Volume 2: Labyrinth
ISBN: 9781682151594

Volume 3: Deal With a Devil
ISBN: 9781682151976

FAITH

Volume 1: Hollywood and Vine
ISBN: 9781682151402

Volume 2: California Scheming
ISBN: 9781682151631

Volume 3: Superstar
ISBN: 9781682151990

Volume 4: The Faithless
ISBN: 9781682152195

Faith and the Future Force:
ISBN: 9781682152331

GENERATION ZERO

Volume 1: We Are the Future
ISBN: 9781682151754

Volume 2: Heroscape
ISBN: 9781682152096

HARBINGER

Volume 1: Omega Rising
ISBN: 9780979640957

Volume 2: Renegades
ISBN: 9781939346025

Volume 3: Harbinger Wars
ISBN: 9781939346117

Volume 4: Perfect Day
ISBN: 9781939346155

Volume 5: Death of a Renegade
ISBN: 9781939346339

Volume 6: Omegas
ISBN: 9781939346384

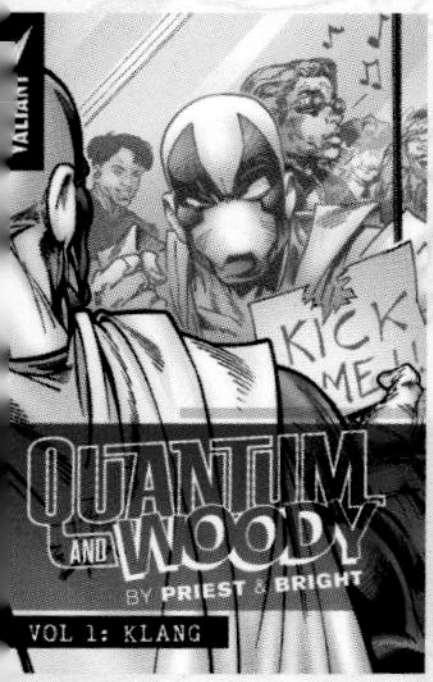
VALIANT
KICK ME
QUANTUM AND WOODY
BY PRIEST & BRIGHT
VOL 1: KLANG
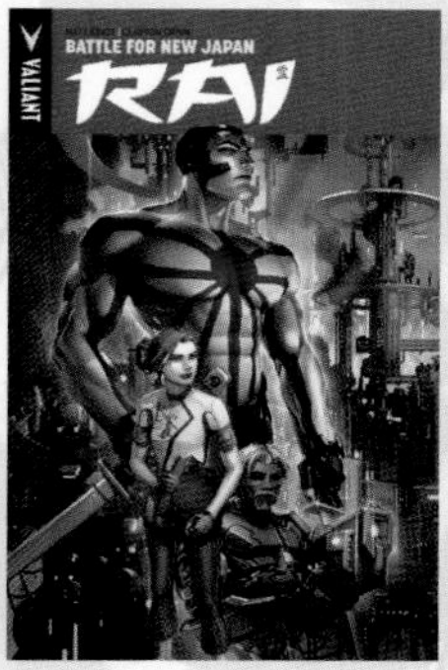
VALIANT
BATTLE FOR NEW JAPAN
RAI
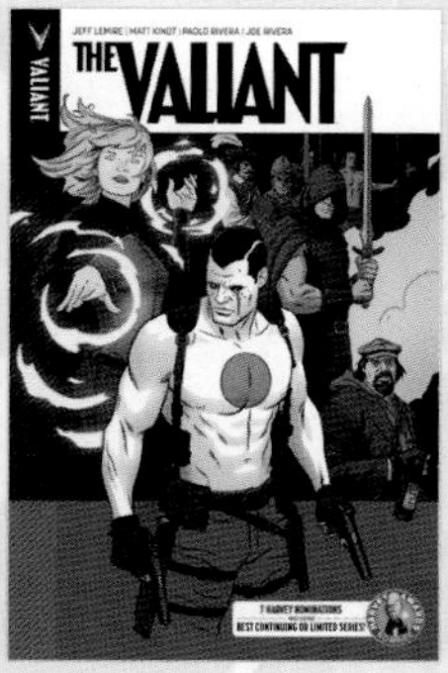
VALIANT
THE VALIANT
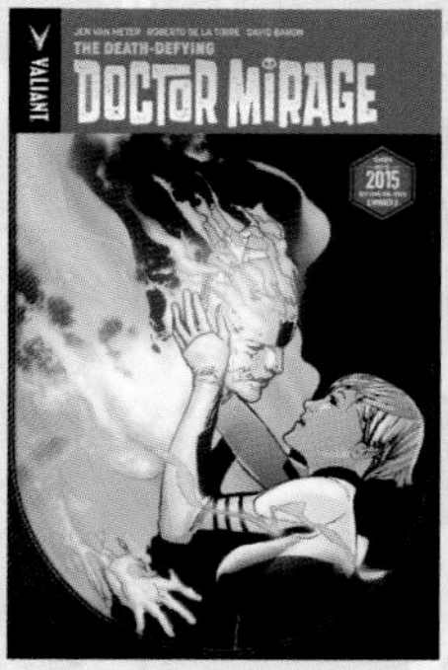
VALIANT
THE DEATH-DEFYING
DOCTOR MIRAGE
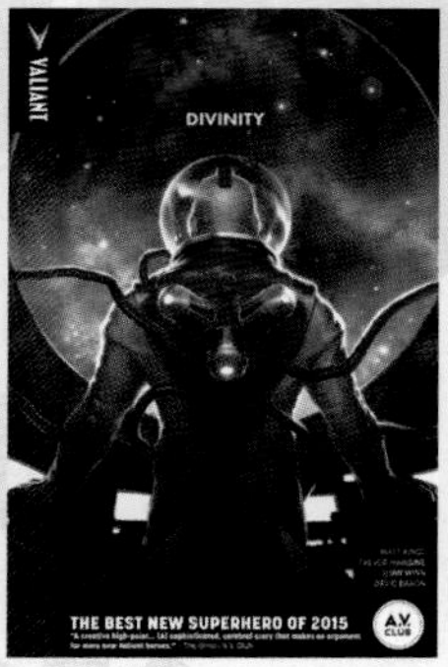
VALIANT
DIVINITY
THE BEST NEW SUPERHERO OF 2015
A.V. CLUB

IARBINGER RENEGADE
olume 1: The Judgment of Solomon
SBN: 9781682151693
olume 2: Massacre
SBN: 9781682152232

IARBINGER WARS
arbinger Wars
SBN: 9781939346094
loodshot Vol. 3: Harbinger Wars
SBN: 9781939346124
arbinger Vol. 3: Harbinger Wars
SBN: 9781939346117

MPERIUM
olume 1: Collecting Monsters
SBN: 9781939346759
olume 2: Broken Angels
SBN: 9781939346896
olume 3: The Vine Imperative
SBN: 9781682151112
olume 4: Stormbreak
SBN: 9781682151372

INJAK
olume 1: Weaponeer
SBN: 9781939346667
olume 2: The Shadow Wars
SBN: 9781939346940
olume 3: Operation: Deadside
SBN: 9781682151259
olume 4: The Siege of King's Castle
SBN: 9781682151617
olume 5: The Fist & The Steel
SBN: 9781682151792
olume 6: The Seven Blades of Master Darque
SBN: 9781682152119

UANTUM AND WOODY
olume 1: The World's Worst Superhero Team
SBN: 9781939346186
olume 2: In Security
SBN: 9781939346230
olume 3: Crooked Pasts, Present Tense
SBN: 9781939346391
olume 4: Quantum and Woody Must Die!
SBN: 9781939346629

UANTUM AND WOODY Y PRIEST & BRIGHT
olume 1: Klang
SBN: 9781939346780
Volume 2: Switch
ISBN: 9781939346803
Volume 3: And So...
ISBN: 9781939346865
Volume 4: Q2 - The Return
ISBN: 9781682151099

RAI
Volume 1: Welcome to New Japan
ISBN: 9781939346414
Volume 2: Battle for New Japan
ISBN: 9781939346612
Volume 3: The Orphan
ISBN: 9781939346841
Volume 4: 4001 A.D.
ISBN: 9781682151471

RAPTURE
ISBN: 9781682151891

SAVAGE
ISBN: 9781682152256

SECRET WEAPONS
ISBN: 9781682152294

SHADOWMAN
Volume 1: Birth Rites
ISBN: 9781939346001
Volume 2: Darque Reckoning
ISBN: 9781939346056
Volume 3: Deadside Blues
ISBN: 9781939346162
Volume 4: Fear, Blood, And Shadows
ISBN: 9781939346278
Volume 5: End Times
ISBN: 9781939346377

SHADOWMAN BY ENNIS & WOOD
ISBN: 9781682151358

IVAR, TIMEWALKER
Volume 1: Making History
ISBN: 9781939346636
Volume 2: Breaking History
ISBN: 9781939346834
Volume 3: Ending History
ISBN: 9781939346995

UNITY
Volume 1: To Kill a King
ISBN: 9781939346261
Volume 2: Trapped by Webnet
ISBN: 9781939346346
Volume 3: Armor Hunters
ISBN: 9781939346445
Volume 4: The United
ISBN: 9781939346544
Volume 5: Homefront
ISBN: 9781939346797
Volume 6: The War-Monger
ISBN: 9781939346902
Volume 7: Revenge of the Armor Hunters
ISBN: 9781682151136

THE VALIANT
ISBN: 9781939346605

VALIANT ZEROES AND ORIGINS
ISBN: 9781939346582

X-O MANOWAR
Volume 1: By the Sword
ISBN: 9780979640940
Volume 2: Enter Ninjak
ISBN: 9780979640995
Volume 3: Planet Death
ISBN: 9781939346087
Volume 4: Homecoming
ISBN: 9781939346179
Volume 5: At War With Unity
ISBN: 9781939346247
Volume 6: Prelude to Armor Hunters
ISBN: 9781939346407
Volume 7: Armor Hunters
ISBN: 9781939346476
Volume 8: Enter: Armorines
ISBN: 9781939346551
Volume 9: Dead Hand
ISBN: 9781939346650
Volume 10: Exodus
ISBN: 9781939346933
Volume 11: The Kill List
ISBN: 9781682151273
Volume 12: Long Live the King
ISBN: 9781682151655
Volume 13: Succession and Other Tales
ISBN: 9781682151754

X-O MANOWAR (2017)
Volume 1: Soldier
ISBN: 9781682152058
Volume 2: General
ISBN: 9781682152171

EXPLORE THE VALIANT UNIVERSE

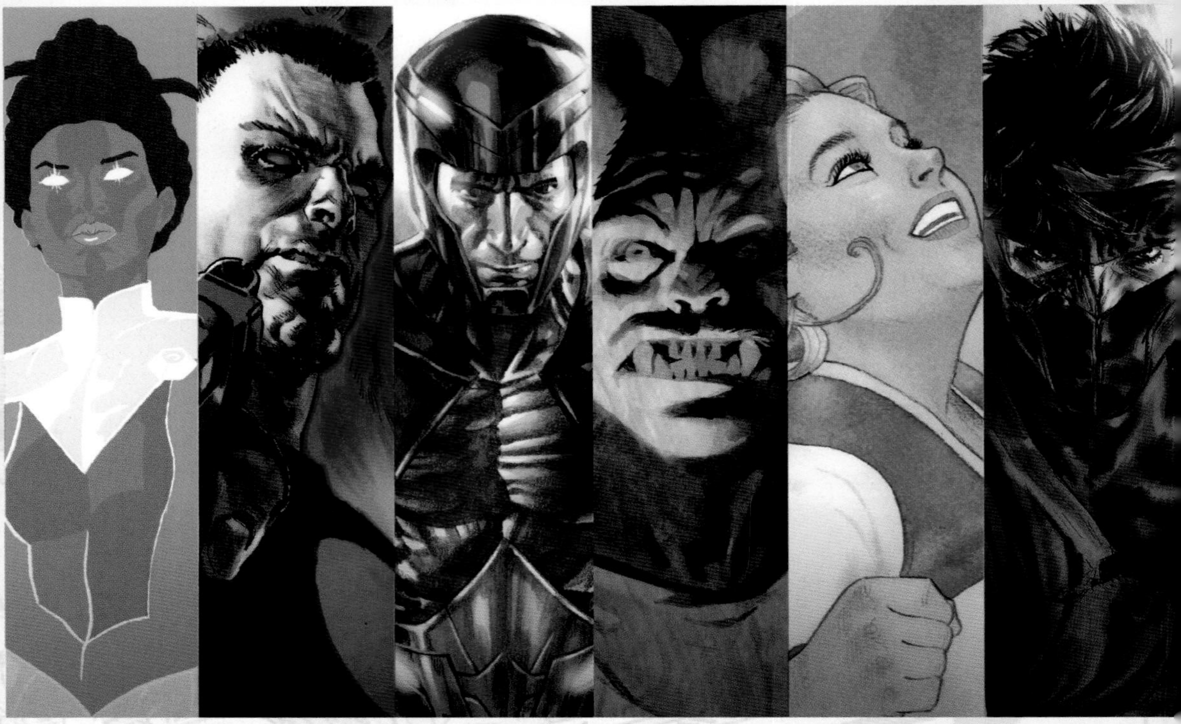

4001 A.D. DELUXE EDITION
ISBN: 978-1-68215-193-8

ARCHER & ARMSTRONG DELUXE EDITIONS
Book 1: ISBN: 978-1-939346-22-3
Book 2: ISBN: 978-1-939346-95-7

ARMOR HUNTERS DELUXE EDITION
ISBN: 978-1-939346-72-8

BLOODSHOT DELUXE EDITIONS
Book 1: ISBN: 978-1-939346-21-6
Book 2: ISBN: 978-1-939346-81-0

BLOODSHOT REBORN DELUXE EDITIONS
Book 1: ISBN: 978-1-68215-155-6
Book 2: ISBN: 978-1-68215-227-0

BOOK OF DEATH DELUXE EDITION
ISBN: 978-1-68215-115-0

THE DEATH-DEFYING DOCTOR MIRAGE DELUXE EDITION
ISBN: 978-1-68215-153-2

DIVINITY DELUXE EDITION
ISBN: 978-1-939346-92-6

FAITH: HOLLYWOOD & VINE DELUXE EDITION
ISBN: 978-1-68215-201-0

HARBINGER DELUXE EDITIONS
Book 1: ISBN: 978-1-939346-13-1
Book 2: ISBN: 978-1-939346-77-3

HARBINGER WARS DELUXE EDITION
ISBN: 978-1-939346-32-2

IVAR, TIMEWALKER DELUXE EDITION
Book 1: ISBN: 978-1-68215-119-8

NINJAK DELUXE EDITION
Book 1: ISBN: 978-1-68215-157-0

QUANTUM AND WOODY DELUXE EDITION
Book 1: ISBN: 978-1-939346-68-1

RAI DELUXE EDITION
Book 1: ISBN: 978-1-68215-117-4

SHADOWMAN DELUXE EDITION
Book 1: ISBN: 978-1-939346-43-8

UNITY DELUXE EDITION
Book 1: 978-1-939346-57-5

THE VALIANT DELUXE EDITION
ISBN: 978-1-939346-91-9

X-O MANOWAR DELUXE EDITIONS
Book 1: ISBN: 978-1-939346-10-0
Book 2: ISBN: 978-1-939346-52-0
Book 3 : ISBN: 978-1-68215-131-0
Book 4: ISBN: 978-1-68215-183-9
Book 5: ISBN: 978-1-68215-215-7

VALIANT CLASSIC

ARCHER & ARMSTRONG: THE COMPLETE CLASSIC OMNIBUS
ISBN: 978-1-939346-87-2

QUANTUM AND WOODY: THE COMPLETE CLASSIC OMNIBUS
ISBN: 978-1-939346-36-0

Q2: THE RETURN OF QUANTUM AND WOODY DELUXE EDITION
ISBN: 978-1-939346-56-8

VALIANT MASTERS: BLOODSHOT VOL. 1 - BLOOD OF THE MACHINE
ISBN: 978-0-9796409-3-3

VALIANT MASTERS: HARBINGER VOL. 1 - CHILDREN OF THE EIGHTH DAY
ISBN: 978-1-939346-48-3

VALIANT MASTERS: H.A.R.D. CORPS VOL. 1 - SEARCH AND DESTROY
ISBN: 978-1-939346-28-5

VALIANT MASTERS: NINJAK VOL. 1 - BLACK WATER
ISBN: 978-0-9796409-7-1

VALIANT MASTERS: RAI VOL. 1 - FROM HONOR TO STRENGTH
ISBN: 978-1-939346-07-0

VALIANT MASTERS: SHADOWMAN VOL. 1 - SPIRITS WITHIN
ISBN: 978-1-939346-01-8

X-O MANOWAR CLASSIC OMNIBUS
Vol. 1: ISBN: 978-1-939346-30-8

X-O MANOWAR | READING ORDER

X O
MANOWAR
SOLDIER
VOLUME 01
VALIANT

X-O Manowar (2017) Vol. 1:
Soldier

X O
MANOWAR
GENERAL
VOLUME 02
VALIANT

X-O Manowar (2017) Vol. 2:
General

X O
EMPEROR
VALIANT

X-O Manowar (2017) Vol. 3:
Emperor

X O
MANOWAR
VISIGOTH
VOLUME 04
VALIANT

X-O Manowar (2017) Vol. 4:
Visigoth

Read the origin and earliest adventures of Valiant's most enduring icon!

VALIANT
BY THE SWORD
X-O
MANOWAR

X-O Manowar
Vol. 1: By the Sword

VALIANT
ENTER: NINJAK
X-O
MANOWAR

X-O Manowar
Vol. 2: Enter Ninjak

VALIANT
PLANET DEATH
X-O
MANOWAR

X-O Manowar
Vol. 3: Planet Death

VALIANT
HOMECOMING
X-O
MANOWAR

X-O Manowar
Vol. 4: Homecoming

VALIANT
TO KILL A KING
UNITY

Unity
Vol. 1: To Kill a King

VALIANT
ARMOR HUNTERS

Armor Hunters

VALIANT
BOOK OF DEATH
ONE OF THE BEST COMIC BOOKS OF 2015

Book of Death

VALIANT
DIVINITY
THE BEST NEW SUPERHERO OF 2015

Divinity

X-O MANOWAR

VOLUME FOUR: VISIGOTH

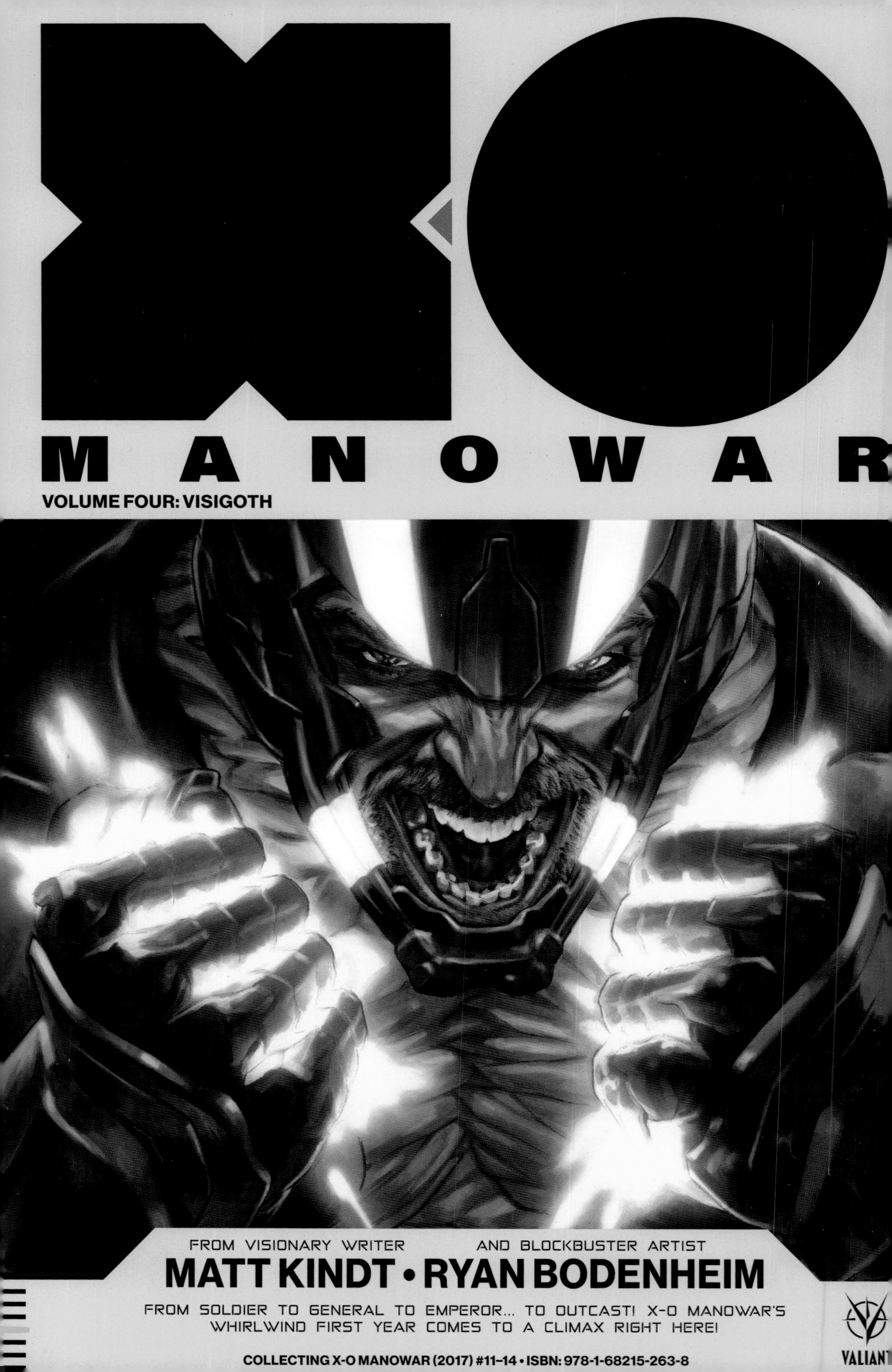

FROM VISIONARY WRITER AND BLOCKBUSTER ARTIST

MATT KINDT • RYAN BODENHEIM

FROM SOLDIER TO GENERAL TO EMPEROR... TO OUTCAST! X-O MANOWAR'S WHIRLWIND FIRST YEAR COMES TO A CLIMAX RIGHT HERE!

COLLECTING X-O MANOWAR (2017) #11–14 • ISBN: 978-1-68215-263-8

VALIANT